Date Due

APR 7 1983		
APR 2 1 1983		
FEB 2 0 1984		

CURRICULUM FOR BETTER SCHOOLS
The Great Ideological Debate

CURRICULUM FOR BETTER SCHOOLS
THE GREAT IDEOLOGICAL DEBATE

Michael Schiro
Boston College
Chestnut Hill, Massachusetts

Educational Technology Publications
Englewood Cliffs, New Jersey 07632

Library of Congress Cataloging in Publication Data

Schiro, Michael.
    Curriculum for better schools.

    Bibliography: p.
    Includes index.
    1. Curriculum planning. I. Title.
LB1570.S33   375'.001   77-17794
ISBN 0-87778-100-1

Copyright © 1978 Educational Technology Publications, Inc., Englewood Cliffs, New Jersey 07632.

Printed in the United States of America.

Library of Congress Catalog Card Number:
77-17794.

International Standard Book Number:
0-87778-100-1.

First Printing: February, 1978.

Second Printing: August, 1980.

Foreword

The number, the scope, and the funds involved in American curriculum development projects since the late 1950's have been unprecedented. Conscious of the extent and velocity of social change in modern industrial societies, the public as well as professional educators recognize the need for corresponding changes in the schools, and the focus of change during the past quarter century has been on the school curriculum.

But neither the public nor the educators have reached consensus regarding the curriculum changes that are necessary and desirable. Students of education may well be confused, even bewildered, by the profusion of different curriculum projects, many of which appear to be in conflict with each other. Most of the articles, books, pamphlets, and brochures which list and describe these various curriculum projects and the products they produce provide, at most, relatively superficial explanations of their characteristics and furnish no basic and comprehensive rationale to aid in understanding important differences. This book is an exception.

The author uses the fundamental ideological orientation of curriculum developers as a basis for classifying their projects and identifying their chief characteristics. He describes and illustrates four major conceptual systems that provide, consciously or unconsciously, the orientation of those who construct curricula. These are the scholar-academic ideology, the social efficiency ideology, the child study ideology, and the social reconstruction ideology. These four ideologies comprise a comprehensive classification of "ideal types." Few, if any, projects represent the full range of characteristics used to define the ideology, but every project is more nearly like one of the types than like any of the other three. For this reason, the identification of a project with the ideology which most nearly characterizes it helps greatly in understanding the nature of important differences among current curriculum projects and the resulting instructional programs. It also provides a basis for predicting the probable features of a proposed curriculum development project when one knows the basic ideological orientation of the curriculum developers involved.

Thus, the reader will find the book helpful in gaining an understanding of the different approaches currently followed in constructing curricula and instructional materials. It is not a manual on curriculum building but an exposition of the implicit as well as the explicit views, assumptions, and guiding principles of the four types of curriculum developers. This enables the student of the school curriculum to sort out the characteristic features of the many contemporary projects and to assess their appropriateness for the purposes and the situations they are intended to serve.

The reader will also find useful the wealth of examples given of curriculum projects in a variety of fields and the unusually complete bibliography included.

Ralph W. Tyler

Preface

During the twentieth century there has arisen within the United States a growing number of educators who have attempted to improve schools by creating a better school curriculum. These educators have taken a variety of approaches to curriculum improvement. Rapidly their approaches coalesced into four curricular ideologies that set forth predictable positions on such issues as the proper goals of curriculum, the nature of good curriculum, and the best ways of creating curriculum. The curricular ideologies were sufficiently different and were pursued with sufficient zeal that their proponents fragmented the field of curriculum into four camps of educators who were almost constantly at odds with each other over curricular issues. Debates among adherents of the different ideologies most frequently arose over particular small issues, such as whether it was more important for schools to teach understandings or skills. The larger conceptual contexts which gave meaning to the smaller issues were rarely debated, for they were only occasionally recognized and then addressed in only the sketchiest manner.

It is the intent of this book to rigorously describe and analyze the larger contexts which influence the particular beliefs and behaviors of educators who act as though one way of improving schools is through curriculum reform. Hopefully the issues raised will provide the reader with a better understanding of both the field of curriculum and his or her thinking in relation to the diversity of conflicting curricular ideologies competing for influence within the field of curriculum.

I should like to acknowledge my indebtedness to the following persons, who are only a few of those who have supported my endeavors in writing this book. To Dr. Stephen Ira Brown, whose understanding provided me with constant support during my explorations. To Dr. Maurice Belanger, whose knowledge of curriculum provided me with a valuable resource. To Dr. Peter James Gaskell, whose interest in my work provided continuous encouragement. To Dr. Ralph W. Tyler, who stimulated me to bring the book to completion. And to Ms. Mettie Whipple, whose patience and editorial aid made her a most understanding wife.

M.S.
April, 1977

Table of Contents

xi

CURRICULUM FOR BETTER SCHOOLS
The Great Ideological Debate

1.
The Curricular Domain:
An Introduction

The field of curriculum is in disarray. This disarray is evident in the inability of curriculum workers to deal effectively with the diversity that exists among themselves as professionals involved in understanding, maintaining, and improving the curricula of educational institutions.

The diversity among curriculum workers becomes obvious upon quickly reading a random selection of the literature they have written. Some curriculum workers speak about accountability and efficiency, others speak about knowledge and discovery, while still others speak about children and their needs. Such diversity is perhaps both healthy and to be expected and would not in itself indicate that the field of curriculum is in disarray.

What illuminates the disarray and what is disturbing is the inability among curriculum workers to meaningfully understand each other's differing approaches to curriculum, the inability among curriculum workers to rationally communicate among themselves about crucial problems they attempt to resolve in different ways, and the inability among curriculum workers to constructively cope with their differing intents for the school curriculum. This inability among curriculum workers to deal effectively with the diversity that exists among themselves is illustrated in the interactions among curriculum developers, one type of curriculum worker. Curriculum developers who attempt to improve schooling by creating textbooks that accurately reflect the contemporary essence of their respective academic disciplines and curriculum developers who attempt to enrich schooling by

3

creating multimedia kits of visual, tactile, and experiential materials designed to further the organic growth of the whole child, tend not to read each other's literature carefully, if at all; they speak about each other as though the other is subjecting the school curriculum to an outdated "evil"; they do not openly share with each other felt needs and concerns about everyday working problems; and they seem not to be able to learn from each other's successes or mistakes. Curriculum developers who believe that salvation for our schools lies in defining clearly specified educational objectives tied to a system of teacher accountability criticize both of these other types of developers for not being "scientific," "efficient," or facing the "real" problems of the schools; and they make little use of the creations and findings of these other types of developers, behaving towards them as though they were adversaries competing for a scarce resource. In general, it is common to find that a curriculum developer who considers it essential to create well-written didactic materials cannot understand why another developer would dedicate himself to creating physical manipulatives for discovery learning; that this latter developer cannot tolerate reading about another developer's attempts to construct skill oriented individualized instruction kits; while this developer, in turn, cannot keep from arguing with still another developer who spends his time stressing the importance of meaningful verbal learning that originates from carefully controlled student-teacher interactions.

The state of disarray within the field of curriculum is evident not only in the inability of curriculum workers to deal effectively with the diversity that exists among themselves, but also in the disoriented manner in which other educators and the general public become embroiled in confusing and self-defeating controversies over curricular issues that originate within the publicized conflicts among curriculum workers. We hear and participate in endless debates about the value of the "traditional" math, the "new" math, the "new-new" math, the "new-new-new" math, and the "back-to-basic-skills" math. We read articles about new instructional materials that are better than the old textbooks and new textbooks that are better than the old instructional materials. We debate about competency-based education and wonder if it must replace the present education. We hear discussions about efficient new ways of teaching large groups of students through the use of computers and television, and about why we must use the more effective and even more recently developed individualized instruction kits. And we argue over how our tax money was recently used to buy new innovative instructional materials that some expert recently said were the by-products of a passing fad that has already died out.

One of the reasons for this disarray within the field of curriculum is that curriculum workers often understand and deal with complex controversies by focusing superficially upon the overt face value of the issues involved in the controversy. Curriculum workers who are concerned with mathematics curricula, for example, might be found debating whether it is more important to teach an *understanding* of multiplication or whether it is more important to teach the *skill* of multiplying. There is nothing intrinsically wrong with debating this issue. The problem is that such debates usually lead curriculum workers to abandon any attempt to meaningfully understand common concerns, to rationally communicate with each other, and to constructively cope with their differences.

This is because there are usually profound disputes over divergent value systems which underlie disagreements over curricular issues, issues that are too often discussed only superficially. These value systems are usually assumed to comprise a curriculum worker's beliefs about such things as the goals of education, the types of content which should be included in the curriculum, the types of learnings the curriculum is to enable the child to acquire, or the instructional procedures that should be imbedded within the curriculum. Curriculum workers who recognize that one must look beyond the superficial level of discourse to the divergent value systems of those in conflict are likely to discuss, for example, with respect to the multiplication issue mentioned above, whether the types of learnings children are to acquire as a result of experiencing a curriculum are understandings or skills; whether the content of a curriculum is to have the form of didactic statements (understandings) or competencies (skills); whether the goal of education is understanding the traditions and discoveries of our culture (understandings), or learning the skills that will enable one to constructively function in adult life (skills);

or whether the role of the teacher is to be a knowledgeable authority who transmits that which is known to those who do not know it (understandings), or a manager/foreman of children who efficiently supervises their learning (skills). Unfortunately, analyzing the controversies among themselves at this level of distinguishing divergent value systems and noting conflicting conceptions of curriculum does not seem to help curriculum workers to better understand each other, communicate with each other, or cope with their differences. But it does help curriculum workers in conflict to agree that they actually *are in disagreement over significant issues* (which is often denied) and it does help them to better discern *what the issues are* that they are in disagreement about (which often eludes curriculum workers embroiled in controversy).

Something else, however, is needed in order to gain insight into the differences among curriculum workers. We must shift our attention from the issues and values to the curriculum workers. We must understand the ideologies of curriculum workers: the driving myths that motivate curriculum workers to take the value positions they do; the theoretical gestalts that cause curriculum workers to conceive of curriculum as they do; and the conceptual frameworks that are utilized by curriculum workers when thinking about and acting upon curricular issues. We must understand, for example, why one curriculum worker sees his job to be one of enculturating children into a particular community of academic scholars by giving the children the understandings and orientation that will allow them to become one of those scholars (understandings), while another curriculum worker sees his job to be one of efficiently fulfilling the needs of society by providing the child with the skills that will enable him to function constructively as a member of society during his adult life (skills). Or, viewing the same ideological positions from another perspective, we must understand why one curriculum worker sees himself as a mini-scholar perpetuating the survival of the academic discipline to which he belongs (understandings), while another curriculum worker sees himself as an unbiased agent of society whose interests he is to promote in an efficient and scientific manner (skills).

In addition—and this is of crucial significance—we must carefully analyze the language of curriculum workers. Much of the disarray within the field of curriculum comes from the wide variety of meanings that curriculum workers attach to words such as knowledge, learning, and teaching. For example, while discussing what should be learned in school, two curriculum workers might both use the word knowledge, with one curriculum worker using the word to mean "cognitive understandings which allow one to comprehend certain things" (understandings), while the other worker uses the word to mean "behavioral capabilities which allow one to do certain things" (skills). What is important here is that the two curriculum workers are likely to become embroiled in disagreement without ever realizing that they are using the word knowledge to mean very different things; with a probable result being that they will develop an inability to meaningfully understand each other, rationally communicate with each other, or constructively deal with their conflicting intents for the school.

In dealing with linguistic issues, we must be careful not to treat the language of curriculum workers in isolation from the ideologies (driving myths, theoretical gestalts, and conceptual frameworks) that allow the curriculum worker to give personal meaning to his language. Similarly, in dealing with the ideologies used by curriculum workers, we must be careful not to treat those ideologies in isolation from the ways in which they are expressed through language and behavior.

It is the intent of this book to provide the reader with the ability to understand some of the disarray within the field of curriculum and to deal effectively with some of the diversity among curriculum workers. To do this, four ideologies representative of the range of different ideologies used by curriculum workers will be examined. In doing so, particular attention will be given to the ways in which the ideologies examined are manifested in the language and behavior of their users.

It is hoped that this book will aid the reader in understanding the field of curriculum in several ways. First, it is hoped that the reader will obtain an overview of the range of different ideologies held by curriculum workers. By doing so, it is hoped that the reader will come to better understand and deal effectively with the diversity of conflicting curricular positions (involving issues and values) competing for influence within the field of curriculum. Second, it is hoped that the reader will obtain insight into the

nature of and ramifications of one of the most important
parameters affecting how curriculum workers behave and speak:
their ideologies. By doing this, it is hoped both that the reader will
come to better understand some of the motives affecting his own
behavior and language and that the reader will acquire
the ability to read between the lines of a controversy over
curricular issues or values to see the motives impelling curricular
combatants to speak and behave as they do. And, third, it is hoped
that this book will enable the reader to make sense out of the
ways in which language is used within the field of curriculum:
there being massive linguistic confusion when terms such as
learning, knowledge, and teaching take on a wide variety of
meanings. It is hoped that the reader will gain the insight into the
meanings underlying both curricular language and his own
language that will enable him to navigate within the field of
curriculum with confidence.

To accomplish this, curriculum developers will be focused upon
as a well-documented, representative, and manageably sized subset
of curriculum workers; and four curricular ideologies used by
them will be described. These curricular ideologies will be entitled
(1) the Social Efficiency Ideology, (2) the Scholar Academic
Ideology, (3) the Child Study Ideology, and (4) the Social
Reconstruction Ideology. In discussing each ideology, this book
will first examine the underpinnings of the ideology. It will next
specify the linguistic and behavioral positions taken by the
representatives of the ideology with respect to their beliefs about
the nature of knowledge, learning, the child, teaching, evaluation,
and their professional role.   After each of the four curricular
ideologies is presented in this way, all four will be jointly
recapitulated, compared, contrasted, and analyzed in the conclud-
ing chapter of this book.

In the remainder of this chapter, two different types of
discussions will be pursued.

First, a brief overview of the four curricular ideologies will be
presented, and the nature of the curricular ideologies will be
further defined.

Second, the diversity and disarray within the field of curriculum
will be further elaborated in order to properly place this study

within the context of the entire field of curriculum and to clearly define its intent and limits.

CURRICULAR IDEOLOGIES

The Social Efficiency Ideology, the Scholar Academic Ideology, the Child Study Ideology, and the Social Reconstruction Ideology are the names given to the curricular ideologies examined within this book. As they are herein elaborated, these ideologies pertain to the programmatic intents of curriculum developers while they engage in the process of curriculum creation.

The Social Efficiency Ideology. The central concern of the Social Efficiency Ideology is "scientific instrumentalism." This concern asserts that curriculum should be developed in a "scientific" manner and that curriculum development should be an "instrument" for fulfilling the wishes of a client.

The ultimate client is taken to be society, and curriculum developers conceive of themselves as being instrumental in perpetuating the functioning of society by preparing the individual child to lead a meaningful adult life within society. Man's essence is believed to lie in the activities or competencies he is capable of performing. The means by which an individual achieves an education is by learning to perform the functions one must perform to be socially constructive.

The curriculum developer's first job is to determine the needs of society—his client. What will fulfill these needs are called the terminal objectives of the curriculum. The developer must then find the most efficient way of producing a product, the educated man, who meets the terminal objectives of the curriculum and thus fulfills the needs of society.

The most efficient way of achieving the terminal objectives of the curriculum is assumed to follow from applying the routines of scientific procedure to curriculum making. Central to the Social Efficiency developer's conception of scientific procedure is the assumption that change in human behavior takes place within a cause-effect, action-reaction, or stimulus-response context. Conceiving of change in human behavior (i.e., learning) within this context requires of the Social Efficiency developer that he predetermine the relationship between cause and effect, action and reaction, or stimulus and response, and that he then plan the causes, actions, or stimuli (i.e., learning experiences) which in a direct and predictable manner will lead to the desired effects, reactions, or responses. As such, two things that play an important role within the Social Efficiency Ideology are the concept of learning (or change in human behavior designed by the curriculum developer) and the creation and sequencing of learning experiences (the causes, actions, or stimuli which will lead to the desirable effect, reaction, or response).

The developer working within the Social Efficiency Ideology conceives of his role in creating curricula to be that of carrying out a task for a client. In doing this he engages in two types of activities. One involves the discovery of terminal objectives for the curriculum (what will satisfy the needs of his client). The other involves the scientific design of learning experiences and a sequencing of those learning experiences to achieve the terminal objectives of the curriculum in as efficient and effective a manner as possible. Within this context, accountability of the developer for the curriculum he creates in order to fulfill the task he undertakes for his client plays an important role; and it is his client to whom the curriculum developer holds himself accountable.

The Scholar Academic Ideology. Curriculum developers working within the Scholar Academic Ideology view curriculum creation from the perspective of the academic disciplines. They assume a loose equivalence between the academic disciplines, the world of the intellect, and the world of knowledge. The central task of education is taken to be the extension of the components of this equivalence. They are to be extended both on the cultural level, as reflected in the discovery of new truth, and on the individual level, as reflected in the enculturation of individuals into civilization's accumulated knowledge and ways of knowing.

An academic discipline is viewed as a hierarchical community of people in search for truth within one part of the universe of knowledge. The hierarchical communities consist of inquirers into the truth (the scholars at the top of the hierarchy), teachers of the truth (who disseminate the truth that has been discovered by the scholars), and learners of the truth (students whose job it is to learn the truth so that they may become proficient members of the discipline).

The aim of education for the Scholar Academic developer is the extension of his discipline by introducing young people into it. This involves making youth members of his academic discipline by first moving them into the discipline as students, and by then moving them from the bottom of the hierarchy towards its top. The means of accomplishing the extension of the discipline is through the transmission of the knowledge of the discipline to students. The curriculum provides the means of doing this. It derives both its meaning and its reason for existence from the academic disciplines. A Scholar Academic developer's major concern is to construct his curriculum in such a way that it reflects the essence of his discipline.

The Child Study Ideology. Curriculum developers working within the Child Study Ideology focus directly upon the child as the central concern underlying their endeavors as they attempt to create curricula that are based on the child's innate nature. They begin not with the needs of society or the academic disciplines but with the needs and concerns of the individual child.

The Child Study developer conceives of the child as containing his own capabilities for growth, as the agent who must actualize his own capabilities, and as essentially good in nature. In addition, the child is viewed as the source of content for the curriculum; his ends and his means are considered to be the appropriate ends and means for the curriculum.

This leads the Child Study developer to treat the concept of growth as the central theme of his endeavors. Growth of the child in terms of his unfolding in conformity with the laws of his being becomes the objective of the developer. As a result, education becomes an affair involving the drawing out of the inherent capabilities of the child. It is a facilitator of the natural growth of the child, and it will produce healthy, virtuous, and beneficial learnings if what is drawn out is allowed to naturally be coaxed out of the child's innate capabilities.

The potential for growth lies within the child. However, the child is stimulated to grow and therefore learn as a result of interacting with his environment. Learning is thus considered a function of the interaction between a child and his environment. And because the particular interactions of the child within his environment are assumed to be unique to the child involved in the interactions, it is further assumed that the result of learning (i.e., knowledge) is also unique to the child.

Within the Child Study Ideology, curriculum is thus thought of as contexts, environments, or units of work within which children can make knowledge for themselves by interacting with other children, teachers, and things. It is the job of the curriculum developer to carefully create those contexts, environments, or units of work which will stimulate growth in students as they create meaning (and thus learning and knowledge) for themselves.

The Social Reconstruction Ideology. Curriculum developers working within the Social Reconstruction Ideology view curriculum creation from a social perspective. First, they assume that society is in an unhealthy condition. Its very survival is believed to be threatened. This is because the traditional mechanisms developed by society to deal with its problems are seen as obsolete and ineffectual. Second, adherents of this ideology assume that something can be done to keep society from destroying itself. This necessitates developing a vision of a society better than the existing one, a society within which the problems and conflicts of the existent society are resolved. Third, this ideology demands that action be directed towards reconstructing society along the lines suggested by the vision of the new society.

Social Reconstruction developers assume that education of "the masses" is the social process through which the society is to be reconstructed. These developers have a supreme faith in the ability of education, through the medium of curriculum, to educate students to understand the nature of their society in such a way that they will develop a vision of a better society, and then act so as to bring that vision into existence.

Because Social Reconstruction developers view education through such a strong social perspective, the nature of society as it *is* and as it *should be* become the determinants of most of their concepts and assumptions. For example, the following three crucial aspects of life are socially defined. First, human experience is believed to be most fundamentally shaped by cultural factors. Meaning in man's life is defined in terms of his relationship to society. Second, education is viewed as a function of the society which supports it. It must be interpreted within the context of a particular culture. Third, truth and knowledge are interpreted as based in and defined by cultural assumptions. They are idiosyncratic to each society and testable with respect to criteria based in social consensus rather than empirical or logical criteria.

As a result, Social Reconstruction developers believe that there is no good individual, good education, truth, or knowledge apart from some conception of the nature of the good society. Since society is undergoing a crisis, it follows that the good man, the good education, truth, and knowledge are also undergoing a crisis.

The aim of the Social Reconstruction developer is to rectify this situation: to eliminate from his culture those aspects which he believes undesirable; to substitute in their place social values which he believes desirable; and by so doing to aid in reconstructing his culture so that it and its constituent members will attain maximum satisfaction of their material and spiritual wants. To accomplish this, the developer directs his energy towards creating a social consensus which rejects the faults of the existing society and which accepts the virtues of the future better society. To develop this social consensus, the developer creates a socio-educational program, a curriculum, that is designed to manipulate society at the point where it inducts the child into the life of the culture. By doing so, it is hoped that society can be greatly improved.

Each of the curricular ideologies has its unique history. Observing the traditions out of which each grew gives an invaluable sense of perspective. Although the origin and evolution of each ideology provides a fascinating enterprise in itself, this book will concern itself with the ideologies only as they have existed since 1880. The nature of the Social Efficiency Ideology will be explored by examining the tradition linking Franklin Bobbitt, W.W. Charters, and Robert M. Gagné. The Scholar Academic Ideology will be examined by simultaneously looking at the period of curriculum development which resulted from the work of Charles Eliot and the Committee of Ten in the 1890's, and by focusing upon the "new curriculum" movement of the 1960's. Evolution of the Child Study Ideology will include an examination of the continuity of belief linking the work of the "early progressives" and the recent "open education" movement. And examination of the Social Reconstruction Ideology will include an investigation of the tradition publicly initiated by George Counts which evolved through the "life adjustment" curricula into the present. These ideologies are not studied with any historical intent. The intent is to savor them within the richness of the traditions out of which they grew rather than to view them solely as they are manifested at the present moment.

The doctrines, opinions, and belief systems of developers have been called *curricular ideologies*. There are two reasons behind the use of the phrase *curricular ideology*. One relates to the choice of the word *ideology*. This word is used because it is necessary to distinguish between motives that underlie behavior and beliefs that are articulated. Our concern is with the former and not the latter. The problem here is that expressed intent is frequently contradicted by actual behavior. Curriculum developers are often not conscious of the major assumptions underlying their actions, just as adherents of most religions or political parties are often not conscious of the motives and impulses that drive them to act within the approved modes of behavior sanctioned by their religion or political party. A distinction needed to be made between the myths, doctrines, opinions, and belief systems motivating curriculum developers to behave as they do and the *verbalizations* that curriculum developers articulate. The word *ideology* is used for this purpose. The phrase *curricular ideology* is thus meant to imply the same type of belief system as religious or political convictions, with the difference that it is occupationally oriented.

The other reason behind the use of the phrase *curricular ideology* relates to the choice of the word *curricular*. It is necessary to distinguish between the curricular domain, pedagogical domain, epistemological domain, learning theory domain, psychoanalytic domain, developmental domain, and so on, when discussing the endeavors of curriculum developers. This is because the curriculum developer often behaves differently when working within these different areas of discourse, just as a teacher often relates differently to his own children and his students. The developer as developer is often different from the developer as psychologist, teacher, or epistemologist. The conceptual context within which a developer works is tied to the role within which he sees himself functioning. As such, *curricular ideologies* refer to endeavors of the curriculum developer while engaging specifically in creating curricula. His behavior while engaging in other roles is excluded from this book.

There are two kinds of classificatory systems useful in illuminating the differences among curriculum developers. These systems are illustrated in Figure 1.1. One classificatory system is designed to map out the entire population of curriculum developers into a finite set of disjoint categories into which any developer can be uniquely classified. Figure 1.1a portrays this kind of classificatory system, in which the entire population of curriculum developers is divided into four separate categories—SE, SA, CS, and SR. Here there is assumed to exist a great deal of uniformity within each category and a great amount of difference between categories. This kind of classificatory system is not useful in distinguishing between the curricular ideologies. For our purposes it is more sensible to use a classificatory system consisting of ideal types that is designed to portray a finite number of positions representing the range of existent practices utilized by curriculum developers. Figure 1.1b portrays this kind of classificatory system, which consists of four ideal types—the four curricular ideologies—which serve as models that approximate the essence of the practices engaged in by curriculum developers. Here each ideal type provides a model that idealizes a particular mode of curriculum development; with the individual practices engaged in by curriculum developers being approximations to the ideal types. In Figure 1.1b, curriculum developers cluster around the ideal types without having to behave exactly in accordance with the characteristics of the ideal types—their distance from an ideal type in a particular direction being an indicator of both how and how much they differ from that ideal type. The four ideologies—ideal types—have been chosen because they offer dramatic alternatives to each other, because they seem to be prototypes around which developers cluster—the density of the set of all curriculum developers in Figure 1.1b being highest around ideal types SE, SA, CS, and SR—and because they seem to represent the range of existent practices utilized by developers. Because the curricular ideologies represent ideal types abstracted from reality, and not reality itself, even though developers are spoken of as behaving in accordance with certain beliefs, it is difficult to find developers

Figure 1.1

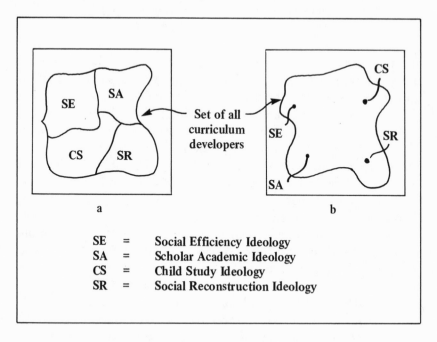

SE = Social Efficiency Ideology
SA = Scholar Academic Ideology
CS = Child Study Ideology
SR = Social Reconstruction Ideology

who *exactly fit* the characterizations; and even though the behavior of most developers approximates the characteristics of only one of the ideal types, there do exist developers whose behavior is a *combination* of the characteristics of more than one ideal type.

Disarray within the field of curriculum is not limited to ideological diversity among curriculum workers. There are many other factors, causes, and symptoms illustrative of the disarray. In the remainder of this chapter three issues to which curriculum workers have generated a diversity of solutions—with which they are incapable of dealing effectively—will be elaborated. These issues are (a) the types of endeavors in which curriculum workers engage; (b) the types of concerns at the heart of the field of curriculum; and (c) the best and proper definition of the word curriculum. Briefly examining these issues will shed some light upon them. It will also provide the vehicle for properly placing this study within the context of the entire field of curriculum, clearly defining its intent and limits.

CURRICULUM WORKERS

There are many different types of endeavors engaged in by people who say, "I work within the field of curriculum." When a curriculum worker describes just exactly what he does, however, his colleagues frequently raise an eyebrow and the look that comes into their faces seems to say, "You are no curriculum worker, because I am a curriculum worker and that is not what I do." Too often discussion then devolves into a territorial dispute over whose efforts are most important or most central to the curriculum field. Such rivalry among curriculum workers should be unnecessary, for there are many different types of curricular endeavors that should supplement each other rather than detract from each other. Included among these is work which is pursued by at least the following five (not necessarily mutually exclusive) sets of people: curriculum practitioners, curriculum disseminators, curriculum evaluators, curriculum developers, and curriculum theoreticians.

Curriculum practitioners are those persons who use curricula within the instructional arena—be they classroom teachers, learning disability specialists, or administrators. A classroom teacher who uses a social studies textbook with children, who implements a reading program in his classroom, or who derives his science program from a science kit is a curriculum practitioner. A learning disabilities specialist who tutors a child individually in reading using specially written materials, or who implements a physical therapy program designed by a local hospital, is a curriculum practitioner. Similarly, an administrator who implements team teaching, who encourages his teachers to use open education techniques, who starts a vocational education program, who insists upon the use of a particular textbook series in a school, or who institutionalizes computerized course assignment of students in his school system according to stratified ability grouping is a curriculum practitioner.

Curriculum disseminators are those persons who make known to curriculum practitioners the existence of and proper methods of utilizing existing curricula. A curriculum disseminator might be a college professor, a salesman, or a school district subject matter specialist. A college professor teaching a methods course in which the newest available curricula were examined would be a curriculum disseminator. A salesman, whether from a non-profit curriculum development agency or a commercial publishing company, who tried to sell a new curricular package to a teacher or school administrator would be a curriculum disseminator. A school district subject-matter specialist who held an inservice workshop for teachers in his school district to expose them to new curriculum materials would be a curriculum disseminator.

Curriculum evaluators are those persons who collect and examine data for the purpose of reporting on the effectiveness, efficiency, and worth of the work done by curriculum practitioners, disseminators, or developers. An evaluator might be employed by a private testing service, a college research department, a school district central administration, a government monitoring agency, the accountability department of a publishing company, or the research staff of a curriculum development agency. His reports are meant to aid in the decision-making process as it concerns curricular issues. His reports might aid in the decision-making process before development begins (for example, by providing a community needs assessment or personnel resource assessment), during the development process (as in the case of a formative evaluation designed to improve an educational experience or product during its developmental phase by providing feedback to those creating it), or at the end of development (as in the case of a summative evaluation designed to provide information to potential consumers on either a program's overall effectiveness with respect to its own goals or on a program's comparative effectiveness with respect to the goals of competing programs). Data collected might refer to the implementation of programs by curriculum practitioners (for example, what happens to pupils in a classroom or teachers in a school), the dispersal of information by curriculum disseminators (for example, the effectiveness of a publisher's salesmen or the most efficient way to get school districts to implement a nationally prescribed program), or the creation of products by curriculum developers (be it a microscope, a mathematics textbook, or a multimedia K to 6 language program).

Curriculum developers are those persons who intentionally prepare curricular materials and strategies for others to use in the instructional arena. Important here is the phrase "for others to use." Curriculum developers can be textbook writers who work for large publishing firms; teachers who get together to prepare a curriculum guide prescribing what should be taught, to whom, and when for their local school district; specialists who work for federally funded curriculum development agencies to prepare curricular materials (such as the National Science Foundation science kits) for use by teachers; or university professors who design curricular systems (such as team teaching) for use by school administrators.

Finally, *curriculum theoreticians* are those persons who examine existing curricula, how curricula are used, disseminated, created, and evaluated; who speculate on what curricula should be like, and how curricula should be used, disseminated, created, and evaluated; and who probe the "whys" of their own examinations and speculations for the purpose of contributing to the general body of knowledge about effective curricular practice, dissemination, development, and evaluation. Be they university professors or researchers working for federally or privately funded research and development curriculum centers, theoreticians are the critics of the curricular enterprise and the overseers of the generalized and specific knowledge created by workers within the field of curriculum.

Effective interaction among curriculum workers is facilitated when those workers recognize that there are many interdependent endeavors to be undertaken within the curriculum field and many types of curriculum workers who undertake them. Effective interaction among curriculum workers is also facilitated when the history of endeavors engaged in by a curriculum worker are understood. For example, the differences between two curriculum theoreticians teaching courses in a university can be more easily appreciated, better understood, and more effectively accommodated when it is known that one began and spent much of his career teaching elementary school, while the other began and spent much of his career evaluating federally funded programs as a curriculum evaluator. Curriculum workers need not be forced into any one of the above mentioned categories, for the categories are neither mutually exclusive nor exhaustive of all possibilities. The categories have been presented both in order to illustrate some of the diversity that exists among curriculum workers (that contributes to their inability to deal effectively with the diversity that exists among themselves), and in order to clearly specify the intents of this book.

This book views the curriculum field from the perspective of the curriculum theoretician. In doing so it focuses specifically upon curriculum developers, because as a subset of curriculum workers they clearly and fairly represent the range of ideological positions held by all curriculum workers; because they are a manageably sized subset of curriculum workers to examine and write about in depth; and because they can be viewed in historical perspective, since their endeavors have been well documented over the last century. This book's applicability is not, however, limited solely to the endeavors of curriculum developers. The reader is encouraged to generalize its contents to the work of curriculum practitioners, disseminators, evaluators, and theoreticians.

Since this study will speak from the perspective of the curriculum theoretician, let us now turn our attention to the endeavors engaged in by curriculum theoreticians. The discussion that follows derives from observation of debates among curriculum theoreticians as to what kinds of concerns are at the heart of the field of curriculum: concerns over the true nature of the endeavor in which they should engage and of the field in which they work.

THE CURRICULAR DOMAIN

What men think affects how they behave, and how men think and behave affects the types of meaning they create. From their conceptions of the nature of the curricular domain have come the questions into which theoreticians have inquired. Having raised questions, curriculum theoreticians have proceeded to conduct research, perform experiments, and develop theories that derive their reason for existence from the questions posed. Having done so, they have given meaning and interpretation to what they have researched, thought, observed, and created—in accordance with the conceptions of the nature of the curricular domain and the nature of the inquiry within the curricular domain.

Man feels comfortable within the worlds of meaning he circumscribes about his life; he feels secure treading well-trodden paths that he knows by heart; he likes to create meaning and think about what he has created and create anew and think upon what he has thought in an endless cycle. By so doing, those who have labored hard and long within the curricular domain have created well-formed positions which dictate the nature of the field. They have created subdisciplines of curriculum theory, each of which has its own well-defined structure.

In order to capture the nature of the subdisciplines of curriculum theory it may be useful to digress into an informal analogy concerning the different types of answers that can be given to the question, "What is the nature of a painting as a work of art?" Some art critics say that a painting must be examined in order to discover its essence the painting must be examined in detail as a physical object. "It is five feet by four feet. It is an oil painting on a burlap canvas. It is composed of two ounces of yellow paint, one ounce of blue paint, five ounces of white paint, etc. It depicts a house in a field next to a barn. In the lower half of the painting the artist used a palette knife and in the upper half he used a number four brush." A painting is conceived of as an object. The way in which one comes to know its essence is by measuring it, weighing it, examining it, analyzing it—in and of itself separate from any context within which it exists.

Other critics disagree, saying that the essence of a painting lies in the feelings and thoughts and emotions and actions and recollections and hopes it inspires in those who view it. These art critics hold that a painting has meaning not in and of itself but because of the actions and interactions it stimulates in the environment within which it exists. "What will you pay for it? It makes me feel happy all over. It brings up memories of that summer we spent together in Paris. When they look at it they become inspired to violent political action in the cause of freedom." Such are the inquiries, the observations, the analyses offered by those who view the essence of art to lie in the actions and interactions it sets up among those who come in contact with it.

A third group of commentators on art might take still another position: that the essence of a painting lies in the intent of the creator. In this view it is what the artist intended to say or to do or to make that is of prime importance. "He was lonely and wanted to express loneliness. He was trying to express his grief over his mother's death. He was trying to inspire us to act in the cause of ecology. He wanted to show us what his childhood was like." From this perspective it is the intent of the artist which defines the essence of a painting. It is the intent of the actor, in and of itself, that is important.

These ways of viewing art—as object, as interaction, and as intent—provide an analogue for the types of inquiry used by curricular theoreticians. They provide three different starting points from which theoreticians begin their work; three different structures of inquiry within which curricular meanings are created; three approaches to the curricular domain that are used by theoreticians as they inquire into the nature of curriculum and the thoughts and actions of curriculum workers.

One group of curricular theorists views curriculum as an object, and curricular activity as activity pertaining to curriculum as an object. Their focus is upon curriculum as a thing unto itself and curricular activity as action having to do with the thing. Another group of curriculum theorists views curriculum as that which occurs in the school room or school house, and curricular activity as activity pertaining to curriculum as interaction. The interactions and the effects of interactions taking place during instruction-related activities provide the essence of curriculum. A third group of curriculum theorists view curriculum as having to do primarily with the intentions and modes of behavior of those attempting to influence and control the education of others. The essence of curriculum is here taken to lie within the intentions of curriculum workers and the manner in which they attempt to actualize their intentions.

Inquirers into curriculum as object begin their inquiry by raising such questions as: "What is the substance of the curriculum, and how is that substance embedded in learning experiences? What is the organization of curriculum in terms of scope, sequence, integration, and continuity? How is the curriculum to be disseminated? What is it that curriculum theoreticians, creators, evaluators, and critics say about curriculum as object?"

Those who view curriculum as interaction begin their inquiries by raising different questions: "What is occurring within the classroom? What is the effect of the curriculum on students and teachers over the long haul? What is the 'hidden curriculum'? How do different curricula affect the instructional arena? What do curricular theoreticians, creators, evaluators, and critics see when they observe instruction?"

Theoreticians who inquire into curriculum as intent begin by raising a third type of question: "What is the nature of the belief systems of curriculum workers? How are different curricula justified? What procedures are used to create and analyze curricula? What do creators of meaning within the curriculum field desire to accomplish through their efforts?"

In each case members of each subdiscipline of curriculum theory, having asked questions which reflect their view of the nature of the curricular domain, proceed to do their research, make their observations, and create their meanings based upon the types of questions which they have asked.

In addition, curriculum theoreticians working within each subdiscipline of curriculum theory tend to lose contact with theoreticians in other subdisciplines of curriculum theory, and tend to pursue their interests as though other types of curriculum theoreticians do not exist. The result is a lack of healthy interaction among curriculum theoreticians, the development of blind spots within their thinking, rivalry among curriculum theoreticians for dominance within the field, and confusion among other curriculum workers as to the comparative worth of the varying messages being delivered by curriculum theoreticians.

In listening to a curriculum theoretician, one is wise to remember that theoreticians tend to view curricular phenomena from the viewpoint of either curriculum as intent, curriculum as object, or curriculum as interaction. One is wise to determine the viewpoint held by the curriculum theoretician so that his biases and blind spots can be kept in mind and compensated for. To coordinate the different messages of curriculum theoreticians, one might remember how physicists resolved the definitional problem surrounding the nature of light. They chose to treat light as waves when it was useful to do so and to treat it as corpuscles when it was useful to do so. Similarly, we should perhaps accept that there are different ways of viewing curricular phenomena, each of which is useful for certain purposes.

This study of the endeavors of curriculum developers views the curriculum field from the perspective of curriculum as intent. The discussion herein deals primarily with the intentions of curriculum workers and the manner in which they attempt to actualize their intentions.

CURRICULUM

This brings us to the point of raising a seemingly insoluble question: What is curriculum? Workers within the field of curriculum have sought for many years to determine a proper definition of the word curriculum. The end result of their endeavors always seems to be the addition of another new improved definition, more debate over the issue, and further criticism of other inadequate definitions. This is not surprising, for each of the many different types of workers within the field of curriculum brings his own biases to his attempts to define the word. To gain insight into the range and multiplicity of meanings attached to the word curriculum, let us use the results of our previous discussions.

It has been shown how curriculum theoreticians tend to view curricular phenomena from one of three viewpoints. Most curriculum workers tend to view curricular phenomena from one of the same three viewpoints: curriculum as object, curriculum as interaction, or curriculum as intent. Workers holding each of these viewpoints use the word curriculum differently. Let us look at some of their conceptions of what a curriculum is.

Curriculum as Object
- a textbook
- a textbook series spanning many grades
- the content that defines the essence of a textbook or textbook series
- the curriculum guide, course of study, or subject syllabi distributed by the superintendent's office
- a box of planned activity cards telling teachers how to conduct exciting learning experiences
- the description of the scope and sequence of learnings children are to encounter in a school
- the program of studies (information, courses, subjects, or

specific course content) students are exposed to while traveling the racecourse of subject matter to be acquired in school
- an outline of a course of study
- the plans for an educational program
- the description of a series of activities designed to change the knowledge and competence of someone or some group of persons
- the design for an educational environment
- a multimedia box of materials including tapes, slides, films, naturalistic objects, books, and records pertaining to a particular subject
- a box of individualized instruction activity cards along with a teacher's guide, answer sheets, and evaluative instruments
- a written plan for action that is designed to guide the teacher during instruction (the plan, not the action)

Curriculum as Interaction
- all of the experiences children encounter within a school
- all of the planned and organized experiences children encounter within a school (this omits learning about smoking in the lavatories)
- all of the planned and organized experiences that are designed for instructional purposes that children encounter within a school (this omits lunchroom, recess, and some extracurricular experiences)
- a series of activities in which children participate that were designed to change their knowledge or competence
- a planned intervention in a child's life during school designed to accelerate the education (behavioral competence) of the child
- everything that actually occurs during the administration, planning, teaching, and learning in a school

Curriculum as Intent
- the sets of intended outcomes an educational system desires to produce
- a set of intended learnings for an instructional program
- the goals or objectives that an educational system hopes its learners will achieve

- the plans for future occurrences within an educational program that include a needs assessment, educational objectives, learning experiences, an organizational schema, and evaluative instruments
- a planned set of behavioral goals that are organized in a manner to facilitate evaluation of learner outcomes
- the design for the future of an educative environment
- the blueprint of experiences that is planned for students.

As can be seen, there are a multiplicity of meanings attached to the word curriculum. The manner of organizing these meanings that was just presented—by focusing on those meanings pertaining to curriculum as object, interaction, or intent—is just one of many ways of organizing them. Another approach to organizing the variety of existing meanings would be to focus upon the meanings given to the word curriculum by the different types of curricular workers—practitioners, disseminators, developers, evaluators, and theoreticians. This would be an alternate approach because each of these workers views the field of curriculum from a slightly different perspective. However, this approach is not very useful because of the enormous internal variation of occupations within each of the categories of curriculum workers herein delineated.

But there is something to be learned from the way in which the types of endeavor engaged in by a curriculum worker affect the meaning he attaches to the word curriculum. To demonstrate how occupation affects the meaning given to the word, let us illustrate some ways that, for example, different types of curriculum practitioners attach meaning to the word curriculum.

A classroom teacher might believe that curriculum is "all of the planned and organized experiences designed to help children learn that take place within the school." A school guidance counselor might assert that curriculum is "all of the experiences children encounter within the school—be they planned or unplanned, organized or unorganized, instructional or non-instructional." A remedial reading teacher might assume curriculum to be "the reading skills it is hoped that poor readers will acquire." A vice-principal in charge of supplies for the school might think that curriculum is "all of the instructional materials—books, tapes, films, learning kits, etc.—used within the school by teachers to help children learn." A school principal might say that "curriculum consists of the curriculum guides or course syllabi published by the school district and distributed by the superintendent of schools." A subject matter specialist for a school system (such as a mathematics coordinator) might consider curriculum to be the "textbook series ordered by the school board for the school system on recommendation of the subject matter specialists." The school superintendent might believe curriculum is "a set of behavioral goals it is hoped the school system's students will achieve." The chairman of the school board might consider curriculum to be "a community-purchased bundle of teacher-pupil interactions produced by combining school buildings, instructional and non-instructional supplies, time of administrators and auxiliary personnel, time of teachers, and time of pupils."

It can be seen that the types of endeavors engaged in by a curriculum worker can affect his understanding of the word curriculum—just as it has been indicated that a person's perspective on the curriculum field can affect the way in which he attaches meaning to the word curriculum. Similarly, a person's conception of what the word curriculum means affects his perspective on the field of curriculum and the types of working roles in which he can see himself engaging.

Some curriculum writers have claimed that the definitional issues surrounding the word curriculum are of little significance, and that no matter how the word curriculum is defined, the definition does not significantly affect the types of issues and problems dealt with by either curriculum workers or the curriculum field as a whole. This may be true to the extent that curriculum workers go about their work somewhat in disregard of the precise manner in which they verbalize their several definitions of curriculum, and to the extent that there is a great deal more haggling over precise wording of the definitions than is warranted. However, it is certainly not true to the extent that a person's internalized definition of curriculum dramatically affects the ways he deals with curricular issues and problems, and the types of curricular issues and problems with which he deals. It seems appropriate to accept the definitional problem as a real and necessary one and to accept the existence of multiple meanings for the word curriculum, each of which has its own justifiable origins, purposes, and reasons for existence.

Given this general background on the meaning given to the word curriculum, we are now faced with the task of formulating a meaning for curriculum that can be used within this study. The meaning we will assign to the word curriculum is determined by two factors: first, that the meaning be suited to discussing the programmatic endeavors of curriculum developers; and, second, that the meaning be sufficiently broad to encompass all meanings given to the word by curriculum developers. The definition offered is created for the purpose of facilitating this study. It is not necessarily intended to have any broader purpose.

Within this book we will use the word curriculum to mean "that output of the curriculum development process that is intended for use in planning instruction." There are several implications of this definition. First, there is an implicit distinction made between the curriculum development process and the instructional process. Curriculum theoreticians debate what the nature of and relationship between these processes is, should be, or might be. For our purposes it is sufficient to note that the curriculum development process pertains primarily to what curriculum *developers* do, while the instructional process pertains primarily to what curriculum *practitioners* do; to note that the curriculum development process is characterized by the word *planning*, while the instructional process is characterized by the word *execution*; to note that curriculum is thus both conceived of as an *output* of the curriculum development process and as an *input* into the instructional process; and to note that there is an overlap of endeavor among these two processes, and that similar types of activity are carried out within both of them. Second, curriculum is an output of the curriculum development process. It must be *planned* before implementation takes place. Curriculum as interaction is considered to be curriculum only if it is planned to be such before it is implemented. Third, curriculum is created with the intention that it will be used sometime in the future. Curriculum implies anticipated future use and excludes after-the-fact accounts of what occurred during instruction that simply have a function of reporting what occurred. Finally, this definition of curriculum distinguishes between all of the products of the curriculum development endeavor and those intended for use in instruction. A curriculum developer may produce such things as articles on learning theory, formative evaluation instruments, piles of memos, and various types of magazine advertisements, but within this study, only that material which was produced for use in planning instruction will be considered to be curriculum.

2.
Scholar Academic Ideology

CURRICULUM AND THE DISCIPLINES
Disciplines as Curriculum

Curriculum developers working within the Scholar Academic Ideology view curriculum creation from the perspective of the academic disciplines.[1] The induction of the child into an academic discipline is the goal of each of their curricula. They create curricula by working within the domains of their academic disciplines as though they are functionaries of their disciplines. And they attempt to make each curriculum an epitome of its parent discipline. The following statement gives the flavor of the way in which these curriculum developers see the world through the eyes of an academic discipline.

> Initiation into the disciplines of knowledge, our vehicle for becoming fully human, is the worthwhile activity for the curriculum of general education. It provides the base upon which the person as a person can develop to realize his full stature as a free mind and as a citizen. All this is not to imply that the individual and society are not important, but they become, temporarily at least, secondary, as we endeavor to establish a framework of objectives for selecting kinds of learning experiences which will inculcate knowledge and abilities of most worth. The curriculum must therefore draw upon analyses of the nature of knowledge and the inherent human abilities it develops in order to determine its nature, prior to analyses of society, the learner, and the

learning process. The last three will at least add very
useful glosses to the framework, but should not determine it . . . . We should therefore ground our curricular
objectives in the distinctive disciplines of knowledge,
rather than in social needs, theories of personality, or in
a notional base knowledge for "living in the modern
world." For it is the disciplines themselves which
predetermine these important factors, as well as our
underlying ethical conception of what is good and what
is worthwhile.[2]

Our discussion of the Scholar Academic Ideology will now follow
the course of elaborating upon the larger meaning of some of the
phrases within this statement.

Initiation into the Disciplines

Initiation of children into the disciplines of knowledge is the
underlying motive of curriculum developers working within the
Scholar Academic Ideology. On one hand, this involves *initiating*
children into an academic discipline at the level at which it is being
taught—that is, for example, helping ten-year-old children behave
as ten-year-old novice mathematicians, physicists, or economists.
On the other hand, it involves enculturating (or inducting)
children into an academic discipline in such a way that when they
grow up they will (if they have the potential and so desire)
become active members of that discipline—that is, for example,
preparing a ten-year-old child to become a chemist, linguist, or
historian. What is crucial here is that the developer creates his
curriculum so that the child who encounters it will learn to know,
think, and behave in the same way as the university academician
does. This involves more than simply creating an educational
program designed to inform the child about an academic discipline. A curriculum is to initiate and enculturate children *into* a
discipline and not inform them *about* a discipline. As such, the
Scholar Academic developer tries to create curriculum in such a
way that, for example, "The schoolboy learning physics *is* a
physicist"[3] performing the same type of intellectual activity as is
performed by the professional physicist. This means that the
curriculum must convey more than just the knowledge of an
academic discipline. It must also convey such things as the

academician's ways of thinking and feeling about things. Bruner hints at this when he writes:

A body of knowledge, enshrined in a university faculty and embodied in a series of authoritative volumes, is the result of much prior intellectual activity. To instruct someone in these disciplines is not a matter of getting him to commit results to mind. Rather, it is to teach him to participate in the process that makes possible the establishment of knowledge. We teach a subject not to produce little living libraries on that subject, but, rather, to get a student to think mathematically for himself, to consider matters as an historian does, to take part in the process of knowledge-getting.[4]

As such, curricula created by Scholar Academic developers do not embody a back-to-the-basics, get-tough, content-oriented approach to education. To think of them as such is to misunderstand the developer's endeavors—endeavors directed toward translating a discipline as academicians know it into viable experiences that allow children to behave as the academicians do, in an attempt to enculturate children into the discipline by enabling them to think, behave, and feel as academicians do.

Grounding Curriculum in a Discipline

In grounding his curriculum in a distinctive academic discipline, the developer attempts to construct his curriculum so that it becomes a reflection of, or epitome of, the academic discipline. J. Myron Atkin's descripton of the basic flavor of curriculum development efforts in a number of disciplines illustrates this:

When one talks with the initiators of such projects, particularly at the beginning of their efforts, one finds that they do not begin by talking about the manner in which they would like to change pupils' behavior. Rather they are dissatisfied with existing curricula in their respective subject fields, and they want to build something new. If pressed, they might indicate that existing programs stress concepts considered trivial by those who practice the discipline. They might also say that the curriculum poorly *reflects* styles of intellectual inquiry in the various fields. Press them further, and they might say that *they want to build a new program that more accurately displays the "essence" of history, or physics, or economics or whatever.* Or a program that better transmits a comprehension of the elaborate and elegant interconnections among various concepts within the discipline.[5]

The developer conceives his curriculum as embodying a portion of the discipline itself. He tries to make his curriculum reflect the nature of the discipline in such a way that students coming in contact with the curriculum will be exposed to the essence of the discipline itself.

Drawing upon the Discipline's Knowledge

In formulating the substance of their curricula, Scholar Academic developers "draw upon analyses of the nature of knowledge" within a discipline. In doing so they focus solely upon what they perceive to be the intrinsic nature of the discipline. As King and Brownell phrase it,

We can summarize the first task of any curriculum planning group, committee, or person as the definition of the nature of the discipline of which the course or courses is a part. The task can be accomplished by (1) establishing the most characteristic view and the range of views of man and nature held by the members of the discipline; (2) describing the mode of inquiry, skills, and rules for truth used by the discoursers; (3) identifying the domain of the discipline and the aspect or perspective characteristic of it; (4) determining the key concepts of the discipline; (5) characterizing the substratum languages and the particular terminology and notation of the discipline; (6) noting the linguistic heritage and communications network of the discipline; (7) setting forth the tradition and history of the idea of the discipline; and (8) explicating the instructive character of the discipline.[6]

As such, "The initial guideline for curriculum construction . . . is the discipline itself."[7] In addition, the curriculum becomes a representation or characterization of the discipline under examination. It becomes a translation of what is already known and

accepted as authoritative within the discipline. Connelly clarifies
further what is considered to be the ideal process for consulting a
discipline in order to derive from it the essence of a curriculum:

> one of the first jobs of the curriculum maker, [is] namely
> to study the discipline in a detail and manner which will
> allow him to characterize the variety of forms of
> knowledge of the discipline. A sound study of text-
> books is not sufficient since mere statements of knowl-
> edge are only partially transparent to the terms with
> which they were generated. Rather, what is required is a
> study of the enquiries—the research reports—from which
> the statements of knowledge have been abstracted.[8]

Many curriculum developers, especially those on the local level,
have neither the resources nor the training to do what Connelly
suggests. They consult, instead, textbooks or memories of courses
taken during their academic training. Thus Harvard Project Physics
began when

> Dr. F. James Rutherford, an experienced high school
> science teacher and administrator in California, under-
> took the preparation of a trial draft of a new course
> text, based on a widely used college textbook, *Introduc-
> tion to Concepts and Theories in Physical Science*, by
> Gerald Holton, Professor of Physics at Harvard Univer-
> sity.[9]

Those developers who are scholars need only reflect upon their
own research and training. In any case, the origins of the
curriculum lie outside of the curriculum development process,
within the existing research endeavors of the academic discpline,
and the first task of the developer is to consult this source and to
gain an understanding of the discipline upon which his curriculum
is to elaborate.

The statement that the origins of the curriculum lie outside of
the curriculum development process implies that a distinction is
made between sources lying outside of the curriculum development process and sources lying within the curriculum development
process—between constructing new knowledge, constructing new
knowledge while constructing curriculum, and constructing curriculum. The origins of the knowledge upon which the curriculum
is based lie within the accepted possessions of the discipline *per*

se. It is not the job of the developer to generate new knowledge specifically for the purpose of its being used within the curriculum; nor is it his function to create new knowledge while developing curriculum. He is not, as curriculum developer, to engage in basic research. His job is to create curricula by consulting already existing knowledge that has been sanctioned as acceptable by an academic discipline. A developer may, of course, be an academician or may enlist an academician to help in the development of the curriculum. However, new knowledge generated by that person is first attributed to belong to an academic discipline and sanctioned by that discipline before it can be legitimately used as an input into curriculum development. The creation of knowledge is thus separate from the process of curriculum construction.

Priorities

Focusing solely upon existing elaborations of an academic discipline while formulating the essence of a curriculum means that curricular concerns other than those embodied within the discipline itself are excluded from contributing to the development of the essence of the curriculum. It means that the essence of the curriculum is formulated "prior to analyses of society, the learner, and the learning process." Phenix phrases the spirit with which concerns others than those residing within the academic disciplines are excluded from contributing to the essence of a curriculum when he writes,

> My thesis, briefly, is that *all* curriculum content should be drawn from the disciplines, or, to put it another way, that *only* knowledge contained in the disciplines is appropriate to the curriculum .... This means that psychological needs, social problems, and any of a variety of patterns of material based on other than discipline content are not appropriate to the determination of what is taught—though obviously such nondisciplinary considerations are essential to decision about the distribution of discipline knowledge within the curriculum as a whole.[10]

This belief, that concerns other than those deriving from the academic disciplines must not be high priorities for the curriculum developer while creating the essence of his curriculum, is further noted by Schwab (1964) when he expresses the prevalent belief among Scholar Academic developers that,

> Of the four topics of education—the learner, the teacher, the milieu, and the subject matter (that which is intended to be taught or learned)—none has been so thoroughly neglected in the past half century as the last. We have had more than enough scrutiny, discussion, and debate about the learning and teaching process, thanks to the popularity of psychological investigations. Class, community, the political state, and school organization have similarly been defined and redefined, studied and reexamined. Only subject matter, among the four, has been relegated to the position of a good wife: taken as familiar, fixed, and at hand when wanted.[11]

Scholar Academic developers change this. They make "subject matter," which they conceive to be the essence of the academic disciplines, their central concern while creating curricula. In doing so, other concerns about "the learner, the teacher, the milieu" become of secondary importance. These other concerns, however, do have a role to play once the essence of the curriculum is formulated. It is to help put the essence of the curriculum into a form suitable for use during instruction. But the priorities are clear: "subject matter" comes first and "The choice of curriculum content [subject matter] can be made *independent* of instructional methods [the effect of applying concerns about student teacher and milieu], but the choice of instructional method is *dependent* upon the nature of the curriculum content"[12] and becomes a concern of the developer only after curriculum content is delineated.

Two implications for the schools of the developer's practice of basing curriculum upon the academic disciplines in this way must be spelled out. First, Scholar Academic developers assume that the *subjects* that are taught within the schools must be selected from among the academic disciplines—that for every school subject there must be a corresponding academic discipline (although for every academic discipline there need not be a school subject). It is also believed that the *subject matter* taught within schools must be drawn from among the academic disciplines and only from among them—that the knowledge taught within the schools must be selected from among the knowledge embodied within the academic disciplines.[13] Second, it is believed that the concerns of the schools are to be identical with the concerns of the academic disciplines—that both are to be concerned solely with the development of the intellect through the pursuit of knowledge and that the immediate demands of physical, social, economic, and political life are not to influence them. This belief arises because many special interest groups are constantly making demands upon the schools. Scholar Academic developers believe that the only demand that should be allowed to influence the school program is the one that "provides the base upon which the person as a person can develop to realize his full stature as a free *mind*"—that is, the intellectual demands as embodied within the academic disciplines. This means that the school must protect itself from allowing its program to be influenced by special interest pressures that insist that man, in addition to being an intellectual creature, is also an *occupational* creature who works to support himself, his family, and his society, a *physical* creature who requires good health to lead a constructive life, a *political* creature who lives within a family, community, nation, and world, a *social* creature whose meanings are defined by his society and who must live within a society, and a *religious* creature who is sustained through his life by a faith and hope in something beyond himself. The school is to have at its highest priority the cultivation of the human mind as expressed within the academic disciplines, and only pressures to influence the school program that support this priority are to be allowed within the school door. Within this context, Scholar Academic developers are particularly concerned that the school does not submit to pressures to include occupational training for children—pressures designed to force the school to include curricula designed to teach professional, vocational, commercial, agricultural, business, industrial, or homemaking education.[14]

Disciplines, Intellect, Knowledge

Underlying the Scholar Academic Ideology is a belief that man's essence is summed up by his ability to think, to understand, to know, to reason, to reflect, to remember, to question, to ponder—in short, to exercise the intellectual capabilities of his mind in search for meaning. It is believed that the fundamental human motivation that raises man above the lower animals is his search for meaning and his ability to use his intellect in that search. This intellectual perspective on man is assumed to provide the basic motive underlying all educational endeavors: that education's rightful purpose is to "provide the base upon which the person as a person can develop to realize his full stature as a free *mind.*" But Scholar Academics do not stop here. They make a further critical assumption. They assume that there exists a loose equivalence between the world of the intellect, the world. of knowledge, and the academic disciplines.

The world of the intellect contains those ways of thinking, reasoning, understanding, and reflecting that allow individuals to make meaning out of their encounters with their world and it contains the institutionalized ways of knowing, remembering, questioning, and deliberating that are passed from one generation to the next. For both the individual and the culture: "Intellect has become, through its organization of all that is known and its search for the unknown, that best and perhaps only bridge to meaning."[15] The world of knowledge contains everything the individual has come to understand and know about his world and all of the meanings that the culture as a whole has accumulated over the centuries and preserved in its traditions. The world of knowledge contains not only that which is known, but also such things as the ways of knowing and postures toward knowledge that have been developed, codified, and preserved by the culture. And the academic disciplines are the consequences of the direct pursuit of meaning by individuals within the culture and the culture as a whole; they are the definers, depositories, and disseminators of the culture's existing knowledge and ways of knowing. In general, the academic disciplines reside within the universities and organize their meanings under the guardianship of communities of academicians bearing such names as mathematics, physics, history, philosophy, economics, and psychology.

What is important is that curriculum developers working within the Scholar Academic Ideology assume that there is a loose equivalence between the world of the intellect, the world of knowledge and the academic disciplines: that the three are essentially one and the same. They assume that the contents of the world of the intellect are essentially the same as the contents of the world of knowledge, and that the contents of the academic disciplines include the contents of both of them. That is, they assume that everything worthy of inclusion in the world of knowledge is contained in the academic disciplines, and that everything included within the academic disciplines is contained in the world of knowledge. Similarly, they assume that everything worthy of inclusion within the world of intellect is contained in the academic disciplines and that everything included in the academic disciplines is contained in the world of the intellect. In addition, and this is crucial, they assume that *those things not included in the academic disciplines are not worthy of being contained in the world of the intellect or the world of knowledge* and that those things not contained in either the world of intellect or the world of knowledge are not worthy of being included within the academic disciplines. Thus, the world of the intellect, the world of knowledge, and the academic disciplines are viewed as roughly equivalent (the same, or equal), both in terms of what they *include* and *exclude*.

This equivalence between disciplines, intellect, and knowledge is further clarified by seeing how each can be described in terms of the other. The academic disciplines encompass the organized accumulation of civilization's knowledge, the modes within which man generates knowledge using his intellect, and the intellect's systems of symbols and thoughts. The academic "disciplines *are* the intellect's systems of symbols and thoughts, the means by which men's minds master nature and grasp ideas."[16] The "intellect is man's schooled power of knowing, of understanding."[17] It is the means by which men understand their world through the generation of knowledge. It grows and develops only "according to the forms of the disciplines."[18] And knowledge is the very substance of the academic disciplines. It is the embodiment of man's intellectual achievements. It is the result of intellectual inquiry within the academic disciplines into the nature of the world.

What is important for the schools is that this equivalence between intellect, knowledge, and the disciplines is assumed to contain its own reason for existence as the prime concern of the curriculum. As King and Brownell phrase it,

We defined intellect as the schooled capacity for knowing accomplished through mastery of symbolic systems. We further asserted that the processes and products of man's symbolic efforts to make his experience with the world intelligible are the disciplines of knowledge. The prime claim of the intellect [on the schools], then, is best met in the schools when the disciplines of knowledge are the fundamental content of the curriculum—its resources and its responsibility.[19]

Education as Extension of
Disciplines, Intellect, Knowledge

The central task of education within the schools is thus taken to be the extension of the components of the equivalence class containing the academic disciplines, the world of intellect, and the world of knowledge. They are to be extended both on the cultural level as reflected in the discovery of new truth and on the individual level as reflected in the enculturation of individuals into civilization's accumulated knowledge and ways of knowing. The curriculum provides the means of enculturating the young into the world of knowledge, the world of the intellect, and the academic disciplines. It derives both its meaning and its reason for existence from the academic disciplines, the world of the intellect, and the world of knowledge. The central concern of the curriculum developer is the extension of these worlds by introducing the young into them.

In addition, the theory of the nature of the equivalence becomes the model for a theory of curriculum and a theory of curriculum creation. That is, the theory of the nature of the academic disciplines, the theory of the nature of the world of knowledge, and "the theory of the nature of the world of intellect becomes the model for a theory of the curriculum"[20] and a theory of curriculum creation. In other words, what Scholar Academic curriculum developers perceive to be the nature of knowledge, intellect, and the disciplines is to dictate their conception of both what curriculum is and how curriculum is to be created. This occurs on two levels: on the global level where the equivalence between knowledge, intellect, and the disciplines ranges over the whole universe of knowledge and on the local level where the equivalence between knowledge, intellect, and the disciplines takes on its particular meaning within each academic discipline.

Disciplines, Knowledge, Intellect: Global Considerations

One of the striking characteristics of the modern view of the world of the disciplines, knowledge, and intellect is that there exist "*distinctive* disciplines of knowledge." There is not just one academic discipline. There is not just one type of knowledge. There is not just one way of knowing.

There are many distinct and separate academic disciplines bearing such names as mathematics, philosophy, history, economics, psychology, and biology. Each discipline is autonomous. It determines the nature of its own knowledge and ways of knowing. It can be judged only according to its own criteria. Each is self-governing and none is responsible to any authority outside or beyond itself. There is no superior body of knowledge or common way of knowing to which the disciplines are subordinate. The living place of the academic disciplines is more of a multiversity than a university.[21]

The world of knowledge is viewed as consisting of a variety of distinct, separate, and discontinuous clusters of locally organized knowledge and ways of knowing. It is not viewed as homogeneous and uniform. Each of the diverse clusters of knowledge is uniquely and intrinsically organized, and each is identifiable as an academic discipline. The plurality within the world of knowledge thus parallels the plurality among the disciplines.

There are many different ways of making meaning within the world of the intellect. There are many distinct traditions of thinking and knowing in which a person's mind can be trained. The ways of understanding that are characteristic of axiomatic mathematics, analytic philosophy, interpretative history, experimental psychology, or statistical economics are viewed as basically different in nature. Each of the many ways of knowing within the world of the intellect has been developed to its highest level of refinement by an academic discipline, and each academic discipline has its characteristic modes of reasoning that it trains its members to use. The plurality within the world of the intellect thus parallels the plurality of the disciplines.

At the global level, the theory of the nature of the equivalence among academic disciplines, the world of knowledge, and the world of the intellect thus demands the necessity for autonomy among the disciplines; and it demands the necessity for a pluralism among the disciplines, within the world of knowledge and within the world of the intellect. These assumptions—of the autonomy of the disciplines and the plurality of disciplines, knowledge, and intellect—are in sharp contrast with pre-twentieth century assumptions of the hegemony of philosophy over the disciplines and the reliance on philosophy for the meaning of knowledge. These assumptions provide unique guidelines for a model of a theory of curriculum and curriculum making. The guidelines follow directly from the assumptions of the autonomy of the disciplines and the plurality of disciplines, knowledge, and intellect.

First, curriculum should consist of separate subjects, each of which represents and reflects a single partition of the world of knowledge as represented by an academic discipline. And, second, the responsibility for curriculum creation within each subject belongs solely to members of the representative discipline who are acquainted with their aspect of the world of knowledge and intellect. No outside extra-disciplinary authority is to legislate the behaviors appropriate for members of the disciplines to engage in while creating curricula.

Disciplines, Knowledge, Intellect:
Local Considerations

At the local level, curriculum development is an intradisciplinary affair. The theory of the nature of each discipline indicates how the developer is to go about creating curricula so as to be in resonance with the nature of inquiry within that discipline. The theory of the nature of each discipline "can be used to reflect back on each discipline in search of its clues for curriculum"[22] in order to make the curriculum a reflection of the discipline "as the scholar himself regards that discipline."[23]

The members of each discipline have sole responsibility for that component of the total curriculum representative of their discipline. They create curriculum as active members working within their disciplines. They create curriculum so that it will reflect their conception of the nature of their discipline. As a result, curriculum development at the local level becomes a provincial affair, where the developer's prime concern is with the individual discipline which his curriculum is to reflect. Bellack indicates this when he writes:

> The focus of attention in each of these [curriculum] projects is an individual discipline. Little or no attention is given to the relationships of the individual fields to each other or to the program of studies within which they must find their place. National committees in the fields of chemistry, physics, and biology have proceeded independently of each other, the projects in economics, geography, and anthropology are unrelated to one another.[24]

THE ACADEMIC DISCIPLINES

Let us now examine how developers working within the Scholar Academic Ideology view the nature of their disciplines. In order to convey the spirit of the conceptual framework within which these developers work, the discussion will be somewhat allegorical.

The Discipline as a Community

One of three basic descriptions has generally been used to define the nature of an academic discipline. Such include describing an academic discipline (1) as "a defined area of study (i.e., history, botany, etc.)"[25]; (2) as the "network of facts, writings, and other works of scholars associated with the field"[26]; and (3) as a "community of individuals whose ultimate task is the gaining of meaning"[27] in one domain of the world of knowledge. We will view an academic discipline as a community of people in search for truth within one partition of the universe of knowledge. As a community, each discipline has characteristics, such as a tradition and a history, a heritage of literature and artifacts, a specialized language, a communications network, and a valuative and affective stance. The members of a discipline share a specialized grammar and logic for expression of ideas, and a "territorial possession" over a particular set of concepts, beliefs, and knowledges.

The primary reason for the existence of a discipline, the motivation drawing people to participate in a discipline, and the cohesive force holding people together within a discipline is the discipline's search for truth. At the very core of each discipline is the problem of self-extension through the pursuit of knowledge and truth. This is manifested in the central concern of each discipline being its own growth: both in terms of the discovery of new truth and thus the enlargement of its domain of inquiry (epistemic development) and in terms of passing on to others that which is already known—thereby enlarging both the amount and level of knowledge within the community making up the discipline (community development). The disciplines are thus not to be understood as static communities concerned only with preservation of "what was" but as dynamic communities concerned with their own extension into "what will be."

The Discipline as a Hierarchical Community

Disciplines are viewed as hierarchical communities consisting of inquirers into the truth, teachers of the truth, and learners of the truth. See Figure 2.1. At the top of the hierarchy are the scholars. They rule over the discipline as scholar-kings, much as Plato's philosopher-kings were to rule over the Republic. It is their function to search for truths which are yet unknown. At the next

Figure 2.1

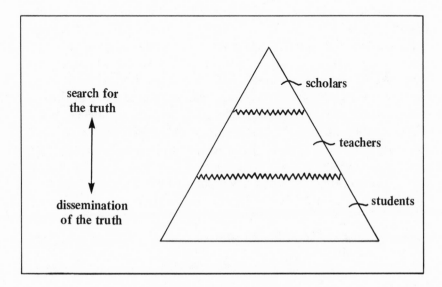

level of the hierarchy are the teachers. They disseminate the truth that has been discovered by the scholars. And at the bottom of the hierarchy are the students. Neophytes in their encounters with the discipline, it is their job to learn the truth so that they may become proficient members of the discipline. The jagged lines separating the major hierarchical levels in Figure 2.1 are to be taken to mean that the boundaries between the levels of the hierarchy are not clear and precise and that there is overlap between the categories of scholar, teacher, and student.

Within each category there are many gradations of placement: from fluid inquirers to static inquirers,[28] from university professors to preschool teachers, and from doctoral candidates to nursery schoolers. The criteria ranking members of the discipline within the hierarchical ordering are primarily intellectual ones involving the member's ability to contribute to the extension of the discipline and involving how much of the knowledge of the discipline a member has acquired. A member's ranking is directly proportional to his prestige, which is in turn directly proportional to how close he is to the apex of the hierarchical pyramid. It is to be noted that there are fewer members of the discipline close to the pyramid's apex than to its base. It is also important to note that scholars, teachers, and students are all viewed as members of the discipline—each being engaged at his own level and in his own way in the extension of the discipline. As Bruner puts this crucial point:

> intellectual activity anywhere is the same, whether at the frontier of knowledge or in a third-grade classroom. What a scientist does at his desk or in his laboratory, what a literary critic does in reading a poem, are of the same order as what anybody else does when he is engaged in like activities—if he is to achieve understanding. The difference is in degree, not in kind. The school boy learning physics *is* a physicist, and it is easier for him to learn physics behaving like a physicist than doing something else.[29]

The Learning ↔ Teaching Dynamic
of the Discipline

The dynamic of the discipline is inherent in the dual activity of "search for truth" ↔ "dissemination of truth" that is present at all levels of the intellectual hierarchy. See Figure 2.1. The discipline as a whole and the members of the discipline as individuals are constantly motivated in an upward direction in search of the unknown, be they scholars in search for as yet unknown truth or students in search for truths unknown to them but known to the discipline. And the discipline as a whole and the members of the discipline as individuals are constantly motivated in a downward direction to disseminate the known, be they scholars reporting what they have discovered or teachers conveying what they have learned. The knowledge of the discipline is viewed as having two characteristics: it can be learned and once learned it can be taught. For "the distinguishing mark of any discipline is that the knowledge which comprises it is instructive—that it is peculiarly suited for teaching and learning."[30] And active members of the discipline—be they scholars, teachers, or students—are viewed as constantly engaged in the dual activity of learning ↔ teaching.

The Educative Process Within the Academic Community

Developers within the Scholar Academic Ideology view education as a process of enculturating students into a discipline. This view of education entails a concern with the student's acquisition of the discipline's knowledge, way of knowing, attitudes towards itself, and traditions. It involves making the student a member of the discipline by first moving the student into the discipline and then moving him from the bottom of the hierarchical ordering towards the top of the hierarchical ordering.[31]

The aim of education is to make the student a member of the discipline. It is to give him a participant's knowledge of the discipline and not an observer's knowledge about the discipline. Membership within the discipline is the result of education within a discipline. And one becomes a member of a discipline by learning to participate in the discipline. King and Brownell hint at this in *The Curriculum and the Disciplines of Knowledge* when they write: "The view of knowledge used as the basis of this book places the increasing ability to participate in the discourse or characteristic activity of the several disciplines of the curriculum as the focal point for instruction."[32] Bruner suggests this when he writes: "To instruct someone in these disciplines is . . . to teach him to participate in the process that makes possible the establishment of knowledge. We teach a subject . . . to get a student . . . to take part in the process of knowledge getting."[33] And Grobman implies something similar in writing about the Biological Sciences Curriculum Study (BSCS) when he says: "Dr. Brandwein suggested we use the word 'science' as a verb and said that students should be 'sciencing' rather than learning about science."[34]

Because the disciplines are viewed as communities with lives of their own and because education is thought of as enculturation into the academic communities, it is assumed that "education for the discipline" is the same as "education for life."[35] Elementary school curricula within a discipline are developed with the intent of preparing the student for high school work in that discipline, and school curricula within a discipline are developed in order to prepare the student for university work within the discipline, and university study within a discipline is to prepare the student for a life of study and work within the discipline.[36]

Education for the discipline involves entering the discipline at the lowest level of the discipline's hierarchy and working one's way towards the top of the hierarchy. It involves learning the knowledge of the discipline and teaching what one has learned to others. And it involves dropping out of the discipline when one can no longer function as a constructive member of the discipline.

The "territorial imperative" is constantly at work.[37] It is at work in two senses. First, education outside of the discipline is discouraged and frowned upon. Potential members of the discipline are not to be lost to "technical education" or "vocational education"; educators within the disciplines have no desire to share the domain of schooling with rivals. All students are viewed as potential property of the disciplines and encouraged to pursue a life dedicated to the search for truth within them. Second, education within the disciplines involves the special cultivation of those members of the discipline most likely to spend their lives within the discipline and most likely to make contributions to the discipline.[38] Those students who show lack of interest in the discipline or who lack the ability to contribute to the discipline (the lower 60 percent of the student body at any level of schooling) are largely ignored by curriculum developers within the Scholar Academic Ideology and encouraged either to "drop out" of the academic community or to stabilize themselves at a particular level within the hierarchy (for example, perhaps by becoming elementary or secondary school teachers). Curricula are designed to preserve the hierarchical nature of the academic community by producing an intellectual elite through the selective promotion of students in such a manner that increasingly more members of the discipline will exist at the bottom of the hierarchy portrayed in Figure 2.1 than at the top of it. Curricula are thus not only developed so as to be primarily relevant to further work within the discipline but also so as to be primarily relevant to students who will be doing further work within the discipline, as was the case with the curricula developed by the Physical Science Study Committee (PSSC), the School Mathematics Study Group (SMSG), and the Biological Sciences Curriculum Study (BSCS).[39]

CURRICULAR ISSUES

Thus far this chapter has outlined several characteristics of the conceptual framework underlying the Scholar Academic Ideology. It has shown how developers using the Ideology view curriculum creation from the perspective of the academic disciplines; from the perspective of "education as initiation into the disciplines" and "curriculum creation as elaboration on a discipline." It has also indicated the nature of the equivalence between the academic disciplines, the world of intellect, and the world of knowledge. And it has portrayed the nature of the equivalence at the local level (within each academic discipline, each segment of the world of the intellect, and each partition of the world of knowledge) as having characteristics which can be summed up in phrases such as "hierarchical community," "community with a tradition," "extensions through a search for and dissemination of the truth," "domain of inquiry within one partition of the world of knowledge," "education through enculturation," and "enculturation into a hierarchical community." Let us now look at three issues raised by this conceptual framework for Scholar Academic developers: the issue of the classification and selection of disciplines (a global issue), the issue of having the curriculum reflect the discipline (a local issue), and the issue of curriculum improvement.

Classification and Selection of Disciplines

The world of knowledge is not homogeneous and uniform. There exists a pluralism in the representation of knowledge. Paralleling this pluralism is a multiplicity of disciplines. Each discipline is autonomous unto itself. There is no superior discipline governing all other disciplines. As a result, the problem arises of identifying the separate disciplines, of determining the nature of each of the disciplines, and of deciding upon the relationship among the disciplines. This is called the problem of the classification of the disciplines. Paralleling this problem is that of the classification of the world of knowledge: determining how the world of knowledge is to be broken up into clusters, what the essence and value of each cluster is, and how the different clusters are related to each other.

From the Scholar Academic viewpoint, it is impossible to determine what knowledge should be taught in the schools until the world of knowledge is classified. Similarly, until the problem of the classification of the disciplines is resolved, one cannot determine which disciplines should be taught in the schools or when they should be taught in the schools. Determination of the school program is thus dependent upon answers given to these problems. "The significance of this set of problems to education is obvious enough. To identify the disciplines which constitute contemporary knowledge is to identify the various materials which constitute the resources of education and its obligations."[40]

The issue of classification arises (a) because there exist different ways of classifying the disciplines and the world of knowledge;[41] (b) because within any classification there exist more disciplines and knowledge than there is room for in the schools;[42] (c) because inherent in different classifications are different conceptions of the nature of the well-educated man;[43] and (d) because within different classifications there are different assumptions about which knowledge and which disciplines have the greatest value.[44] The solution of the problems of classification is crucial in determining the proportional representation (including omission) of the different disciplines and knowledges within the school program.

The problem of classifying the disciplines and the world of knowledge into different "realms of meaning"[45] (as Phenix calls them) is not a trivial one. As Schwab says: "What is important about each one [classification scheme] is not so much the list of disciplines and definitions which it may provide but rather: (a) the distinctions it uses to distinguish disciplines [and clusters of disciplines—each of Phenix's 'realms of meaning']; and (b) the educational problems and issues which these distinctions raise to visibility."[46]

Classifications can be radically different. For example, Comte's classification is based upon dependency relationships among disciplines (biology is dependent upon chemistry, which is dependent upon physics, which is dependent upon mathematics, etc.), while Aristotle's classification is based upon the distinction between theoretical (to intellectualize), practical (to do), and productive (to make) types of knowledge.[47]

What is important is that significantly different types of educational problems arise from different classifications. For example, under Comte's classification, the issue of vocational education is easily dismissed, while under Aristotle's classification, it is difficult not to include vocational education within the schools. Today the issue of vocational education can be easily dismissed within the Scholar Academic Ideology, because the scheme utilized for classifying the world of knowledge into disciplines is a hierarchical one that takes account primarily of "theoretical" types of knowledge (in the Aristotleian sense of the phrase) and that considers "practical" types of knowledge as dependent upon and derivative from "theoretical" types of knowledge (in the sense of the Comtian interpretation). As such, different classifications suggest significantly different solutions to considerations such as what disciplines should be included in the curriculum,[48] how much time should be given to each discipline,[49] and what disciplines "may be joined together for purposes of instruction, what should be held apart, and in what sequence they may best be taught."[50]

Most developers, of course, do not bother themselves with questions about the classification of the disciplines or the world of knowledge. They unknowingly accept the assumptions taught them by their disciplines. They then argue the case for the representation of their discipline within the schools, and design their curricula based upon assumptions that they have not rigorously thought out; assumptions that derive from the impulse of their individual academic communities to preserve themselves and extend themselves (both with respect to community development and epistemological development). However, conflicts often do arise among the disciplines as they vie for representation within the school program. And these conflicts are often dependent upon assumptions about the classification of knowledge and are often argued, unknowingly, around such assumptions. This was the case in the replacement of Latin and Greek in the schools by social studies, civics, and English language study (1880-1950). And it might be the case in the replacement of social studies and civics in the schools by sociology, psychology, and anthropology (1950-).[51]

Curriculum as Reflection of the Discipline

At the local level the curriculum developer works solely within his own discipline. The major concern of the Scholar Academic developer at this level of endeavor is one of constructing curriculum that reflects the essence of his discipline. It is believed that curriculum that accurately reflects its representative discipline facilitates enculturating students into the discipline as it authentically exists.

Having the curriculum reflect the essence of its representative discipline means that the curriculum "(1) must be an epitome of the discipline; (2) must have an approach and sequence in conformance with and in support of the discipline; and (3) must be alike in fundamental concepts and mode of inquiry."[52] Curricula which are appropriately created are thus to reflect their disciplines in every conceivable way.

Accompanying the concern that curriculum reflect its representative discipline are assumptions such as the following: that the developer's attention while creating curriculum be focused solely upon his discipline;[53] that the only source for curricular content is the discipline itself;[54] that the sole criterion for selection of curricular content is that such content reflect the authentic structure of "the discipline in question as the scholar himself regards that discipline";[55] that the curriculum "should be determined by the most fundamental understanding that can be achieved of the underlying principles that give structure to" or are inherent in the discipline;[56] that questions about the relationship of curriculum to existing educational resources, teachability, and learnability are to be dealt with after the scope and sequence of the curriculum are detailed;[57] that the needs of children and of society have little place in determining the content of the curriculum;[58] and that advice from social sciences such as psychology, sociology, and anthropology is to be sought only after the essence of the curriculum is determined.[59]

In speaking about the tasks involved in identifying the essence of a discipline and simulating that essence within a curriculum, the Scholar Academic developer often uses the phrase "structure of the discipline."[60] The curriculum is to reflect the structure of the discipline, and the process of curriculum creation is to reflect the structure of the discipline. The phrase "structure of the discipline" usually means little other than the essence of the discipline. However, it identifies a set of problems involving the determination of the essence of the discipline which the curriculum developer must appropriately resolve if he is to satisfactorily create curriculum.

Three such problems are (a) deciding upon what is meant by the phrase "structure of the discipline," (b) deciding what the structure of the discipline actually is, and (c) coping with the problem of the changing nature of the structure of any discipline. Let us examine each of these problems in turn.

First, the developer must identify what he means by the structure of his discipline. This problem is not as easy as it sounds. Each discipline has several different types of structures, and there is considerable disagreement as to what any one type of these structures consists of. For example, one category scheme separates structures into conceptual structures and ideological structures, while another scheme favors the categories of substantive, methodological, and attitudinal structures. Deciding upon the type of structure the curriculum is to reflect is only half of the problem, for there are many interpretations of the nature of each type of structure. For example, the substantive structure of a discipline may be any of the following: the discipline's collection of ideas; collection of facts; collection of concepts; collection of principles; collection of relations among facts, concepts, and principles; collection of patterns organizing facts, concepts, principles, and relations among such; or collection of generalizations from which, as Bruner says, the facts, concepts, principles, ideas, relations, and patterns of the discipline can be "regenerated."[6][1]

Whichever type of structure the developer decides to have his curriculum reflect and whatever interpretation is given to that type of structure, it is crucial that the curriculum reflect the structure of the discipline so that the student can be appropriately enculturated into the discipline. As Schwab says, the "structure determines what questions we shall ask in our enquiry; the questions determine what data we wish; our wishes in this respect determine what experiments we perform. Further, the data, once assembled are given their meaning and interpretation in the light of the conception which initiated the enquiry."[6][2]

Having determined the type of structure his curriculum will reflect, the developer must next decide what the structure of his discipline is so that he can have his curriculum reflect it. This is not easy, for there are usually differing positions as to the essence of any discipline. For example, is ecology summed up by the phrase "set of antecedent-consequent events," "structures and functions," or "homeostatic mechanism?"[6][3] Perhaps each phrase provides a different view of the nature of ecology. Deciding which position to take can pose a problem for curriculum developers, especially if they create curricula as a team. The Biological Science Curriculum Study (BSCS) resolved its disagreements by fragmenting into three commissions, each of which developed its own curriculum: the green version (ecological), the blue version (molecular), and the yellow version (cellular).

Having decided upon what is meant by the structure of his discipline and what the nature of that structure is, the Scholar Academic developer is faced with a third problem. This problem results from the refusal of the disciplines—as vital communities—to remain static. The disciplines are constantly growing, and thus their natures are constantly changing. Unknown truths are discovered and reorganized in terms of ever more sophisticated paradigms. Their very structures thus change over time. For example, in the 1890's the substantive structures of the scientific disciplines could be described as taxonomic, morphological, classificatory, macroscopic, and static, while in the 1960's their substantive structures were best described by terms such as microscopic, dynamic, structural, relational, and functional.[64] It is quite appropriate that 1890 curricula were different from 1960 curricula, for the disciplines themselves have been evolving.[65] The fundamental belief about curricula—that they should be constructed so as to reflect the structure of the disciplines that they represent—has not changed.[66]

In identifying the structure of his discipline, the Scholar Academic developer also discovers things such as how students should learn the discipline. He discovers this because "the structure, or logic, of each of the scholarly disciplines offers a way of learning the discipline itself"[67] and because "the disciplines themselves, understood as ways of making knowledge, not merely as knowledge already made, offer suggestions about how they may themselves be learned."[68] Accompanying this type of discovery are hypotheses such as the one that affirms that the theory of learning that is appropriate for use in developing a curriculum within a discipline is unique to the discipline and is to be a reflection of the discipline.

Combining hypotheses such as the one just mentioned with other characteristics of the conceptual system held by Scholar Academic developers lead to a variety of implications for a theory of curriculum creation. Two interesting implications result from combining this hypothesis with (a) the assumption of the plurality and autonomy of the disciplines, and (b) the assumption that each discipline has its own unique method of extending its epistemic development through the generation of new knowledge. The first implication is that each of the multiplicity of disciplines has its own learning theory inherent within itself and that there is thus not "a simple theory of learning leading to one best learning-teaching structure for our schools ... but ... a number of different ... [learning theories] each appropriate or 'best' for a discipline."[69] The second implication is that children should learn the discipline in a manner that parallels the way in which the discipline obtains new knowledge and new ways of knowing: that children learning the discipline should engage in the same type of activity as the scholar doing research.[70]

These are but a few of the issues raised by the phrase "structure of the discipline." Others relate to concerns such as the following: that the medium of the curriculum reflect the medium used for inquiry and reporting of inquiry within the discipline and that the learning experiences constituting the curriculum be consonant with those experienced by practicing members of the discipline.[71] The overarching concern in every case, however, is that the curriculum reflect the discipline in every way possible.

Curricular Improvement

Curriculum developers working within the Scholar Academic Ideology view curriculum improvement as taking place within the existing socio-administrative structure of the educational establishment. Their concern is with the knowledge structure of the school—primarily with the scope and sequence of what is taught, and secondarily with the methodology used in teaching—and not with the nature of the school as an institution of socialization. Thus, curriculum developers may speak of out-of-date content or poor teachers but never of corrupt lay control or the complex power structure within and without the schools which influences them. They see the school as an "ideal" institution whose primary purpose is the enculturation of the able student into the world of knowledge and not as a social institution which is functioning within the socio-psychological, eco-environmental, and politico-administrative structure of its society.[72]

The two primary media used to stimulate curricular improvement are the conference and the textbook. The conference is a meeting among scholars, or scholars and teachers, or teachers which results in reports that make recommendations about what should be taught within schools. The textbook is a daily program prepared by a member of the discipline which prescribes what is to be taught within the schools. Textbooks can be accompanied by laboratories, movies, or field trips. Conferences are usually of one of two types: interdisciplinary, such as the Committee of Ten, where global issues are focused upon, or intradisciplinary, such as the Cambridge Conference on School Mathematics, where local issues are focused upon. The intent behind the conference is to bring about curricular improvement by producing a prestigious report which affects the knowledge structure of the curriculum by pressuring either the schools or textbook preparers to implement the recommendations of the report. As Harold Rugg writes of the Committee of Ten, the Committee of Twelve, and other national committees of the 1890's, they have exerted a tremendous influence in shaping the school curriculum. The prestige of their reports was so great that, once published, their recommendations were copied into entrance requirements of universities and they constituted the outline to which textbooks had to correspond if the authors and publishers expected widespread adoption. Both state and local, town and city systems came to base their syllabi definitely upon the recommendations of the committee.[73]

Textbook writing is an intradisciplinary affair. It can result in a text for students, a curriculum guide for teachers, or both. Textbook writing is viewed as improving education by affecting what is taught within a course on a day-by-day, month-by-month, and year-by-year basis. It is to be noted that these mechanisms for curriculum improvement parallel closely two modes of communication utilized by members of the academic disciplines: the conference and the textbook-research report.

Let us now shift from examining the context within which the Scholar Academic developer works to examining the following things which mold the manner in which the developer creates curriculum at the local level within his discipline: the developer's conceptions of his professional aims for himself, the nature of knowledge, the nature of the child, the nature of learning, the nature of teaching, and the nature of evaluation.

AIMS OF THE CURRICULUM DEVELOPER

The aim of the Scholar Academic developer is to extend his discipline by transmitting its essence to students who are being enculturated into it. The extension of the discipline by enculturating new members into it serves the long range purposes of (a) preserving the existence of the discipline by guaranteeing that there exist members of the discipline who will carry on its traditions and further its epistemic development, and (b) building literacy about the discipline within the general population so that its members will benefit from the truths discovered by the discipline and so that they will support the endeavors of the discipline.

These long range aims are rather vague and intangible—they do not specify why a particular item is included in a textbook or laboratory exercise. As a result, developers working within the Scholar Academic Ideology are often charged with an overconcern with the means of accomplishing an unspecified and vague end to the exclusion of concern with the ends of the educational endeavor within which they are engaged.[74] In essence, this charge reduces to the claim that Scholar Academic developers have neither aims for their curricula nor justifications for the existence of the substantive aspects of their curricula. These claims are not justifiable. The fact that a person does not specify verbally his aims and clarify his justifications does not mean that they do not exist. For example, Scholar Academic developers assume *a priori* that the benefits of being enculturated into the world of the intellect need no pragmatic defense; they assume *a priori* that the benefits of preserving the culture's ways of knowing by extending the disciplines are central to the preservation of civilization; and they assume *a priori* that the extension of the world of knowledge within the minds of students is the defined mission of the school. If one remembers that the theory of curriculum and curriculum creation utilized by Scholar Academic developers is a reflection of the theory of the nature of their discipline, it should be easier to understand (if not accept) why these developers lack the impulse to specify and justify the extension of their disciplines through the curriculum.

The means of accomplishing the extension of the discipline is through the transmission of the knowledge of the discipline to students. The transmission of knowledge is the immediate task faced by the developer on a daily basis. It is often mistaken as the primary aim (end) rather than the secondary aim (means) of the developer. Because it is the immediate task which he faces continuously, the transmission of the knowledge of the discipline tends to become the guiding light which molds the behavior of the developer. It is often taken by the developer to be equivalent to enculturating the student into the discipline.

KNOWLEDGE
Nature of Knowledge
The primary characteristic of the knowledge which Scholar Academic developers consider to be potential content for curriculum is that it is claimed by one of the academic disciplines as

belonging to its domain. For these developers "The only really useful knowledge is that which conforms to the structures revealed in the cognitive disciplines."[75] Knowledge is that which is recognized by a discipline as essential for its search for truth. And knowledge which is of most worth is that upon which the epistemic development of a discipline depends and which contributes most to community development within the discipline. Knowledge thus derives its value and its claim to being knowledge from its ability to contribute to the extension of an academic discipline.

Form of Knowledge

Several characteristics of the form which knowledge takes need elaboration. First, knowledge takes the form of both "content" and "process."[76] When the word knowledge is used it means both "that which is known" and "the way in which something is known." A bit of knowledge is viewed as implicitly carrying both substantive and methodological aspects of a discipline. A man possessing a bit of knowledge possesses both the "information" and the "ways of knowing" representative of that knowledge.

Second, knowledge has a form which is called instructive or didactic.[77] As such, it is capable of being transmitted from one human to another, of being retained in the mind of the person to whom it is transmitted, and of being used by the person to whom it is transmitted to give meaning to yet unknown truths. Didactic knowledge is repeatable and impersonal. It can be repeated without losing its point; the occasions for delivering it are not fixed; and special circumstances are not needed for its transmission. Any suitably trained teacher can transmit knowledge to any suitably trained student. This means that information tied to particular non-recurring circumstances, such as a particular item of conversational, bargaining, reassuring, or prosecuting information, is not considered to be knowledge. It also means that personal information that cannot be communicated without losing its point, such as feelings of competence, power, self-esteem, or love, is not considered to be knowledge.

Finally, knowledge is a representation of reality and not reality itself. Whether reality is taken to be an idea—as Plato, the humanistic developers, and Harvard Project Physics believed to be the case—or whether reality is taken to be a physical occurrence— as Aristotle, the realist developers, and the Physical Science Study Committee believed to be the case—knowledge is a representation of reality and not the reality itself. Students learn about reality, they do not learn reality. Teachers transmit knowledge of reality, they do not transmit reality. And a person possesses knowledge of reality, he does not possess reality. The relationships between reality and knowledge are illustrated in Figure 2.2 and Figure 2.3.

Arrow a in Figure 2.2 indicates that knowledge has its source in reality; arrow b indicates that its receptacle is the human mind (or community of human minds); and arrow c indicates that knowledge is capable of being checked by comparing it directly with reality through validity experimentation. Figure 2.3 represents the history of a bit of knowledge from conception to inclusion within a curriculum: it originates in reality, it is discovered by a member of an academic discipline, the discipline sanctions its existence, and it is made available to the curriculum developer by the discipline.

Knowledge and Objective Reality

What is implicit in the above comments needs to be stated explicitly. Scholar Academic developers accept the duality between the "subjective reality within each individual's mind" and the "objective reality outside of each person's mind." Knowledge can originate within either "subjective reality" or "objective reality." However, only that knowledge which can be externalized, objectified, and impersonalized within objective reality is of worth. Knowledge that is suitable for curriculum content must be observable within objective reality. That which is known only within the mind of an individual and incapable of being presented, observed, scrutinized, and acquired by the members of the disciplines as a community is not of worth to the curriculum developer. It is thus held that objective reality is the more important of the two realities for curricular purposes, and that knowledge of worth is knowledge of objective reality and not subjective reality. Truth exists outside of man and independent of man. Knowledge is that body of truth discovered by the discipline to exist within objective reality.

Figure 2.2

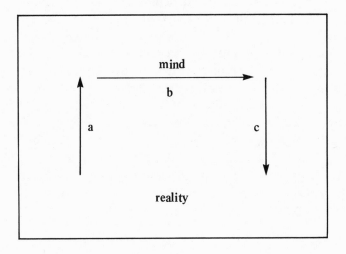

Figure 2.3

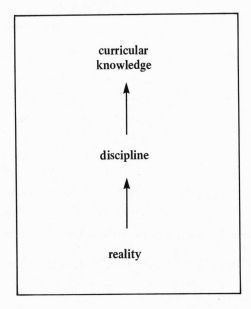

Origin of Curricular Knowledge

The process of obtaining curricular knowledge is thus conceived to be one which requires that (a) something comes to exist within objective reality; (b) the academic discipline discovers that something and sanctions its existence by making it part of the domain of the discipline; and (c) the developer selects that something from the items within the domain of the discipline because he believes it reflects the structure of the discipline. Having collected curricular knowledge, the developer can then imbed it within a curriculum and transmit it to students. This is represented in Figure 2.4. It is important to note that the source for curricular content is the discipline and that the test for the worth of knowledge depends upon how well it reflects the essence of the discipline.

Figure 2.4

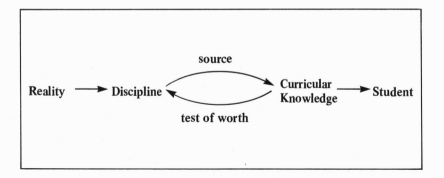

THE CHILD
The Child as Mind

Developers within the Scholar Academic Ideology seldom speak of the child. When they do speak of the child, they speak of the child's mind. In particular, they speak of the rational or intellectual aspects of the child's mind. Man—the child and the student—is viewed as a creature of intellect. Other aspects of his nature are of little concern to these developers. As King and Brownell assume,

> Man is the symbolizing animal. He reasons. He remem-
> bers. He reflects. He meditates. He imagines. He
> cultivates his mind by acquiring, retaining, and extend-
> ing knowledge. He struggles to control his emotions and
> actions with reason. He makes knowledge a virtue and
> ignorance an evil. He questions appearances in search of
> reality . . . . These aspects of intellect distinguish man
> from other creatures. The intellect is man's schooled
> power of knowing, of understanding.[78]

The child is thus viewed as a mind, the important aspects of that
mind being those "powers" which are capable of being "schooled"
within the academic disciplines.

The Child as Memory and Reason

The mind of man is viewed as consisting of two facilities: one
facility is for storage and the other is for performing mental
operations upon that which is stored. The former is often called
memory and the latter reason. The former is capable of being
filled and the latter is capable of being trained.

The Incomplete Child

From this perspective the Scholar Academic developer views the
student as a neophyte in the disciplines of knowledge:

> The student is a neophyte in the encounters with the
> [academic] community of discourse; he is, nevertheless,
> to be considered a member of the community, im-
> mature to be sure, but capable of virtually unlimited
> development. He is learning the ways of gaining knowl-
> edge in the discipline . . . *seeking always to gain meaning*
> through the ensemble of fundamental principles that
> characterize the discipline.[79]

The Scholar Academic developer views the student as an immature
member of an academic discipline who is capable of growth,
development, and enculturation within that discipline by "gaining
meaning through the discipline." He views the student as a mind at
the bottom of the academic hierarchy which is capable of being
drawn upward into that hierarchy. The child is at the bottom of
the academic hierarchy and capable of growth because his mind is
missing something that it is capable of acquiring. Whether the view

is that the mind is empty and capable of being filled, blank and capable of acquiring meaning, evil and capable of being made good, naive and capable of being made sophisticated, untrained and capable of being trained, or unexercised and capable of being exercised, the student is viewed as missing something that exists outside of his mind and that is capable of being transmitted into his mind.[80] The student is thus viewed as a mind, consisting of memory and reason, which is incomplete but susceptible of being made less incomplete.

LEARNING
The Teaching ↔ Learning Dynamic

The teaching ↔ learning dynamic is at the very core of both civilization and the academic disciplines. Civilization is viewed as an organization of communal intelligence whose central socialization process centers around its formal teaching ↔ learning function. Academic disciplines are viewed as communities of intellects whose central dynamic is that of its learning ↔ teaching function. As a result, a learning ↔ teaching atmosphere pervades all activity within the Scholar Academic Ideology. Man is viewed as an animal designed both to learn and to teach what he has learned. Similarly, society is viewed as a community whose major function is one of communal extension through teaching.

Direction Within the
Teaching ↔ Learning Dynamic

However, while creating curricula, developers working within the Scholar Academic Ideology think of learning as a function of teaching. Learning results from teaching, and how a person learns is a consequence of how a person is taught. In its starkest simplicity, learning is viewed from the perspective of "x teaches y to z" rather than from the perspective of "z learns y from x." Here the process "teaches y" determines the process "learns y," and the phrase "teaches y to z" comprises the experiences encountered by and learned by the student.[81] Learning is thus viewed from the perspective of the transmitter rather than from the perspective of the receiver of learning.

Active and Receptive Agents of
the Teaching ↔ Learning Dynamic

Within the teaching ↔ learning relationship, the teacher is viewed as active and the learner is viewed as receptive. It is appropriate to view the student as being drawn into the discipline but not appropriate to view the student as joining the discipline. A discipline can "take . . . hold on the minds of pupils" but the minds of pupils cannot take hold on the discipline.[82] It is appropriate to view the student's memory as being filled, but not to view the student as filling his memory. It is the minds of students which are "stored" and not the students who "store" their minds. And it is appropriate to view the student's mind as being trained but not appropriate to view the student as training his mind.

Within the Scholar Academic Ideology, learning is the result of an intentional activity initiated by the teacher and aimed at a deliberate equipping of the student. The active agent is the teacher. The receptive agent is the learner. And that which is learned is primarily a result of activity on the part of the teacher and secondarily a result of activity on the part of the learner.

Teaching ↔ Learning Dynamic
and Objective Reality

That which the teacher teaches and that which the student learns has its source within the academic discipline—outside of the mind of the student and the mind of the teacher, and outside of subjective consciousness. It has its source within objective reality. As such, teaching is the process of directing stimuli, having their origin within objective reality, at the student so as to bring about his learning. And learning is what results from the reception of the stimuli. This model of teaching ↔ learning is illustrated in Figure 2.5, in which the arrow of direction and activity leads from the discipline to curricular knowledge to the mind of the student. Within this model of teaching ↔ learning the differential importance of the receptive nature of mind versus the operative nature of mind accounts for different theories of "thinking" which are postulated by Scholar Academic developers. In Figure 2.6 an attempt is made to illustrate different positions which might be taken by Scholar Academic developers with

Figure 2.5

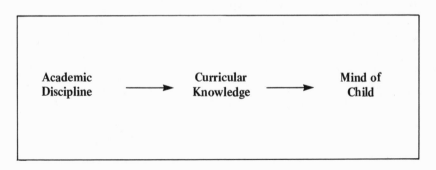

respect to the degree of receptivity versus operativity of the child's mind during learning. Figure 2.6 (a) represents major emphasis upon knowledge impressing itself upon mind, and Figure 2.6 (b) represents major emphasis upon mind giving meaning to the knowledge impressed upon it. In both cases the source of knowledge lies outside of the student and is actively directed at the student by a teaching agent rather than actively grasped by the learning agent.

Learning Theory as Reflection of the Discipline

One of the central hypotheses of the Scholar Academic Ideology is that the theory of learning appropriate for use in developing curricula within an academic discipline (a) is unique to the discipline, and (b) is to be a reflection of the structure of the discipline and derived from the nature of the discipline itself. The belief is that the theory of learning to be used in construction of curriculum is not separate from the discipline but an integral part of the discipline. The belief is that the structure of the discipline carries inherent within itself a methodology for teaching and learning.

Lack of Concern with Formal Learning Theory

As a result, developers working within the Scholar Academic Ideology make a clear distinction between the work that they are engaged in and the work learning theorists (social scientists) and

Figure 2.6

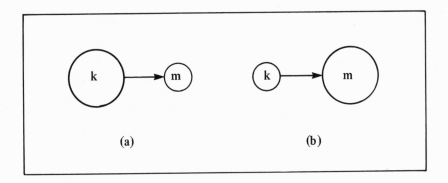

epistemologists (philosophers) are engaged in. Although developers profess an interest in the writings on learning theory produced by philosophers and social scientists, they tend to ignore such writings while creating curricula. As the curriculum developers who participated in the Cambridge Conference on School Mathematics wrote about their endeavors, "The conference should deal primarily with the goals of school mathematics, leaving aside the relationship of these goals of existing educational resources"[83] and thus "We made no attempt to take account of recent research in cognitive psychology."[84] The Scholar Academic developer is interested in reflecting the structure of his discipline within curriculum, and in so doing there is no need for a learning theory separate from the discipline, for it is held that the very nature of the discipline dictates the way in which it is to be learned and taught. When developers do engage in inquiry into the nature of learning, it is usually with respect to curricula that they have already developed. And when they do elaborate upon the learning theory that they utilize, it is usually in justification of the learning theory that was used while creating a curriculum rather than the projection of a learning theory that will be used while creating a curriculum. Thus, generation and elaboration of learning theory by Scholar Academic developers both takes place in conjunction with a particular body of knowledge and is an endeavor which tends to be a *post hoc* justification that follows rather than precedes curriculum development.

Many Theories of Learning

One of the implications of the belief that the structure of every discipline carries inherent within itself a unique theory of learning ↔ teaching which is particularly suited to itself is that the Scholar Academic developer assumes that there exist many different theories of learning rather than one general theory of learning.[85] Each of the many disciplines has its own unique theory of learning ↔ teaching that reflects its nature. And the determination of the mode of learning ↔ teaching to be utilized within a curriculum is to be directly linked to the nature of the discipline which the curriculum reflects.[86]

Learning to Parallel Inquiry

Another implication of the belief that each discipline carries inherent within itself its own theories of teaching ↔ learning is the assumption that children should learn the discipline in a manner that parallels the way in which the discipline obtains new knowledge and new ways of knowing: that is, that children learning the discipline should engage in the same type of activity as the scholar doing research.

Scholar Academic developers customarily use the term inquiry to denote the method used by a discipline to promote its epistemic development and the method used by the scholar within the discipline to search out new truths. The term interpretation may, however, be more appropriate to the humanistic disciplines. It should be noted that the term inquiry does not refer to how children should learn—e.g., "by inquiring" or "through inquiry"—but to how the discipline obtains new knowledge and new ways of knowing.[87]

The assumption of the Scholar Academic developer is that student learning within a discipline should parallel and reflect the modes of inquiry utilized by the discipline. The student should be taught to learn a discipline in a manner identical to the way in which the scholar learns new information while doing research. Student learning of already existent knowledge should be identical to the learning which brings into existence hitherto-unknown knowledge. As Phenix states: "Education should be conceived as a guided recapitulation of the processes of inquiry which gave rise to the fruitful bodies of organized knowledge comprising the established disciplines."[88]

There are often both methodological and substantive aspects to be seen in this assumption. For instance, there are the beliefs that the child's method of learning should be the same as the scholar's and that the knowledge taught to the child should be the same as the knowledge used by the scholar—ideas popular in the 1960's. Similarly, there are the beliefs that the sequence of methods of learning taught to the child should parallel the sequence of methods of learning discovered by scholars, and that the order in which knowledge is learned by the child should parallel the sequence in which knowledge was generated by the discipline— ideas popular in the 1890's. The aim is always to get the student to learn and know as members of the discipline learn and know, so that the student can function as a member of the discipline.[89] This often involves having students undergo experiences similar or identical to those undergone by scholars: having them analyze historical documents as scholars do (e.g., the Educational Development Corporation Social Studies Project); helping them to "discover" mathematics through intuition as mathematicians do (e.g., Zoltan P. Dienes' Multi-Base Arithmetic Blocks); or having them do physics experiments as physicists do (e.g., the Physical Science Study Committee).

The Changing Nature of Learning Theory

One of the problems which the Scholar Academic developer must cope with in the long run is that the structure of his discipline is constantly evolving, and thus that the nature of his teaching ↔ learning theories must also be constantly evolving. In order to give some insight into the form which Scholar Academic learning theory takes, and the types of shifts which occur over time, it is appropriate to compare faculty psychology—the learning theory of the 1890's—with the "structure of the disciplines" psychology—the learning theory of the 1960's.

Faculty psychology viewed man's mind as made up of faculties or mental muscles (such as logic, neatness, thrift). Learning consisted of exercising these muscles. The exercising came from studying the disciplines which, because of their particular natures, were thought to have differential "disciplining" power. Sully sums this up when he says: "The great law underlying the process of development is that the faculties or functions of the intellect are strengthened by exercise" within the disciplines.[90] "Structure of the disciplines" psychology views man's mind as uniform. The academic disciplines represent the different "ways of knowing" accumulated by the culture. Learning consists of accumulating within the mind competencies in using the different "ways of knowing" or modes of inquiry. Foshay sums this up when he says: "The function of instruction is to develop in the student's mind several modes of inquiry."[91]

In both faculty psychology and "structure of the disciplines" psychology the aim is to produce in the student's mind different "ways of knowing." For faculty psychology these begin as properties inherent in the student's mind while for "structure of the disciplines" psychology they begin as properties inherent in the disciplines (the cultural representation of mind). In faculty psychology the different "exercising powers" of the disciplines are what stimulate learning while in "structure of the disciplines" psychology the different modes of inquiry of the discipline stimulate learning. In both cases something from the disciplines impinges upon the minds of students to cause learning.[92]

Two last points need to be discussed with respect to the Scholar Academic view of learning.

Learning as Mechanistic or Cybernetic

First, one of the common beliefs held by developers working within the Scholar Academic Ideology is that man's mind consists of memory and reason. Accompanying this view is one in which learning is viewed as a process of storing memory and a process of training reason. This view of learning tends to allow developers to think of mind during learning as a machine or computer in operation. This analogy does not provide a black box model of learning but rather either a mechanistic or cybernetic model of learning in which gears, levers, storage bins, memory cells, or electrical circuits are filled and exercised. It is in accordance with these types of analogies that Scholar Academic developers tend to act towards learning.

Readiness

The final point for consideration arises from Bruner's statement "that any subject can be taught effectively in some intellectually honest form to any child at any stage of development."[93] A variety of elaborate interpretations of what this means has been offered.[94] The statement has been used to justify a variety of curricular practices, such as the use of "a spiral curriculum, in which the same subject arises at different times with increasing degrees of complexity and rigor."[95] It is possible that Bruner meant the statement to say just what it states. It is also possible that the statement is a fair interpretation of how Scholar Academic developers approach readiness issues while creating curricula: that is, solely in terms of direct and linear simplification of topics initially too difficult for children to understand.[96]

TEACHING

Most of what has to be said about teaching has already been covered. Several points deserve mention, however.

First, teaching is that function within the discipline which enables students to learn the discipline. The aim of teaching is to get the knowledge of the discipline into students' minds. And the act of teaching is viewed as one of transmitting the discipline to the student.

Teaching is viewed within the context of the discipline. Its functions are function of the discipline. Its methods are methods inherent in the communications system of the discipline. Its functionaries are functionaries of the disciplines. And its successes and failures are the strengths and weaknesses of the discipline.[97] Particularly important here is the belief that:

> The teacher's qualification as a member of one or more disciplines is basic. The teacher is ideally an exemplar of the discipline to his students and to his colleagues; he is the embodiment of its values, its language, its skills, its ways of finding meaning.[98]

> Most importantly he is a continuing member of the discipline who has reflected on the nature of that discipline, its traditions, its ways of gaining knowledge, its assumptions about what can be known and how it can be known.[99]

Second, the primary medium of teaching is didactic discourse. This is the mode of communication utilized by the academic disciplines to report their findings in journals and reports. It takes the form of language which is utilized in either formal or informal lectures. It has the following characteristics: it is intended to be kept in mind (rather than responded to or acted upon); it is intended to better the mind of the recipient (through strengthening its power or improving its storage rather than simply interesting the recipient, soothing the recipient, or stimulating the recipient); and it is impersonal and non-situational in that it can be transmitted to any suitably prepared student in any situation (rather than needing a special recipient and a specially prepared environment as in the case of love communications).[100]

In addition, the method of teaching (and thus the manner in which the student learns) that is embedded within the curriculum is to reflect the structure of the discipline and the nature of inquiry within the discipline:

> For example, the primary *method* of teaching history at any level is that of historiography, or the *method* of the mature professional [working within the discipline] .... Each material, reading, and lesson sequence [making up the curriculum] should be consistent with a warranted interpretation ... of the characteristic elements of the discipline ... therefore every [aspect of the curricular] plan must have *an approach* and *a system* or *sequence* in conformance with the discipline.[101]

The belief is that the method of teaching that is imbedded within the curriculum is to be a reflection of the discipline itself.

Third, the teacher is viewed by the Scholar Academic developer as a mediator between the curriculum and the student, as one who transmits the curriculum to the student. He is not viewed as an artist, a creator, a manager, a counselor, or a motivator. He is viewed as a transmitter of the discipline as reflected in the curriculum. The teacher is a minischolar who has chosen to devote himself to the problems of interpreting and presenting the discipline to the student rather than to the creation of new knowledge.[102]

And fourth, both what *ought* to be taught and what *can* be taught are derived from the academic disciplines themselves. As Scholar Academic developers participating in the Cambridge Conference on School Mathematics wrote:

The question of what is or is not worth teaching must
be approached, initially at least, in terms of all the
possibilities that are inherent in the subject matter [of
the discipline]; the question of what is teachable and
what is not depends largely upon the organization of
that subject matter.[103]

Note the shift from what is worth teaching (what ought to be
taught) to what is teachable (what can be taught). Both are
derived from the academic discipline, and both tend to be
considered together; with little differentiation being made between what is "worth teaching" and "what is teachable." This
merging of what is "worth teaching" and "what is teachable" is
reinforced by the curriculum developer's tendency to ignore
existing educational resources until after the essence of his
curriculum is created and to act "on the assumption that if a
teachable program were developed, teachers would be trained to
handle it."[104]

EVALUATION
Student Evaluation
Evaluation of the student is concerned with the student's ability
to re-present to members of the discipline that which has been
transmitted to him through the curriculum. This evaluation rests
upon a correspondence theory of knowledge: the extent to which
that which is in one's mind reflects the discipline is the extent to
which one possesses knowledge. The purpose of student evaluation
is to certify those students who are rising within the occupational
hierarchy of the discipline. Evaluation has as its intent the
rank-ordering of evaluees: its intent is to assign evaluees a
sequential ordering from best to worst within the test group. The
rank ordering is determined through an *a posteriori* norm-refer-
enced test which determines the results of evaluation after
students have been evaluated. It is not used to separate
students according to what they know but according to
who knows it best.

Curricular Evaluation
Curricula are evaluated in terms of how well they reflect their
disciplines. Evaluation based upon analysis by scholars is assumed

to be as significant as evaluation based upon teacher and student use. Summative evaluation of the curriculum is measured in terms of how well the curriculum (a) reflects the discipline, and (b) prepares the student for further work within the discipline. Formative evaluation takes place with respect to the overall effect of a unit, rather than with respect to the particular effect of components of a unit; it provides feedback of the form "more refinement is needed" or "things are fine" rather than providing feedback of a form that would comment in detail on the particular successes and failures of each individual component of a unit.

Within the Scholar Academic Ideology there are two aspects of curricular evaluation: one pertains to the "content" or "essence" of the curriculum, and the other pertains to the "learning experiences" that embody the "essence" of the curriculum in the "physical materials" that are used during instruction. Evaluation of the "essence" or "content" of the curriculum is carried out by scholars (or in the absence of scholars by persons behaving as they believe scholars would) through the use of logical analysis to determine the degree to which the curriculum reflects the discipline. It is carried out using "rational" modes of thought and criteria corresponding to those of the discipline. Ferris' comment about the high school science courses created by Scholar Academic developers in the early 1960's gives the flavor of this type of evaluation:

> Because of the *eminence* of the scientists who have been
> involved in the development of each of these new high
> school science courses, it can be *presumed* that the
> course content is accurate and authoritative.[105]

Evaluation of the "learning experiences" or "physical materials" that are used during instruction is carried out both through rational analysis to determine how well they embody the "essence" of the curriculum and through field testing to determine their effectiveness in helping teachers to teach and students to learn the discipline. During field testing the "learning experiences" or "instructional materials" are evaluated primarily in terms of the teacher's ability to use the curriculum with students (through informal reports from teachers of what does or does not work in the classroom) and secondarily in terms of the student's ability to learn from the curriculum (through formal objective achievement tests). In both cases the curriculum developer behaves towards the results of evaluation as though "the greatest service evaluation can perform is to identify aspects of the course where revision is desirable."[106] Thus, curriculum evaluation is based upon analysis by scholars—or mini-scholars—(as to its "essence"), observation by teachers (as to its teachability), and use by students (as to its learnability), with priorities following in that order.

Notes

[1] This is often interpreted as viewing curriculum from the perspective of subject matter. There have been two great subject matter reform movements within the field of curriculum creation. The first took place between 1890 and 1910. Much of its impetus came from the standardization and reorganization of the high school and the work of the Committee of Ten. Three sources which discuss this period from different points of view are: Edward A. Krug. *The Shaping of the American High School: 1880-1920.* Madison: University of Wisconsin Press, 1969; Theodore R. Sizer. *Secondary Schools at The Turn of the Century.* New Haven: Yale University Press, 1964; and John Elbert Stout. *The Development of High School Curricula in the North Central States from 1860 to 1918.* Chicago: University of Chicago Press, 1921. Krug's book contains an excellent bibliography. The second major subject matter reform movement took place between 1950 and 1970. It has popularily been called the "new curriculum movement." The curriculum projects funded by the National Science Foundation and known as the "alphabet-soup projects," such as Physical Science Study Committee (PSSC), Biological Sciences Curriculum Study (BSCS), School Mathematics Study Group (SMSG), Chemical Bond Approach (CBA), and Harvard Project Physics (HPP), are representative of this movement. Minor movements between 1910 and 1950 continued to produce developers who worked within the Scholar Academic Ideology. William C. Bagley's "Essentialist Movement" emanating from Columbia University from 1920 to 1940 is an example of one such "minor" movement.

[2] Richard C. Whitefield (Ed.) *Disciplines of the Curriculum.* London: McGraw-Hill, 1971, p. 12. Copyright © 1971 McGraw-Hill Book Co. (UK) Ltd. Reproduced by permission.

[3] Jerome S. Bruner. *The Process of Education.* Cambridge: Harvard University Press, 1960, p. 14.

[4] Jerome S. Bruner. *Toward a Theory of Instruction.* Cambridge: Harvard University Press, 1966, p. 72.

[5]J. Myron Atkin. "Behavioral Objectives in Curriculum Design: A Cautionary Note." *The Science Teacher*, Vol. 35 (May, 1968), pp. 28-29. (The italics are mine.)

[6]Arthur R. King and John A. Brownell. *The Curriculum and the Disciplines of Knowledge*. New York: John Wiley, 1966, pp. 187-188.

[7]Dorothy M. Fraser. *Current Curriculum Studies in Academic Subjects*. Washington, D.C.: National Education Association, 1962, p. 231.

[8]F. Michael Connelly. "Philosophy of Science and the Science Curriculum." *Journal of Research in Science Teaching*. Vol. 6 (January, 1964), p. 111.

[9]*Harvard Project Physics: Newsletter 1*. Cambridge: Harvard Project Physics, 1969, p. 5.

[10]Philip H. Phenix. "The Disciplines as Curriculum Content." In A. Harry Passow (Ed.) *Curriculum Crossroads*. New York: Teachers College Press, 1962, pp. 57, 57-58.

[11]Joseph J. Schwab. "Problems, Topics, and Issues." In Stanley Elam (Ed.) *Education and the Structure of Knowledge*. Chicago: Rand McNally, 1964, p. 4.

[12]George A. Beauchamp and Kathryn E. Beauchamp. *Comparative Analysis of Curriculum Systems*. Wilmette: Kagg Press, 1967, p. 80. (The italics are mine.)

[13]Jane R. Martin. "The Disciplines and the Curriculum." *Educational Philosophy and Theory*. Vol. 1, No. 1 (1969).

[14]King and Brownell, *loc. cit.*, ch. 1.

[15]*Ibid.*, pp. 22-23.

[16]*Ibid.*, p. 24.

[17]*Ibid.*, p. 20.

[18]Philip H. Phenix. "The Architectonics of Knowledge." In Stanley Elam (Ed.) *Education and the Structure of Knowledge*. Chicago: Rand McNally, 1964, p. 50.

[19]King and Brownell, *loc. cit.*, p. 37.

[20]*Ibid.*, p. 67.

[21] Clark Kerr. "The Multiversity: Are Its Several Souls Worth Saving?" *Harpers*, No. 227 (November, 1963). It is interesting to note that the 1880's brought both the concept of departmentalism, as a symbolic statement of the disunity of knowledge, to the university and the first major reform movement within the Scholar Academic Ideology. Interesting speculations can be postulated about the parallel rise of the disciplines as reflected in departmentalism and the formulation of the Scholar Academic Ideology. A discussion of the rise of university departmentalism can be found in: Frederick Rudolph. *The American College and University*. New York: Alfred A. Knopf, 1962.

[22] King and Brownell, *loc. cit.*, p. 95.

[23] *Goals for School Mathematics: The Report of the Cambridge Conference on School Mathematics.* Boston: Houghton Mifflin, 1963, p. vii. From the foreword by Francis Keppel.

[24] Arno A. Bellack. "The Structure of Knowledge and the Structure of the Curriculum." In Dwayne Huebner (Ed.) *A Reassessment of the Curriculum.* New York: Teachers College Press, 1964, p. 27.

[25] King and Brownell, *loc. cit.*, p. 68.

[26] Harry S. Broudy. *Building a Philosophy of Education* (second edition). Englewood Cliffs: Prentice-Hall, Inc., 1961, p. 291.

[27] King and Brownell, *loc. cit.*, p. 68.

[28] Schwab discusses the importance of the difference between fluid enquiry (the "e" is one of Schwab's trademarks) and static enquiry in Joseph J. Schwab. "The Structure of the Natural Sciences." In G.W. Ford and Lawrence Pagno (Eds.) *The Structure of Knowledge and the Curriculum.* Chicago: Rand McNally and Co., 1964. Roughly, fluid enquirers are those who bring about paradigm changes within a discipline while static enquirers are those who fill in the fine structure of existent paradigms. Thomas S. Kuhn's *The Structure of Scientific Revolutions.* Chicago: University of Chicago Press, 1962, is a theoretical essay on fluid enquiry. James Dewey Watson's *The Double Helix.* New York: Atheneum, 1969, provides an example of static enquiry.

[29] Bruner. *The Process, loc. cit.*, p. 14.

[30] Phenix. "The Disciplines," *loc. cit.*, p. 57.

[31] Hiller Krieghbaum and Hugh Ranson. *To Improve Secondary School Science and Mathematics Teaching.* Washington, D.C.: U.S. Govt. Printing Office, 1968, p. 3.

[32]King and Brownell, *loc. cit.*, p. 79.

[33]Bruner. *Toward a Theory, loc. cit.*, p. 72.

[34]Arnold B. Grobman. *The Changing Classroom: The Role of the Biological Sciences Curriculum Study.* New York: Doubleday, 1969, p. 80.

[35]Sizer, *loc. cit.*, p. 132.

[36]Grobman, *loc. cit.*, p. 74; Harry O. Gillet and William C. Reavis. "Curriculum-Making in the Laboratory Schools of the School of Education, The University of Chicago." *The Twenty-Sixth Yearbook of the National Society for the Study of Education.* Bloomington: Public School Publishing Co., 1926, p. 263; Arthur W. Foshay. *"How Fare the Disciplines?" Phi Delta Kappan*, Vol. LI, No. 7 (March, 1970), p. 352; and Gloria Dapper and Barbara Carter. "Jerrold R. Zacharias: Apostle of the New Physics." *Saturday Review* (October 21, 1961), pp. 53-65.

[37]Robert Ardrey. *Territorial Imperative.* New York: Atheneum, 1966.

[38]Dapper, *loc. cit.*, p. 53. She says that PSSC Physics was, in fact, directed towards students in the top quarter of their class, students who definitely intended to go to college.

[39]Judson B. Cross. "Some Notes on the Philosophy of P.S.S.C." Miscellaneous paper circulated at Education Development Center, Newton, Massachusetts, July 10, 1963. On page 1 Cross suggests that PSSC Physics should be a course that challenges the best high school students—in fact, the future Nobel Prize winners.

[40]Schwab. "Problems, Topics, Issues," *loc. cit.*, p. 7.

[41]Joseph J. Schwab. "The Concept of the Structure of a Discipline." *The Educational Record*, Vol. 43, No. 3 (July, 1962).

[42]Both Sizer, *loc. cit.*, and Krug, *loc. cit.*, argue that the irradication of the 40 different subjects taught in the high school and the standardization of the curriculum in such a way that it consisted of no more than a half dozen disciplines was one of the major motives underlying the Committee of Ten, the many lectures of Charles Eliot, and the first school reform movement within the Scholar Academic Ideology (1880-1910).

[43]Daniel Bell. *The Reforming of General Education.* New York: Columbia University Press, 1966.

[44]National Education Association. *Report of the Committee of Ten on*

Secondary School Studies. New York: American Book Company, 1894. For example, this prestigeous report states that "If twice as much time is given in a school to Latin as is given to mathematics, the attainments of the pupils in Latin ought to be twice as great as they are in mathematics, provided that equally good work is done in the two subjects; and Latin will have twice the educational value of mathematics." A copy of the report exists in the appendix of Sizer, *loc. cit.* This quote comes from pages 252-253 of the Sizer reprint.

[45] Philip Phenix. *Realms of Meaning.* New York: McGraw-Hill, 1964.

[46] Schwab. "Problems, Topics, Issues," *loc. cit.*, pp. 11-12.

[47] Schwab. "Problems, Topics, Issues," *loc. cit.*, and King and Brownell, *loc. cit.*, both present discussions of this.

[48] Krug, *loc. cit.*, ch. 10, discusses this issue with respect to the question of vocational education versus the disciplines in the schools from 1880-1920.

[49] *Report of the Committee of Ten, loc. cit.*, provides a discussion of this issue with many diagrams and charts.

[50] Schwab. "Problems, Topics, Issues," *loc. cit.*, p. 7.

[51] The issue of how one goes about classifying the disciplines, in contrast to the issue of the need to classify and the issue of the uses of the classification, has not been discussed. Two different types of procedures seem to be used: what might be called the Schwab scheme and the Phenix scheme. The Schwab scheme goes something like this: first, assume each discipline has many different structures and generate them; second, generate the classification scheme from the needs of society, children, etc.; third, fit the disciplines to the classification scheme in order to determine the nature of the school program. The Phenix scheme goes something like this: first, postulate the classification scheme according to some personal hunch; second, assume each discipline has one and only one structure and state it; and, third, fit the disciplines to the classification scheme according to the reasons used to construct the classification scheme. The Phenix scheme is by far the most popular.

[52] King and Brownell, *loc. cit.*, p. 190.

[53] *Ibid.*, pp. 187-188.

[54] Phenix. "The Architectonics," *loc. cit.*, p. 51.

[55] *Goals for School Mathematics: The Report of the Cambridge*

Conference on School Mathematics. Boston: Houghton Mifflin, 1963, p. viii, from the foreword by Francis Keppel.

[56] Bruner. *The Process, loc. cit.*, p. 31.

[57] *Goals for School Mathematics, loc. cit.*, pp. 2-4.

[58] Fraser, *loc. cit.*, p. 23.

[59] King and Brownell, *loc. cit.*, pp. 105-110. Joseph J. Schwab. "On the Corruption of Education by Psychology." *The School Review*. Vol. 67 (Summer, 1958).

[60] Joseph S. Lukinsky. " 'Structure' in Educational Theory." *Educational Philosophy and Theory*. Vol. 2, No. 2 (October, 1970), pp. 15-31.

[61] A term used by Bruner in *The Process of Education.*

[62] Schwab. "Problems, Topics, Issues," *loc. cit.*, p. 9.

[63] F. Michael Connelly. "Conceptual Structures in Ecology with Special Reference to an Enquiry Curriculum in Ecology." Chicago: University of Chicago, unpublished doctoral dissertation, 1968.

[64] Schwab. "The Concept," *loc. cit.*, Schwab. "Problems," *loc. cit.*; and Bellack, *loc. cit.*

[65] In both *BSCS Biology Teachers Handbook*. New York: John Wiley, 1964, and "Problems, Topics, and Issues," Joseph Schwab talks about the changing nature of biology and the other sciences. He makes a definite point to indicate that the textbooks of the period 1890 to 1929 were correct for their time because they corresponded to the structure of science at that time—which were taxonomic, morphological, classificatory, and microscopic. The textbooks for the period 1930 to 1960 were not "right" for their time, however, because they reflected a picture of the nature of the scientific disciplines that no longer existed. The purpose of BSCS was to rectify the situation by updating the picture of science presented in high school biology courses by developing curricula that reflected the present nature of biology—which was microscopic, dynamic, structural, relational, and functional.

[66] Because disciplines evolve over time, the problem arises of how to minimize the gap between what occurs at the top of a discipline's hierarchy and the bottom of the discipline's hierarchy—between the work of scholars at the forefront of the disciplines and the work of students in the schools. The noticeable parallelism between the generation of new knowledge by a

discipline and the teaching of certain knowledges at earlier and earlier grades within the schools is the reflection of yet another problem of the structure of the disciplines.

[67] Arthur W. Foshay. "How Fare the Disciplines?" *Phi Delta Kappan*, Vol. 51, No. 7 (March, 1970), p. 349.

[68] Schwab. "The Concept," *loc. cit.*, p. 197.

[69] *Ibid.*

[70] Phenix. "The Disciplines," *loc. cit.*, pp. 64-65.

[71] Robert B. Davis. "Discovery in the Teaching of Mathematics." In Lee S. Shulman and Evan R. Keislar (Eds.). *Learning by Discovery: A Critical Appraisal.* Chicago: Rand McNally, 1966, p. 116.

[72] Sizer, *loc. cit.*, p. 72, speaks of this while Grobman, *loc. cit.*, p. 73, provides an example of the manner in which developers do so.

[73] Harold Rugg. "The Foundations and Techniques of Curriculum Construction." *The Twenty-Sixth Yearbook for The National Society for the Study of Education: Volumes I and II.* Bloomington, Ill.: Public School Publishing Co., 1927, p. 64.

[74] John I. Goodlad. *The Changing School Curriculum.* New York: The Fund for the Advancement of Education, 1966. John I. Goodlad. *School Curriculum Reform in the United States.* New York: The Fund for the Advancement of Education, 1964.

[75] Phenix. "The Architectonics," *loc. cit.*, p. 51.

[76] Schwab. "Problems, Topics, Issues," *loc. cit.*, p. 31; and Bruner, *The Process, loc. cit.*, p. 72.

[77] Gilbert Ryle. *The Concept of Mind.* London: Hutchinson, 1949, pp. 310, 311; and Phenix, "The Use," *loc. cit.*, p. 274.

[78] King and Brownell, *loc. cit.*, p. 20.

[79] *Ibid.*, p. 212.

[80] The traditional phrase back to which the incompleteness idea is traced is John Locke's (*Essay Concerning Human Understanding*, Book II, Chapter I, Section 2): "Let us then suppose the mind to be, as we say, white paper, void of all characters, without any ideas..." Israel Scheffler, "Philosophical

Models of Teaching." *Harvard Education Review*, Vol. 35, No. 2 (Spring, 1965), discusses three different deficiency models of the nature of man and the accompanying models of teaching.

[81] Fletcher Watson. "Approaching the Design of Science Curricula." Cambridge: unpublished paper at the Harvard Graduate School of Education, 1962, p. 1.

[82] *Report of the Committee of Ten, loc. cit.*, p. 225.

[83] *Goals for School Mathematics, loc. cit.*, p. 2.

[84] *Ibid.*, p. 3.

[85] Schwab. "The Concept," *loc. cit.*, p. 197.

[86] Philip Phenix. "Curriculum and the Analysis of Language." In James B. MacDonald and Robert R. Leeper (Eds.) *Language and Meaning*. Washington, D.C.: Association for Supervision and Curriculum Development, 1966, p. 31.

[87] *BSCS Handbook, loc. cit.*, pp. 30, 39-47; and Mary E. Diederich. "Physical Sciences and the Processes of Inquiry." *Journal of Research in Science Teaching*. Vol. 6, No. 4 (Feb., 1969), p. 309.

[88] Phenix. "The Disciplines," *loc. cit.*, p. 63.

[89] Bruner. Toward, *loc. cit.*, p. 72; and Grobman, *loc. cit.*, p. 80.

[90] James Sully. *Teachers Handbook of Psychology*. New York: Appleton, 1886, p. 49.

[91] Foshay, *loc. cit.*, p. 349.

[92] Many sources exist that describe faculty psychology. The following is one: Walter B. Kolesnick. *Mental Discipline in Modern Education*. Madison: University of Wisconsin Press, 1962. This book is interesting because it makes the claim that faculty psychology flourishes today under only a slightly different guise than used in the 1890's.

[93] Jerome Bruner. "Needed: A Theory of Instruction." *Educational Leadership*, Vol. 20, No. 8 (May, 1963), p. 529. See also: Bruner. *Toward, loc. cit.*, p. 33.

[94] Lee S. Shulman. "Psychological Controversies in the Teaching of Science and Mathematics." *The Science Teacher*. Vol. 35, No. 6 (September, 1966), p. 38.

[95] *Goals for School Mathematics, loc. cit.*, p. 13.

[96] Harold Ordway Rugg and John Roscoe Clark. "Scientific Method in the Reconstruction of Ninth-Grade Mathematics: A Complete Report of the Investigation of the Illinois Committee on Standardization of Ninth-Grade Mathematics: 1913-1918." *Supplementary Educational Monographs*, Vol. II, No. 1 (April, 1918).

[97] *The Scholars Look at the Schools: A Report of the Disciplines Seminar*. Washington, D.C.: National Education Association, 1962, p. 53.

[98] King and Brownell, *loc. cit.*, p. 157.

[99] *Ibid.*, p. 121.

[100] Ryle, *loc. cit.*, p. 310.

[101] King and Brownell, *loc. cit.*, pp. 160, 189.

[102] *Ibid.*, pp. 121, 197.

[103] *Goals for School Mathematics, loc. cit.*, p. 2.

[104] *Ibid.*, p. 3.

[105] Frederick L. Ferris. "Testing in the New Curriculums: Numerology, Tyranny, or Common Sense." *The School Review*, Vol. 70 (Spring, 1962), p. 162.

[106] Lee J. Cronbach. "Course Improvement Through Evaluation." *Teachers College Record*, Vol. 64, No. 8 (May, 1963), p. 675.

3.
Social Efficiency Ideology

A SCIENTIFIC TECHNIQUE OF
CURRICULUM MAKING

In 1913 Franklin Bobbitt launched the Social Efficiency Ideology by demanding that educators apply to their endeavors the techniques of scientific engineering developed by industry.[1] In 1918, in *The Curriculum*—the book that dates the birth of the field of curriculum—Bobbitt further declared that the educational "task preceding all others is the determination of . . . a scientific technique" of curriculum making.[2] It is the quest after and utilization of this "scientific technique" that underlies the Social Efficiency Ideology. In *The Curriculum* Bobbitt described the underpinnings of the scientific technique of curriculum making this way:

> The central theory is simple. Human life, however varied, consists in the performance of specific activities. Education that prepares for life is one that prepares definitely and adequately for these specific activities. However numerous and diverse they may be for any social class, they can be discovered. This requires only that one go out into the world of affairs and discover the particulars of which these affairs consist. These will show the abilities, attitudes, habits, appreciations, and forms of knowledge that men need. These will be the objectives of the curriculum. They will be numerous, definite, and particularized. The curriculum will then be that series of experiences which children and youth

must have by way of attaining those objectives . . . that
*series of things which children and youth must do and
experience* by way of developing abilities to do the
things well that make up the affairs of adult life; and to
be in all respects what adults should be.[3]

In 1949 Ralph W. Tyler presented the essence of Bobbitt's
scientific technique of curriculum making in its broadest form in
Basic Principles of Curriculum and Instruction.[4] He did so by
presenting four basic questions which must be answered while
developing any curriculum. They are:

1. What educational purposes should the school seek to
   attain?
2. What educational experiences can be provided that
   are likely to attain these purposes?
3. How can these educational experiences be effectively
   organized?
4. How can we determine whether these purposes are
   being attained?[5]

Let us briefly examine the nature and significance of each of these
questions within the Social Efficiency Ideology, as they are
expressed by Tyler in *Basic Principles of Curriculum and Instruction.*

Tyler's first concern is with "What educational purposes should
the school seek to attain?" These "educational purposes" are what
Franklin Bobbitt called the "objectives of the curriculum" in *The
Curriculum.* Determination of the objectives of the curriculum is
an essential and unavoidable first task for curriculum developers
within the Social Efficiency Ideology, for as Tyler says,

if an educational program is to be planned . . . it is very
necessary to have some conception of the goals that are
being aimed at. These educational objectives become the
criteria by which materials are selected, content is
outlined, instructional procedures are developed and
tests and examinations are prepared.[6]

As a result, during the early stages of curriculum development one
finds the Social Efficiency developer "devoting much time to the
setting up and formulation of objectives, because they are the
most critical criteria for guiding all the other activities of the
curriculum-maker."[7] Social Efficiency developers believe, in fact,

that one cannot proceed to other phases of the curriculum development process until after objectives have been formulated, for as Tyler puts it, "All aspects of the educational program are really means to accomplish basic educational purposes."[8] The importance of determining curricular objectives in a systematic and scientific manner can be partially gathered from noting that approximately 50 percent of *Basic Principles of Curriculum and Instruction* is devoted to discussing how to determine the objectives of a curriculum. Tyler's basic assumption about the source from which curricular objectives should be drawn is summed up in his statement that "no single source of information is adequate to provide a basis for wise and comprehensive decisions about the objectives of the school."[9] What is important is to use systematic and scientific methods to draw curriculum objectives from a wide range of sources, such as the nature of the culture, the desires of members of society, studies of learners, and the beliefs of academicians and subject matter specialists—in short, from all relevant aspects of the "world of affairs," as Bobbitt put it.

Important to Tyler and other adherents of the Social Efficiency Ideology is the nature of educational purposes as expressed in the way in which curricular objectives are phrased. The objectives of the curriculum are to be stated in behavioral terms: as observable human skills, as capabilities for action, as activities that man can perform, as demonstratable things that a person can do. Stating objectives in behavioral terms is important for several reasons. First, the phrasing of objectives reflects the Social Efficiency developer's conception of the nature of man. The essence of man is expressed in the specific behaviors he can perform. Important here is both the *behavioral* conception of man and the conception of man as a bundle of *specific* skills. As Bobbitt summed it up in 1918, "Human life, however varied, consists in the performance of specific activities." Although Tyler does not fully accept this, it is crucial to the working content surrounding the ideology. Second, the phrasing of objectives in behavioral terms reflects the Social Efficiency developer's conception of the nature and purpose of education. Tyler describes the nature of education this way: "Education is a process of changing the behavior of peo- ple . . . educational objectives, then, represent the kinds of changes in behavior that an educational institution seeks to bring about in its students."[10] Tyler describes the purpose of education similarly: "Since the real purpose of education is . . . to bring about significant changes in the students' patterns of behavior, it becomes important to recognize that any statement of the objectives of the school should be a statement of changes to take place in students."[11] The essence of education is thus summed up by the phrase "changing of behavior." And, third, the phrasing of curricular objectives in behavioral terms allows them to be stated in a form which facilitates the efficient and scientific development of the curriculum: both in a form that "provides clear specifications to indicate just what the educational job is"[12] and "in a form which makes them most helpful in selecting learning experiences and in guiding teaching."[13]

Tyler's second concern is with "What educational experiences can be provided that are likely to attain these purposes?" These "educational experiences" of Tyler's are the same as Bobbitt's learning "experiences which children . . . must have by way of attaining those objectives." Here the "experiences" from which the child learns comprise the substance of the curriculum and are the means to attaining the ends of the curriculum as defined in its "objectives." Learning experiences have this place within the curriculum because it is believed that "for a given objective to be attained, a student must have [learning] experiences that give him an opportunity to *practice the kind of behavior implied by the objective*."[14] Here, "the term 'learning experience' refers to the interaction between the learner and the external conditions in the environment to which he can react."[15] There are two aspects of this concept of learning experiences that are crucial to Tyler and the Social Efficiency Ideology. First, Tyler believes that "Learning takes place through the active behavior of the student; it is what he does that he learns."[16] Second, Tyler believes that "learning takes place through the experiences which the learner has; that is, through the reactions he makes to the environment in which he is placed."[17] From this viewpoint, both the learner and the conditions for learning provided by the learning experiences are crucial. The learner is crucial to the learning process because he "himself must carry on the action which is basic to the experience"[18] from which he learns: because "it is the reactions of the learner himself that determine what is learned."[19] The conditions for learning which comprise the learning experience are crucial because the actions and reactions of the learner are controlled, molded, or shaped through the interactions that he has with the environment in which he is placed. The significance of this for the behavior of the curriculum developer follows directly. He must control the learning experiences that the student has by "manipulation of the environment in such a way as to set up stimulating situations—situations that will evoke the kind of behavior desired."[20] In particular, he must contrive an educational environment that contains the stimulus conditions which will elicit, stimulate, reinforce, and support the behavior (actions and reactions) desired of the student as specified by the objectives of the curriculum.

Tyler's third concern is with "How can these educational experiences be effectively organized?" This is similar to Bobbitt's concern with creating an effective *"series* of experiences" that children must encounter as they run the curriculum. It is important for educational experiences to be effectively organized, for as Tyler says,

In order for educational experiences to produce a cumulative effect, they must be so organized as to reinforce each other. Organization is thus seen as an important problem in curriculum development because it greatly influences the efficiency of instruction and the degree to which major educational changes are brought about in the learners.[21]

Important here is the word efficiency as it relates to the words sequence and objectives. To effectively organize learning experiences is to *sequence* them so that they *efficiently* facilitate transfer of learning from prior experiences to later ones, and *efficiently* facilitate transfer of learning from experiences in one area of endeavor to those in another so that educational *objectives* can be attained as *efficiently* as possible. The crux of the matter for Social Efficiency developers is to *sequence* learning experiences so that "each successive experience builds upon the preceding one"[22] in such a way as to allow the objectives of the curriculum to be reached in the most *efficient* manner possible by allowing learning to take place in the most *efficient* manner possible.

Tyler's fourth concern is with curricular evaluation: "How can we determine whether these purposes are being attained?" For Tyler and adherents of the Social Efficiency Ideology "the process of evaluation begins with the objectives of the educational program"[23]—with the educational purposes—and "is essentially the process of determining to what extent the educational objectives are actually being realized by the . . . curriculum."[24] Since "educational objectives are essentially changes in human beings,"[25] it follows that "evaluation is the process for determining the degree to which these changes in behavior are actually taking place."[26] Important here is that the behavioral conception of man and education that resulted in educational purposes being stated as behavioral objectives also ends up resulting in a concept of evaluation that is limited solely to the overt behavior of the evaluee and that is limited solely to the specific behaviors stated in the educational objectives. Since, as Bobbitt says, "the objectives of the curriculum . . . will be numerous, definite, and particularized," it follows that evaluation "will be numerous, definite, and particularized."

In summary, the scientific technique of curriculum making underlying Bobbitt's and Tyler's assumptions can, in the broadest of terms, be said to consist of scientifically determining "educational purposes," "educational experiences . . . to attain these purposes," an effective organization of these experiences, and evaluative measures to "determine whether these purposes are being attained" in accordance with a behavioral interpretation of the nature of man.

THE PROGRAMED CURRICULUM
AND THE BEHAVIORAL ENGINEER

The type of curriculum created by Social Efficiency developers can be called programed curriculum, partially because of the careful attention paid to the sequencing of events within it. There are many different ways of delivering the programed curriculum. Such range from sophisticated computerized teaching machines on which students work individually to programed courses taught to large groups of students at the same time; from mechanical teaching machines that offer students few learning choices to individually prescribed instruction where student interests, abilities, learning styles, and learning rates are to be accounted for through the writing of individual learning prescriptions; from environment simulators where the student does not need the aid of a teacher to curriculum packages where the teacher is the center of attention and where every utterance and action of the teacher is prescribed; from programed textbooks which present only written learning experiences to programed courses which present a wide variety of multimedia learning experiences that require the learner to engage in many different types of behavior. Describing one of these types of delivery systems, the assumptions underlying it, and the procedures used in creating its programed curriculum will make more concrete the scientific technique of curriculum making thus far described. The delivery system to be described is the mechanical teaching machine. Within the following discussion teaching machines are offered as an example of only one of many possible types of delivery systems for the programed curriculum. The purpose is not to limit the breath of the Social Efficiency Ideology but rather to illustrate only *one* of many ways in which it is manifested through its concrete application. It is, of course, quite feasible to deliver a programed curriculum without any mechanical or electronic means whatever.

One type of mechanical teaching machine consists of a large metal box with five touch-sensitive windows on its front surface. One large rectangular touch-sensitive window covers the upper half of the box's front surface and displays one item of information to which the learner must respond. Four smaller touch-sensitive square windows occupy the lower half of the box's front surface and display the learner's possible responses. To use this teaching machine the learner must match the information displayed in the rectangular window with the appropriate response displayed in one of the four square windows. First, the learner is presented with some information in the rectangular window. For example, the window might display the statement: "A number times ten is written by putting a zero to the right of the number as in 2 x 10 = 20, 3 x 10 = 30 or 8 x 10 = 80. What is 5 x 10?" When he is ready to respond, the learner presses the rectangular window, and the possible responses appear in the four square windows. For example, they might be "05," "50," "55," "40." The learner must now press the square window that he thinks contains the appropriate response. If the learner responds correctly, all five windows momentarily turn green as the information disappears from them, the next piece of information appears in the rectangular window, and the learner continues the above process. If the learner responds incorrectly, a buzzer sounds, only the possible responses disappear, the learner must press the rectangular window again to get the possible responses to reappear, and he then has a second opportunity to choose the correct response. This sequence is repeated until the correct response is chosen. Underlying the operation of this teaching machine is a program, or programed curriculum, that consists of a carefully sequenced set of frames, each frame consisting of one item of information and its corresponding possible responses. The frames that make up the program are designed and sequenced in such a way as to gradually lead the learner from incompetence to competence in a particular skill.

This description of a teaching machine "should not be allowed to obscure the truly important feature of the new technology, namely, the application of methods for behavioral control in developing programs for teaching."[27] The "new technology of teaching . . . is not simply the mechanization of teaching, but instead . . . a behavioral engineering of teaching procedures."[28] Such a behavioral engineering of teaching procedures contains both a conceptual component that explains how the teaching machine actually teaches and a methodological component that dictates how the programed curriculum for the teaching machine should be created. Underlying both is the curriculum developer's conception of himself as a "behavioral engineer."

Understanding how a teaching machine teaches requires an understanding of the nature of teaching. The behavioral engineer views teaching as a process of shaping a learner's behavior through the use of rewards or reinforcements. The learner's behavior is to be shaped in such a way that the occurrence of a specific stimulus automatically results in the learner emitting a desired response. The stimulus that the teaching machine described above produces for the learner is the information presented within the rectangular window. The learner's response is his pushing of a square window. The reinforcement or reward provided the learner for a correct response consists of the touch-sensitive windows immediately turning green followed by the presentation of the next frame in the program. And the learner's behavior is shaped both by arranging the rewards of learning in such a way that they reinforce the connection between the desired response and the specific stimulus upon which it is to be contingent, and by not letting the learner proceed to more advanced frames until he automatically emits the desired response to a specific stimulus. Underlying this view of teaching are several crucial assumptions.

First, it is assumed that learning consists of a change in behavior, the new behavior being the emitting of a response to a stimulus that would not otherwise have taken place. Something is learned from the teaching machine when a learner responds to a stimulus—the information in the rectangular window—in a way he would not have before exposure to the machine.

Second, it is assumed that learning takes place only through the learner having the opportunity to practice the behavior he is to learn, for it is what one does that one learns. On the teaching machine the learner practices the behavior he is to learn because he is required to respond to the stimulus by actually emitting the desired behavior by pushing a square touch-sensitive window.

Third, it is assumed that learning is specific with respect to particular stimuli: that learning consists of acquiring specific responses that are associated with specific stimuli, and that it does not consist of acquiring vague and general responses to vague and general stimuli. For example, it is assumed that one does not learn to "multiply" in general but that one learns such things as "multiplying a one digit number by ten." This is inherent in the nature of the frame of the teaching machine that presents one item of clearly defined information to the learner at a time, to which there is only one specific and clearly defined response.

Fourth, it is assumed that a learner can acquire complex behaviors only gradually by slowly building up ever more complex repertoires of behavior out of simpler ones. Teaching machines support this assumption because their programs move the learner in finely graded steps through many unitary frames, each of which develops a single behavior in such a way that successive, more complex behaviors build upon the simpler behaviors preceding them. In addition, the teaching machine guarantees that the learner actually does slowly build up ever more complex repertoires of behavior because it does not allow him to advance to subsequent levels of complexity until after he has demonstrated that he has mastered the preceding prerequisites. It does this by evaluating the learner's response to each frame in the program and by allowing him to proceed further only after he has shown his ability to respond to that frame correctly.

And, fifth, it is assumed that all aspects of learning can be dealt with within the context of the above mentioned view of teaching. Complex behaviors, such as learning how to fly an airplane, simply require the development of complex teaching machines, such as the computerized flight simulators developed by the U.S. Air Force. Skills not so seemingly overtly behavioral, such as intellectual skills, simply require that in dealing with them we accept that

> we are actually referring to a verbal repertoire controlled by the same laws as other behavior. The old, defunct explanatory concepts of knowledge, meaning, mind, or symbolic processes have never offered the possibility of manipulation or control; but behavior, verbal or otherwise, can be controlled with ease and precision.[29]

Equating such things as intellectual skills with verbal behavior allows the behavioral engineer to assume that through shaping verbal behavior he is also shaping the corresponding intellectual skills. Thus, by shaping a learner's ability to respond appropriately in a verbal manner to verbal stimuli relating to logic, it can be assumed that the learner's intellectual skills in logical reasoning are also being shaped. The power of equating intellectual skills and other such seemingly inaccessible human behaviors with verbal behavior comes in the ease with which verbal behavior can be dealt with on a teaching machine that requires only that written (verbal) stimuli be presented and written (verbal) responses be made.[30]

Underlying the mechanical functioning of a teaching machine is a programed curriculum, or program. The "behavioral engineering of teaching procedures" dictates how programed curricula for teaching machines are to be developed by behavioral engineers. There are four basic tasks in which the behavioral engineer must engage while developing a program.

The first task that the behavioral engineer must undertake in designing a program is to obtain the "educational purposes" of the program he is to develop. These specify the exact terminal performances the learner is to acquire as a result of performing the behaviors demanded by the sequence of frames making up the program. Educational purposes are obtained from the clients for whom the program is being designed—they are not invented by the behavioral engineer himself. Depending upon the circumstances surrounding the particular program being created, such clients might be society as a whole, a scholarly organization (such as the American Association for the Advancement of Science), a single academician, a group of concerned parents, a group of teachers, a school administrator, a publishing company, or a number of children. In obtaining educational purposes from the client for whom he or she works, the behavioral engineer must help the client phrase them in a form that is helpful in guiding his or her endeavors while creating the program. The form to be used is a behavioral one: such purposes "must be phrased in terms of observable behaviors of pupils and must be so specific as to refer both to the exact ability [the pupil is to acquire] and the exact content to which it [the ability] is to be applied."[31]

The second task the behavioral engineer must undertake is to carefully analyze the "educational purposes" of the program into a sequence of extremely specific behavioral objectives, each of which represents one stimulus-response contingency that the learner must acquire in order to be gradually moved from incompetence to competence by the teaching machine. This analysis is often referred to as task analysis, activity analysis, or construction of a learning hierarchy. It "requires that the behaviors that lead to terminal behaviors are carefully analyzed and sequenced in a hierarchical order such that each behavior builds on the objective immediately below it in the sequence and is prerequisite to those that follow it."[32] One Social Efficiency developer, Robert Gagné, describes one of the many existing ways in which such an analysis can be logically accomplished when he writes,

> Analysis of a topic begins with the statement of the terminal objective—the performance or performances one expects the student to be able to exhibit after the learning of that topic has been completed. Once this

objective has been satisfactorily defined, one can proceed to identify a subordinate set of subtopics, each an
individual learning act, that must be considered prerequisites for the learning. Each of these subtopics in
turn may be subjected to the same process of analysis,
until one has arrived at performances that the students
are known to possess, at which point the analysis stops.
Each *subordinate* objective, then, is derived by systematically applying to the *next higher objective* the
question, "What must the student already know how to
do, in order to learn this performance?" The description
of what the student must know—in other words, the
prerequisite capabilities he must have—identifies the
subordinate objectives.[33]

This is not a simple endeavor, for to create a program of any
length requires defining and sequencing hundreds of extremely
specific behavioral objectives in such a way that the learner is
continuously and gradually led from incompetence to competence
with the least amount of difficulty.[34] Once the specific behavioral
objectives are constructed and appropriately sequenced, the
behavioral engineer begins his third task.

The third task that the behavioral engineer must undertake in
designing a program is to create and organize the learning
experiences that the learner will encounter while using the
teaching machine. The learning experiences are the program's
frames, which consist of stimuli and their associated possible
responses. The organization of learning experiences is the linear
sequence of frames within the program. Each frame or learning
experience that is created corresponds to one of the clearly
specified behavioral objectives previously defined. The linear
sequencing of the frames or learning experiences that is created to
form the program parallels the sequence of specific behavioral
objectives previously defined. In the end,

The actual instructional content of a program consists
of a sequence of learning tasks or activities (e.g., frames,
steps), through which a student can proceed with little
outside help, and provides a series of small increments in
learning that enables the student to proceed from a
condition of lack of command of the terminal behavior
to that of command of it.[35]

The fourth task that the behavioral engineer must undertake is to design evaluative measures that accompany each and every learning experience or frame that the learner encounters. These evaluative measures are designed so as to be inherent in the response the learner makes to each frame in the program, and they simply indicate whether or not the learner has acquired the desired behavior which the frame was designed to impart. These evaluative measures serve at least the following four functions. They provide "for rather immediate feedback to the student concerning the adequacy of his performance on each frame or element of the program"[36] under the assumption that "learning is enhanced if students receive rather immediate feedback concerning the correctness of their efforts in attempting to approximate a desired behavior."[37] They continually assess whether or not the learner has acquired the desired behavior from each frame—that is, made the correct response to the stimulus presented by the teaching machine; as a result, they determine whether the learner will be allowed to proceed to successive frames within the program or whether he must do additional work before proceeding further— that is, repeat the frame until he performs the correct response. They provide a continual "monitoring function, both for the learner and the teacher"[38] that can keep them both "rather continuously informed regarding his [the learner's] goals and his performance."[39] The evaluative measures provide the behavioral engineer with information that can be used to determine the effectiveness of the program itself in obtaining the educational purposes for which it is designed. Such information can be used both as a basis for improving either frames or their sequence if such is necessary and as a basis for proving to the client that the program produced to accomplish his purposes does in fact do so.

Inherent in the description just offered of teaching machines, the assumptions underlying its functioning, and the procedures used in creating its program are several factors that are common to most Social Efficiency curricula. First, there is the conception of curriculum as programed curriculum: as a highly structured *"series of experiences,"* as Bobbitt phrased it, designed to shape (or program) the behaviors of the learner. Second, there is the conception of the curriculum developer as a behavioral engineer, as a person who uses a scientific technique of curriculum making.

Third, there is a conception of learning as a shaping process which results in a change in behavior, which takes place through the learner practicing the behavior he is to learn, which is specific with respect to particular stimuli, and which results in complex behaviors being developed only gradually through the accumulation of many small unitary prerequisite behaviors. Fourth, there is a belief that the procedure for constructing curriculum requires that the developer consult a client to obtain the educational purposes for his curriculum which are to be stated as terminal performances; that he analyze the educational purposes into a sequence of very specific behavioral tasks; that he create and sequence learning experiences to enable the learner to attain each of the specific behavioral tasks and eventually the terminal performances; and that he create evaluative measures that continually monitor the behavior of learners who are engaged in experiencing the curriculum.

THE ANALOGY
The Myth

The central myth within the Social Efficiency Ideology is that of "scientific instrumentalism." This myth asserts (a) that curriculum should be developed in a "scientific" manner similar to the way in which industry produces its products, and (b) that curriculum development should be an "instrument" in fulfilling needs disjoint from its own vested interests in a manner similar to the way in which industry fulfills needs disjoint from its own interests. In the opening sentence of the first major work produced by a curriculum developer within the Social Efficiency Ideology, Franklin Bobbitt announced the spirit of "scientific instrumentalism" in 1913:

> At a time when so much discussion is being given to the possibilities of "scientific management" in the world of material production, it seems desirable that the principles of this more effective form of management be examined in order to ascertain the possibility of applying them to the problems of education.[40]

This belief in the "scientific management" of curriculum-making lies at the heart of the Social Efficiency Ideology. It is a belief in a methodology of curriculum making: a belief in a scientific technique of curriculum making. It asserts that the manner in which curriculum is developed is more important than the content of the curriculum or the ends of the curriculum. It embodies two attempts to make education more efficient in meeting its demands: first, it embodies an attempt to be "scientific" by using the tools of science to efficiently construct curricula,[41] and second, it embodies an attempt to turn curriculum making into an instrument for fulfilling the wishes of a client.

The Analogy

In an analogy comparing curriculum development to the industrial manufacture of steel rails, Franklin Bobbitt laid bare the essentials of the Social Efficiency Ideology.[42] The school is compared to a factory. The child is the raw material. The adult is the finished product. The teacher is an operative or factory worker. The curriculum is whatever processing the raw material (the child) needs to change him into the finished product (the desired adult). The curriculum developer is a member of the research department who finds out what the consumer market (society) wants in terms of a finished product and who finds out the most efficient way of producing that finished product.

Role of Curriculum Developer

The curriculum developer, thus, has two functions to perform: he must determine what the consumer market wants in terms of a finished product, and he must determine the most efficient way of producing that finished product. The nature of these two central aspects of the work of the curriculum developer are summed up by Bobbitt in his first two principles of curriculum-making:

> *Principle I.* Definite qualitative and quantitative standards must be determined for the product [the desired adult].
>
> *Principle II.* Where the material [man] that is acted upon by the labor processes [teacher] passes through a number of progressive stages on its way from the raw material [child] to the ultimate product [adult], definite qualitative and quantitative standards must be determined for the product at each of these stages.[43]

The first principle refers to the creation of terminal objectives for the curriculum. Terminal objectives are what Tyler calls educational purposes. Terminal objectives designate the ends of the curriculum and the standards which indicate when the ends have been satisfactorily met. The major curriculum developers active within the Social Efficiency Ideology between 1910 and 1930 focused their efforts upon the endeavors inherent in satisfactory fulfillment of "Principle I." Franklin Bobbitt is an example of such a developer.

The second principle refers to the creation of progressive objectives, which are often termed "interim" or "en route" objectives. Progressive objectives consist of the series of specific behavioral objectives that collectively comprise the terminal objectives. Creating progressive objectives involves determining the means by which terminal objectives are to be accomplished. Such is accomplished both by specifying a series of specific subobjectives, called progressive objectives, which indicate the step-by-step change in the student which must take place for the terminal objectives to be accomplished, and by specifying the standards which indicate when each progressive objective has been accomplished. The major curriculum developers active within the Social Efficiency Ideology between 1940 and 1975 focused their efforts upon the endeavors inherent in satisfactory fulfillment of "Principle II." Robert Gagné is an example of such a developer.

Both the early developers and the modern developers working within the Social Efficiency Ideology recognized the vital importance of both terminal and progressive objectives. However, due to historical trends, to be discussed later, differential emphasis has been placed on the two types of objectives at different times during this century.

Social Orientation and Terminal Objectives

Within Bobbitt's analogy, society is the source from which the terminal objectives of the curriculum are to be determined. Since society does not realize the importance of specifically stating terminal objectives, it becomes the curriculum developer's job to discover them. As such, the curriculum developer, acting as an agent of society, determines the needs of society and the suitable product which will fulfill those needs. Just as a steel mill is no more than a contractor to do a job for railroads in making rails, so the curriculum developer and the schools are no more than contractors to do a job for society in making suitable adults. As Bobbitt puts it:

> It is well to note also, for our purposes, that the standard qualifications of the product are not determined by the steel plant itself. The qualitative and quantitative specifications are determined by those that order the product, in this case, the railroads. The steel mills are but agents of the railroads ... it is the transportation world that determines all qualitative and quantitative standards for this particular product . . . . Now the relation of the school system to the various departments of the world's activity is exactly the same as the relation of the steel plant to the transportation industry. . . . It is the need of the world of affairs that determines the standard specification for the educational product. A school system can no more find standards of performance within itself than a steel plant can find the proper height or weight per yard for steel rails from the activities within the plant. . . . This principle is fundamental. . . . The standards must of necessity be determined . . . by those that use the product, not by those who produce it. . . . Standards are to be found in the world of affairs, not in the schools.[44]

Progressive Objectives

This is not the case with respect to progressive objectives. Although society states specifically what product is to be produced by the schools, it is the curriculum developer who determines the most efficient way of producing it. As Bobbitt states:

> The standards for the educational product required by the first principle stated at the head of this section must necessarily be socially determined by matters that lie outside of the school system. The progressive standards required by the second principle must be psychologically and experimentally determined by expert educa-

tional workers within the school system itself. This is a special professional problem requiring scientific investigation of a highly technical sort. It is a field of work in which the untrained layman can have no opinion and in which he has no right to interfere. Society is to say what shall be accomplished in the ultimate education of each class of individuals. Only the specialist can determine how it is to be done.[45]

Education

Within the Social Efficiency Ideology the production of an educated person through schooling is viewed in much the same way as the production of steel rails. To use Bobbitt's analogy again:

Education is a shaping process as much as the manufacture of steel rails; the personality is to be shaped and fashioned into desirable forms. It is a shaping of more delicate matters, more immaterial things, certainly; yet a shaping process none the less. It is also an enormously more complex process because of the great multitude of aspects of the personality to be shaped if the whole as finished is to stand in full and right proportions.[46]

"Scientific Instrumentalism"

Bobbitt's analogy, in which curriculum-making is compared to the industrial manufacture of steel rails, provides the basic metaphor underlying the Social Efficiency Ideology. Its method of curriculum-making is called "scientific instrumentalism." It is called "scientific" because developers using it have, as William Lovell Patty says, attempted "to apply the routines of traditional scientific procedure ... to education ... assuming an *ipso facto* application of the scientific spirit ... placing their faith in the procedures of current scientific thought and technology. . ."[47] The method is called "instrumentalistic" because developers using it have conceived of themselves as instruments and of their method as an instrument useful in fulfilling an end which is completely disjoint from themselves and their method.

The Social Efficiency Ideology will now be explored by examining the nature of the social orientation, the curricular activity involved in creating terminal objectives, the curricular activity involved in creating progressive objectives, the dichotomy resulting from the separation of activities involving the creation of terminal and progressive objectives, and the major historical trends which provided the impetus for the growth of the ideology.

SOCIAL ORIENTATION
Society

Curriculum developers working within the Social Efficiency Ideology take society as a given. They view human life as capable of existing and flourishing only within the social context. For man, human society is the ultimate necessity. And for education, the social orientation is obligatory.[48] Bobbitt infers this when he writes,

> We are accustomed to say that education is a social process. It is the process of recivilizing, or civilizing anew, each new generation.
>
> Each individual, we are told, is born on the cultural level of one hundred thousand years ago. He is but a bundle of potentialities. He brings with him no portion of our accumulated human culture. Literally, he is born a savage. Education is the process of so conditioning his activities and experiences that, as he grows up, he is shaped into the normally civilized man.
>
> What is true of the individual is true of the whole new generation.... Society has the responsibility of so conditioning the growth of this new generation that it takes over and exhibits in its conduct the high and complex culture activities which man has been slowly inventing, accumulating, and habituating himself to during the long period of human history. Society's performance of this recivilizing function we call education.[49]

Two Social Efficiency assumptions about the nature of society need elaboration. First, society is viewed as consisting of a system of activities. The essence of society lies not in the products of society—in its accumulated knowledge, its accumulated art work, or its accumulated architecture—but rather in the activities which allow the members of the society to interact with each other in a manner which sustains the society. Franklin Bobbitt infers this when he says that "Civilization is a system of activities. . . . Civilization has been a process of inventing and using improved, and usually enlarged, methods of carrying on the activities of life."[50]

Second, developers using the Social Efficiency Ideology view the essence of society to be located in the set of activities engaged in by its mature adult members. Society is defined in terms of the "affairs of the mature world,"[51] and not in terms of the affairs of youth. As Bobbitt says, "note the strategic character of the adult activities. It is here that civilization manifests itself in its highest terms."[52]

Man in Society

Man is not conceived as existing or functioning as an isolated individual but as an integral component of society. Man is first a member of society and second an individual. As a member of society man has two characteristics.

First, man is conceived as an actor within society. He is a bundle of activities. His essence is determined by the activities in which he can successfully engage. His meaningfulness is summed up in the behaviors he can perform. Bobbitt elaborates on this interpretation of the nature of man, while putting it in the context of what developers working within the Social Efficiency Ideology are reacting against, in asserting that man's nature is that of a "doer."

> A recently published book begins with the sentence: "Education is the process of filling the mind with knowledge." In that single sentence we have the central conception of the old education. According to this conception, a human being, as he begins life, is mainly but an empty knowledge reservoir. The business of education is to fill this reservoir with the prepared facts of history, geography, grammar, science, and the rest. . . . Man is not a mere intellectual reservoir to be filled with knowledge. He is an infinitely complex creature of endlessly diversified *action*. His most salient characteristic is not his memory reservoir, whether filled or unfilled, but *action, conduct, behavior*. Action is the

thing of which his life is made. In his activity he lives
and realizes the ends of his existence . . . his behavior is
his life. Primarily, he is not a *knower*, but a *doer*. . . .
Since he is primarily a doer, to educate him is to prepare
him to perform those activities which make up his life.
The method of the new education is not subject storage
but *action*, activity, conduct, behavior.[53]

The conception of man as a "doer" can be interpreted in the sense
of his performing physical activities, emotional activities, social
activities, intellectual activities, activities of all types. In every
sense of the word man is conceived as a "doer," as a bundle of
action capabilities, and not as a reservoir of inert information.

Second, man's essence is viewed as embodied in his mature
adult behavior. As such, childhood is viewed as a stage of
preparation for adulthood. Childhood is not important in and of
itself. It is important because it provides a time to prepare for
adulthood. As Robert Gagné says of science education, "if one is
to begin science education at the earliest school level [kinder-
garten], one must have a rationale that connects adult behavior
with child behavior."[54] Thus, education of the six-year-old is to
prepare for the life of the seven-year-old, this in turn for that of
the eight-year-old, and so on until maturity is reached.[55] As
Bobbitt says:

It is helpful to begin with the simple assumption, to
be accepted literally, that education is to prepare men
and women for the activities of every kind which make
up, or which ought to make up, well-rounded adult life;
that it has no other purpose; that everything should be
done with a view to this purpose.[56]

Modern education has discovered the child and the
potential things within him that are to be cultivated and
made to grow into their mature forms.

It has discovered the child, but it does not see him
merely *as* a child. . . . It sees the man within the child as
clearly as it sees the child. It sees its task as one of
bringing into full and complete being this man within
the child. It cannot see the full-orbed man, however,
except as it sees him in action as he does his part in the
world of active affairs. It therefore sees society and

what man does and must do to live his life fully and well
within the actual society.[57]

The developer always keeps in mind "the man within the child" in
viewing the education of the child as preparation for adulthood
within society, for as Bobbitt insists, "Education is primarily for
adult life, not for child life. Its fundamental responsibility is to
prepare for the fifty years of adulthood, not for the twenty years
of childhood and youth."[58]

Educating Man to Live in Society

The aim of education is twofold; first, to perpetuate the
functioning of society; and, second, to prepare the individual to
lead a meaningful adult life within society. The means by which an
individual achieves an education is by learning to perform the
functions one must perform to be socially functional. And the
educated man is one who acts appropriately in society. Let us
examine each of these statements in turn.

Society as represented within the behavior of its adult members
is taken as a given. The necessity for its perpetuation is accepted
unquestionably. The means of perpetuating society is to prepare
the individuals who will constitute it to fulfill the social roles
needed to sustain its functioning. This is the job of the school.
W.W. Charters indicates this when he says:

> The point of view . . . is a functional one. It presup-
> poses that all subject matter has been created and
> preserved by the race to satisfy needs and solve
> problems, and that in the schools such parts of this
> subject matter as satisfy the most fundamental needs are
> taught.[59]

> Society possesses the right to require that the school
> shall educate its offspring so that they will be prepared
> to carry on the work of society with efficiency.[60]

The first aim of education is thus to perpetuate the functioning of
society.

Society is made up of men. And men take on their meaning, as
well as their fulfillment and pleasure, by participating in society.
The way to prepare the individual to lead a meaningful adult life
within society is to provide him with the skills which will allow
him to be constructively active within the social context. This is

also the job of the school. Robert Gagné and Franklin Bobbitt both hint at this when they say,

It is this social organization [the educational system] that must transform the highly dependent young child into the adult who, in his own individual manner, *lives a life that is satisfying to himself largely because it contributes to the goals of his society.*[61]

The business of education today is to teach to the growing individuals, so far as their original natures will permit, to perform efficiently those activities which constitute the latest and highest level of civilization. Since the latter consists entirely of activities, the objectives of education can be nothing other than activities, and since, after being observed, an activity is mastered by performing it, the process of education must be the observing and performing of activities. The curriculum is that performance of the activities in their earlier stages out of which the matured performance grows.[62]

The second aim of education is to prepare the individual to lead a meaningful adult life within society.

The way in which to educate man so that he perpetuates the functioning of society and so that he is prepared to live in society is through "functional education." The meaning underlying the term "functional education" is twofold. The term applies both to teaching the student to *function in the future activities* in which he will be engaged once becoming a mature member of society, and to teaching the student to act in the desired way by having him *function in the desired way.* "Functional education" thus derives the means by which education is to take place directly from the ends of education: children are to learn to act as they should by acting as they should. Bobbitt clarifies this:

In the functional education toward which we are moving, we are to aim at the power to perform activities, and it is clear that we shall employ the principle that one learns to act in desired ways by acting in those ways.[63]

One learns to act by acting. One learns to live by living. Behavior is not only the end of life but also the

process of life and equally the end and process of
education. . . . Education is preparation for life, and life
is a series of activities. Education, therefore, is preparation for the performance of those activities. Let us
discover what the activities are which make up man's
life and we have the objectives of education. . . .

In discovering the objectives in terms of activities,
however, one is also discovering the fundamental
processes involved in achieving these same objectives,
since, obviously, the way to learn to perform an activity
is to perform it. Activity-analysis [the method of
deriving and sequencing the specific behavioral objectives that lead to terminal objectives or educational
purposes], therefore, discovers both educational ends
and educational processes or, in other terms, both the
objectives of the curriculum and the curriculum itself.
The curriculum, defined as we here use the term, is the
series of pupil activities and experiences which enable
one to achieve one's educational objectives.[64]

Note the manner in which the ends of education in terms of
student behavior are tied to the means or processes of achieving
those ends. Ends consist of the activities the student must perform
as a mature member of society. Means consist of learning to act in
the desired ways by acting in those ways—first, through observation, and second, through performance of the activity one must
achieve proficiency in. It should also be noted, however, that there
is a distinction between the terminal behaviors desired for the
child once he is educated and the aims of education. Most
developers working within the Social Efficiency Ideology verbally
call for the clear specification of the aims of education. However,
in their actions, most developers interpret this to mean specifying
the terminal behaviors desired of students.

Finally, the educated man who functions effectively in society
is the man whose capabilities for action are trained so that when
certain conditions (stimuli) present themselves he will respond
with the appropriate action (response). The ability to act
appropriately when necessary is what is important to learn and not
the knowledge of what the correct action should be. As Bobbitt
puts it, education

has the function of training every citizen, man or woman, not for knowledge about citizenship, but for proficiency in citizenship; not for knowledge about hygiene, but for proficiency in maintaining robust health; not for a mere knowledge of abstract science, but for proficiency in the use of ideas in the control of practical situations. . . . We have been developing knowledge, not function; the power to reproduce facts, rather than the powers to think and feel and will and act in vital relation to the world's life.[65]

Education for a Future Better Society

Developers working within the Social Efficiency Ideology view themselves as instruments stimulating the development of a future society superior to the existent one, and not as proponents of the status quo. Although they see the school as the guardian of the system of values and institutions which the society has already evolved, their aims of education for both the child and the society are phrased in the future tense. As Bobbitt says:

Education under the circumstances has, therefore, a double task to perform: (1) to act as a primary agency of social progress, lifting the . . . world to a higher and more desirable level; (2) to do this by educating the rising generation so that they will perform their . . . functions in a manner greatly superior to that of their fathers. The task is to develop in the rising generation, not merely the degree of proficiency found in the world about them, but to carry them much beyond; to look, not merely to the actual practices, but rather to those that ought to be. It is so to train them that the . . . mistakes, weaknesses, imperfections, maladjustments, etc., that now appear so numerously in the . . . situations of their fathers shall be as fully as practicable eliminated in that more harmonious and more efficient . . . regime that they are to establish and maintain.[66]

The future society is thus prepared for by looking to the existing social situation rather than by looking to a vision of society in terms of a utopian projection disjoint from the existing society.

The preparation of society for the future is viewed in a legalistic manner: it is based upon precedents which exist in the present. The strategy for change is not to look for new behaviors more appropriate than the existent ones, but to reinforce the strengths and desirable traits within the present society and eliminate the weaknesses and deficiencies within the existent society. The assumption is that the evolution of the culture will take place by training growing individuals to do that which is done most efficiently and effectively within the culture and avoid that which is done inefficiently and ineffectively within the culture. By this differential reinforcement-elimination, the betterment, improvement, and evolution of society will be achieved.

TERMINAL OBJECTIVES
Social Orientation and Terminal Objectives

The ends toward which the curriculum developer directs his efforts are the perpetuation of society and the preparation of man to live in society. In order to achieve these ends, the activities needed by society to continue its functioning must be specified, along with the skills needed by an individual in order to function within society. The statements specifying these two sets of needed behaviors are called the terminal objectives of the curriculum. Their discovery and clear specification is the first task that the curriculum developer must undertake. They can be discovered only by referring to the nature of society and the activities engaged in by man within society. As Bobbitt sums up:

> Education has no function except that of leading persons to perform properly the activities which constitute an enlightened, humanistic, civilization. Our first task is to find out with definiteness and certainty what these activities are.[6 7]

> When we know what men and women ought to do along the many lines and levels of human experience, then we shall have before us the things for which they should be trained. The first task is to discover the activities which ought to make up the lives of men and women; and along with these, the abilities and personal qualities necessary for proper performance. These are the educational objectives.[6 8]

Important to note is that the source of terminal objectives lies within society and not within the beliefs of the curriculum developers nor within the endeavor of curriculum creation itself. The nature of terminal objectives can be clarified by answering two questions: first, how does one go about obtaining terminal objectives from society, and second, what is the form of terminal objectives?

Source of Terminal Objectives

Society has not seen the necessity for delivering to schools a complete and definitive list of terminal objectives.[69] As a result, the curriculum developer must act as an agent of society in discovering terminal objectives. Different approaches can be taken. Bobbitt attempted to poll the whole American society as a first step to discovering both what its needs were and how it felt such needs could be satisfied. In so doing he made heavy use of statistics. The developers of *Science: A Process Approach*, as agents commissioned by the American Association for the Advancement of Science (AAAS) to develop an elementary school science curriculum, limited themselves to the assumption that science was a need of society and proceeded to investigate only the needs of scientists. In so doing they made heavy use of personal interviews as a means of collecting data.

The collection of data leading to the formulation of objectives can come from a variety of sources. In *Curriculum Investigations*, Bobbitt makes use of periodical literature, newspapers, encyclopedias, daily language, and the *Literary Digest*. He indicates the varied types of information useful in formulating terminal objectives when he says that curriculum development

> seeks to discover the quite specific types of human activity which men should perform efficiently. For example, it would discover the five or ten thousand words they spell, the several score mathematical operations they perform, the several hundred specific practical home activities in which they engage, the main things they do in the care of their health, the specific things involved in managing a checking account at the bank and the like. For each vocation it discovers the many specific jobs in which the workman should be proficient.[70]

The developers of *Science: A Process Approach* were delineating the specific types of "jobs" that scientists believed workers in science should be proficient in when they specified the eight basic and five integrated processes underlying their science curriculum. They summed them up this way:

> The basic processes of science appropriate for children in the primary grades are identified by the following terms: 1. Observing, 2. Using Space/Time Relationships, 3. Using Numbers, 4. Measuring, 5. Classifying, 6. Communicating, 7. Predicting, 8. Inferring. A principal aim of the program is to develop skill in the careful and systematic use of these processes in the primary grades as a necessary preliminary to undertaking more complex science learning in the later grades.
>
> In the intermediate grades the children confront more complex integrated processes of scientific activity. These integrated processes are identified by the following terms: 1. Formulating Hypotheses, 2. Controlling Variables, 3. Interpreting Data, 4. Defining Operationally, 5. Experimenting.[71]

Developers can spend different amounts of effort in determining terminal objectives. Bobbitt spent almost all of his time determining them. In order to do so he polled society as a whole. Gagné, as a major developer of *Science: A Process Approach*, fairly quickly determined terminal objectives. He did so by surveying only one "department of the world's affairs," science.[72] In both cases, however, the curriculum developer consulted a client whose interests were disjoint from his own.

The Masterlist of Terminal Objectives

The method used in determining the terminal objectives for the curriculum is what Bobbitt calls the construction of the masterlist of terminal objectives. In order to compile the masterlist of terminal objectives, Charles C. Peters states that the curriculum developer should "go out into the field, actually study the men and women as individuals, and generalize on the basis of a numerical count of cases."[73] Essential to the Social Efficiency Ideology are the concepts of "going out into the field" and "numerical count of cases."

The Masterlist: Going Out into the Field

The necessity of "going out into the field" to collect terminal objectives raises questions about the types of reality which are of concern to developers working within the Social Efficiency Ideology. The distinction has long been made between the "subjective reality within man's mind" and the "objective reality in the world outside of man." Social Efficiency developers accept the distinction between these two types of reality and act as though there is a clear dichotomy between them. Their behavior while creating curricula also indicates that they are concerned primarily with objective reality.

As a result the reliable sources for terminal objectives are to be found within objective reality and not within subjective reality. In order to determine terminal objectives, the developer must "go out into the field": "a curriculum-making group should not take its thought second-hand. It should do its own seeing, thinking, judging, and deciding."[74] While in the field the developer must actually study the actions performed by men.[75] It is the actions performed by men and the behavior repertoires needed by mankind to successfully maintain the functioning of society from which terminal objectives are to be drawn, and not the "assumed goings on in the head." For these developers the starting point is always the activities of mankind as manifested in objective behavior, rather than the needs of man as assumed to exist within the subjective mind.

The Masterlist: "Numerical Count"

The necessity of determining terminal objectives through "generalizing on the basis of a numerical count of cases" is central to the Social Efficiency Ideology. This is because the reality conceived to be of worth by Social Efficiency developers is defined in a normative manner and not in an idiosyncratic manner. These developers are concerned with those aspects of reality which accord with what the majority of the members of society conceive to be "real" or "true" or "necessary." Their focus is upon what is common to the majority of the members of society rather than upon what is unique to special individuals within society.

Terminal objectives are thus to be based upon what can be "generalized on the basis of a numerical count of cases," upon

norms within society. This results in emphasis being placed upon
statistical analysis during curriculum creation. It results in an
emphasis being placed on concern for the individual with respect
to achieving normative ends, rather than on concern for the person
with respect to achieving individual ends. It results in developers
placing emphasis upon the contemporary needs of society in
determining terminal objectives. And it results in emphasis being
placed upon what the needs of the society *are* and not what men
think they should be. Bobbitt infers this when he says of some
statistically derived tables:

> The foregoing tables go a long way toward showing the
> things which function in human life *today*. They do not
> show what functioned long ago. They cannot, therefore,
> be used to justify survivals from ancient days. They do
> not show, nor do they attempt to show, what educa-
> tionists, whether old-fashioned or new-fashioned, *think*
> the world should be concerned with. They show what it
> *is* concerned with.[76]

The Masterlist: Atomism

In order to be useful, terminal objectives must be self contained
in nature and unitary in effect. Social Efficiency developers
consider it impractical to attempt to accomplish vague and general
objectives such as teaching citizenship.[77] As Bobbitt phrases it:

> Education cannot take the first step in training for
> citizenship until it has particularized the characteristics
> of the good citizen. The training task is to develop those
> characteristics. It is not enough to aim at "good
> citizenship" in a vague general way. . . . The citizen has
> functions to perform. We are to develop ability to
> perform those functions. But first we must know with
> particularity what they are.[78]

Social Efficiency developers believe that one can only train the
child to elicit specific behavioral responses as a result of
encountering certain types of stimulus conditions. Thus, in
compiling the masterlist of terminal objectives, the developer first
determines "What are the major divisions or field of human
action?" and then determines "in each major field—whether six,
ten, twenty, or fifty—what are the specific adult activities of the

good type?"[79] This involves first specifying the fields of human action and then partitioning each field into a set of specific behaviors, such that each specific behavior can be represented as a terminal objective to be aimed at. Bobbitt describes his way of doing this as follows:

> The first step is to analyze the broad range of human experiences into major fields. . . . The major fields of human action having been defined, the second step is to take them, one after another, and analyze them into their more specific activities. In this analysis, one will first divide his field into a few rather large units; and then break them up into smaller ones. This process of division will continue until he has found the quite specific activities that are to be performed. At all stages of the analysis, attention should be fixed upon the *actual activities of mankind*. . . . As the analyses approach the units that are minute, numerous, and interrelated with each other, and especially when accuracy demands quantitative definition, careful scientific assembling of the facts becomes necessary. The activities once discovered, one can then see the objectives of education. These latter are the *abilities* to perform in proper ways the activities.[80]

In order to put terminal objectives in a self-contained and unitary form, the vague and general aims which the developer might wish to achieve or the complete conglomerate of behaviors which the developer might wish to convey must be broken down into unitary and self-contained entities. This breaking down of a general objective or partitioning of a complex behavior into its smallest unitary actions is called atomism. In creating the masterlist, the developer must atomize the field of action he is preparing individuals to function within. He must break up the field of action into sufficiently small units such that each is of the smallest convenient size. And he must treat the behavior he is formulating into terminal objectives as a set of independent actions, the sum of which make up the complete behavior. This means that one must conceive of human life and human activity as capable of being "broken up into a very large number of specialized activities, for the most part distinctly marked off from each other."[81]

The Masterlist: Priorities

When formulating the masterlist of terminal objectives by surveying the client population, the Social Efficiency developer obtains both a list of potential objectives and an ordering of those potential objectives according to popular vote. Having obtained the ordered list, the curriculum developer proceeds to have "expert judges" reorder the items within that list.[82] There are thus two stages to the construction of the masterlist: the first involves the compilation of an initial ordered list by surveying the client population, and the second involves having competent judges reorder the items of the list. Thus, although the Social Efficiency developer bases his terminal objectives in the normative aspects of the client population, he uses an elitist base to order the priorities of the population.

Form of Terminal Objectives

The terminal objectives created by developers within the Social Efficiency Ideology are one form of what is popularly known as behavioral objectives. The recent widespread debate over behavioral objectives makes it unnecessary to engage in a detailed analysis of the nature or form of terminal objectives. Several points need to be briefly mentioned, however.

First, terminal objectives can take on meaning associated with a variety of types of human activity, be it cognitive, affective, or psychomotor. Bobbitt effectively met the criticism that only certain types of things can be put in the form of terminal objectives in "The New Technique of Curriculum Making" in 1924.

Second, terminal objectives are discoverable. As Bobbitt says in *The Curriculum*:

> However numerous and diverse they may be for any social class, they can be discovered. This requires only that one go out into the world of affairs and discover the particulars of which these affairs consist. These will show the abilities, attitudes, habits, appreciations, and forms of knowledge that men need. They will be the objectives of the curriculum. They will be numerous, definite, and particularized.[83]

The needs and characteristic behaviors of any client population are thus capable of being known and expressed before the curriculum developer constructs his curriculum.[84]

Third, it is the form of terminal objectives that is of primary concern to developers rather than the content of terminal objectives. The developer views himself as an agent of society: it is his task to draw out of society its terminal objectives; it is not his task to determine the content of objectives. However, in formulating terminal objectives, the developer must specify the ends of his curriculum in a form that will facilitate their accomplishment. Thus, objectives must be stated in a special form in order to allow the developer to achieve them efficiently. As such, the content of the objective is not the important factor to the developer but the manner in which the objectives are stated so as to facilitate the creation of a curriculum designed to achieve them. As Mager comments in *Preparing Instructional Objectives*, "This book is not concerned with which objectives are desirable or good. It concerns itself with the form of a usefully stated objective."[85]

Fourth, terminal objectives are to be stated in behavioral terms. The extreme to which developers go in specifying the criteria for acceptable ways of stating objectives in behavioral terms varies. The following statement by Gagné gives a feel for both the nature of behavioral objectives and one set of criteria:

> Behavioral specification is directly related to the criterion of reliability. To "know," to "understand," to "appreciate," to "gain insight into," and so on, are excellent words to convey general purposes, but they are not useful as descriptions of reliably observable behavior; nor are their intended meanings easily agreed upon by a number of individuals. ... The action verbs which are used in the construction of the behavioral objectives for *Science: A Process Approach* are ... *Identify ... Distinguish ... Construct ... Name ... Order ... Describe ... Demonstrate ... State a Rule ... Apply a Rule ...*[86]

And, fifth, developers working within the Social Efficiency Ideology endeavor to state objectives in particularized and standardized form. This is related to their endeavors toward atomization and their focus upon normative behavior. Objectives are not to be vague, idiosyncratic, and general. They are to be specific, standardized, and particularized. Gagné indicates this when he writes that there are

> obvious differences between statements of objectives that are ambiguous, and true definitions of objectives, which are not. What are the characteristics of a definition of an objective? Such a definition is a verbal statement that communicates reliably to any individual (who knows the words of the statement as concepts) the set of circumstances that identifies a class of human performances . . . these are "operational definitions." The kind of statement required appears to be one having the following components: 1. A *verb* denoting observable action (draw, identify, recognize, compute, and many other words qualify; know, grasp, see, and others do not). 2. A description of the *class of stimuli* being responded to (for example, "Given the printed statement ab + ac = a(b + c)"). 3. A word or phrase denoting the *object used for action* by the performer, unless, this is implied by the verb (for example, if the verb is "draw," this phrase might be "with a ruling pen"; if it is "state," the word might simply be "orally"). 4. A description of the *class of correct responses* (for example, "a right triangle," or "the sum," or "the name of the rule").[87]

Terminal Objectives and Scientific Instrumentalism

The primary reasons why objectives must be stated before work on the curriculum begins, and why they must be stated in specific behavioral terms, is a function of the instrumentalistic conception of the nature of curriculum development and the behavioral conception of the nature of man held by developers working within the Social Efficiency Ideology. The conception of curriculum development as an instrument for fulfilling the needs of a client population necessitates that the needs to be fulfilled be clearly specified in the form of objectives, so that the developer will know exactly what his curriculum is to accomplish, and so that he will be able to create the curriculum in the most efficient manner possible. The conception of man as a bundle of actions necessitates that the objectives be stated in behavioral terms.

PROGRESSIVE OBJECTIVES
Progressive Objectives

Franklin Bobbitt defined progressive objectives when he stated that "... the material [man] that is acted upon by the labor processes [teacher] passes through a number of progressive stages on its way from the raw material [child] to the ultimate product [adult] ..."[88] Progressive objectives are the sequence of specific behavioral objectives that designate the particular tasks ("progressive stages") the student must sequentially master ("pass through") in order to achieve competency in the activity inherent in the terminal objective (become "the ultimate product"). Determining progressive objectives and the sequence in which progressive objectives are to be achieved is the primary task of the curriculum developer. The determination of such has often been considered equivalent to the determination of the essence of the curriculum.

Let us first examine the manner in which the sequence of "progressive stages" which transforms the "raw material" into the "ultimate product" is determined. We will then inquire into the assumptions about causation which allow Social Efficiency developers to conceive of directly transforming the "raw material" into the "ultimate product."

Activity Analysis

The process of formulating the "progressive stages" which the student must pass through in moving from incompetence ("raw material") to competence ("finished product") is called activity analysis. Activity analysis exists in a wide variety of forms.[89] Two forms will be briefly discussed: those of Bobbitt and of Gagné.

Franklin Bobbitt's early form of activity analysis is based upon an assembly line model of education. It includes three basic stages. First, the overall job to be completed—the performance necessary to achieve the terminal objective—is broken down into a finite set of tasks that need to be completed, the sum of which result in the accomplishment of the completed job. Second, each task is analyzed in order to find the most efficient way of performing it. The criterion of efficiency used by Bobbitt was elapsed time. Third, a flow chart is created which specifies the manner in which each task is to be performed, the time allowed to complete each task, the standards which each task must meet, and the sequence in which the tasks are to be completed.[90]

Robert Gagné's form of activity analysis begins with the analysis of a terminal objective. Starting with the terminal objective, Gagné asks the question, "What must the learner already know how to do in order to achieve this performance, assuming that he is to be given only instructions?"[91] Let us say that the learner could not perform the task specified by the terminal objective unless he could first perform prerequisite tasks a and b. A pyramid begins, as illustrated in Figure 3.1.

Figure 3.1

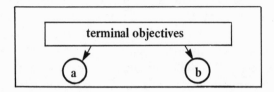

Tasks a and b are now the new objectives to be accomplished. Gagné calls them prerequisite objectives. Bobbitt would call them progressive objectives. They function just like terminal objectives. Gagné now asks the question of each of the prerequisite objectives a and b, "What must the learner already know how to do in order to achieve this performance, assuming that he is to be given only instructions?" Let us say that the learner must be able to perform tasks c and d in order to perform task a, and that the learner must be able to perform tasks e, f, and g in order to perform task b. The learning pyramid grows, as illustrated in Figure 3.2. The process is then repeated, treating c, d, e, f, and g as prerequisite objectives (and thus for purposes of an on going activity analysis as terminal objectives). Each of these objectives is in turn analyzed by asking the question, "What must the learner already know how to do in order to achieve this performance, assuming that he is to be given only instructions?" The result of this next stage of analysis might produce the learning pyramid illustrated in Figure 3.3.

In this manner the curriculum developer builds a very complex

Figure 3.2

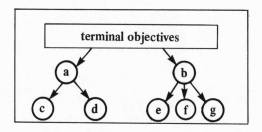

pyramid of prerequisites to prerequisites to prerequisites to . . . to prerequisites to the terminal objective. This process ends when the subordinate performances possessed by every learner for whom the learning program is intended are arrived at. This pyramid of prerequisite objectives capped by a terminal objective is called a learning hierarchy and the diagram of it is called a hierarchy chart.[92] Once the initial learning hierarchy is deductively derived, it is empirically tested to see if it is "psychologically" complete and accurately ordered. Then the two-dimensional hierarchy is

Figure 3.3

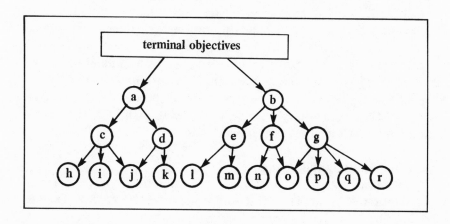

broken down into a one-dimensional learning sequence, which preserves the hierarchical prerequisite nature of the learning hierarchy. In running the curriculum, the student then proceeds through this learning sequence to attain the performance ability inherent in the terminal objective.[93]

Activity Analysis Leads to
Learning Experiences

Once activity analysis is completed and progressive objectives are specified as a sequence of specific behavioral objectives, the Social Efficiency developer is then faced with the task of planning and organizing the learning experiences that will allow a child to progressively acquire the competencies inherent in each specific behavioral objective. By properly planning and organizing learning experiences so that the child will progressively acquire the competencies inherent in each progressive objective, the curriculum developer provides the means by which the child can acquire the terminal performances of the curriculum as specified by its terminal objectives. In planning and organizing learning experiences, three requirements are important: (1) it is important that each learning experience that is created corresponds to at least one of the clearly specified progressive objectives; (2) it is important that each of the progressive objectives be represented by at least one (and perhaps more than one) learning experience and that the learning experiences actually produce in the child the requisite behaviors specified by every progressive objective; and (3) it is important that the sequence of the learning experiences within the curriculum (the organization of learning experiences) parallels the sequence of corresponding progressive objectives as determined by activity analysis. Because of these three important requirements, it can be said that activity analysis leads to the determination and organization of learning experiences as well as the determination and sequencing of progressive objectives.

Activity Analysis and Sequence

Several aspects of activity analysis, as described above, need to be elaborated upon. The most important is sequence. Sequence is the ordering of the progressive objectives which the student must run in order to achieve the terminal objective. It is one of the elements which defines a curriculum, another being the progressive objectives themselves. It is important to note that progressive objectives do not form the essence of the curriculum in and of themselves. The essence of the curriculum lies in the ordering of the objectives.

Bobbitt indicates the central role of sequence in statements similar to the following: "The . . . curriculum . . . is that *series* of things which children and youth must do and experience . . ."[94] and "the objectives and the pupil activities are identical, and *the series is the curriculum.*"[95] The central role of sequence in *Science: A Process Approach*, a curriculum based upon Gagné's form of activity analysis, is indicated when its developers write that "this entire curriculum of science may be characterized by the *sequence* of stated behaviors (the objective), *one building upon another* until the terminal performances for each process are reached."[96]

Perhaps one of the most pointed statements referring to the centrality of sequence within curricula and curriculum-making is the following one by Gagné:[97]

> The planning that precedes effective design for learning [curriculum-making] is a matter of specifying with some care what may be called the *learning structure* [1] of any subject [2] to be acquired. In order to determine what comes before what [3], the subject must be analyzed in terms of the types of learning involved in it. The acquisition of knowledge is a process in which every new capability builds on a foundation established by previously learned capabilities [4]. The convenient escape mechanism that the student is not "mature" enough to learn any particular content needs to be studiously avoided, since it is valid for only the very earliest years of life [5]. A student is ready to learn something when he has mastered the prerequisites [6]; that is, when he has acquired the necessary capabilities through preceding learning [7]. Planning for learning is a matter of specifying and ordering the prerequisite capabilities [8] within a topic to be learned, and later perhaps among the topics that make up a "subject."[98]

Note first the way in which Gagné defines "structure" ([1]) in

terms of sequence: "what comes before what" ([3]) and
"ordering the prerequisite capabilities" ([8]). Note second the
continued use of synonyms for sequence whether describing
curriculum-making ([3] and [8]), knowledge ([4]), or learning
([6] and [7]). Note third the lack of emphasis on content and
subjects ("of *any* subject" [2])—Gagné's vested interests do not lie
here. And note fourth the pointed attack against "readiness" as
defined in terms of human development ([5]). This attack against
"readiness" is significant. It is directed at people like Bruner, [99]
who emphasize (Gagné believes) that sequential development in
terms of human growth is biologically programmed into the
human organism rather than experientially accumulated.

Sequence and Objective Reality

For developers working within the Social Efficiency Ideology,
sequence is not framed within the context of biological evolution
of the human organism—where the emphasis is upon the subjective
development of the individual—but rather within the context of
the experiential background of the human organism—where the
emphasis is upon the objective experiences encountered by the
individual.[100] Man is stimulated to achieve a terminal performance by having him engage in the optimal sequence of activities
which will provide him with the experiential background—not the
biological structures—necessary to achieve the terminal performance.

Sequence, thus, is not determined by initially focusing upon the
nature of the person, but by focusing upon the acts in which the
person will engage. It is not determined by focusing upon
subjective types of reality, but by focusing upon objective types of
reality. This is consistent with the practice among Social Efficiency developers of (a) distinguishing between subjective and
objective reality, while (b) placing their emphasis during curriculum creation upon objective reality. This ultimately results in a
weighted distinction being made between the person *per se* and
the person as a possessor of certain potential action capabilities.

Sequence and Futurism

In addition, the centrality of sequence places curriculum
development within a context in which the developer constantly

conceives of his endeavors as contributing to the next stage of development within the child. The Social Efficiency developer is constantly working on activity n so that activity $n + 1$ can be accomplished and is constantly conceiving of the child engaging in activity n so that he will be able to achieve activity $n + 1$ (where n is a positive integer). The concern is always with the future development of the child in contrast with the present growing of the child. Value thus gets placed upon activities and objectives because they contribute to the worth of the child in the context of the future tense, rather than because they contribute to the worth of the child within the context of the present. The endeavor engaged in by the curriculum developer has value because of its contribution to the future rather than its contribution to the present.

Activity Analysis and Atomism

Another aspect of activity analysis which deserves mention is its atomistic nature. During activity analysis atomism involves the breaking of progressive objectives into small unitary operations for analysis. The first step in Bobbitt's activity analysis involves breaking down the total activity to be completed into a finite number of unitary tasks for analysis. Charters expresses the spirit behind this type of atomism when he uses the word "minuteness" to refer to the size that the unitary tasks are to be.[101] Charters further illustrates what he means by minuteness by analyzing the work of a competent secretary into 871 separate unitary tasks.[102] The completion of the total activity then involves the satisfactory completion of each unitary task, as Bobbitt indicates with respect to learning the many atomistic elements of English: "No one of these factors alone is sufficient to produce correct English. . . . To develop the ability involves the development of each and all of the specific factors."[103]

Gagné's approach to atomism is different. He derives his learning hierarchy by progressively analyzing objectives backward from the terminal objective to the initial objective using a recursive function where prerequisite objective of hierarchical level n is derived from a prerequisite objective of hierarchical level $n + 1$. The prerequisite objective derived at each stage of analysis is unitary and atomistic enough so that the learner can complete it "given only instructions" beyond the next lower level of pre-requisite objectives. The essence of Gagné's process of atomizing is summed up in his belief that in order to create learning hierarchies for topics it is "necessary to *break them down into smaller units* representing fairly specific intellectual skills."[104] During activity analysis the process of transforming the "raw material" into the "finished product" is thus broken up into a finite sequence of unitary stages, each of which is analyzed and treated as an individual atomistic process within the sequence.

Atomism and Objective Reality

While engaging in atomistically delineating progressive objec-tives during activity analysis, Social Efficiency developers keep their attention focused upon the actions of man. This focus upon the actions of man as manifested in progressive objectives excludes a focus upon man as separate from his actions or man as inclusive of his actions. This results in a partitioning of the individual from his actions: it results in the Social Efficiency developer dealing with the individual's capabilities for action as an entity separate from the individual. This is one consequence of making a weighted distinction between objective reality and subjective reality, with objective reality being favored.

Here, the developer atomistically delineates progressive objec-tives while objectively focusing upon man's action capabilities in such a manner that the subjective aspects of man as manifested in his person tend to be ignored. Here only those objective aspects of man which can be analyzed atomistically are focused upon, with the subjective aspects of man fading into the background because of the difficulty in dealing with them in an atomistic manner. Here the very nature of the differentially weighted dualism between objective reality and subjective reality is highlighted as the developers' actions indicate that values are *achieved by* man's activity rather than being *realized in* man's activity.

Activity Analysis: Efficiency,
Performance, and Empiricism

Three other aspects of activity analysis need to be mentioned. First, the criterion used in making decisions during activity analysis is that of efficiency. It is always efficiency that is sought.

The essence of how efficiency permeates all aspects of decision making is summed up in the following four statements. Gagné: "Such a procedure should, if systematically followed, bring about the required learning in the most *efficient* possible manner."[105] Gagné: "the mechanics (or 'logistics') of education . . . should be determined by the requirements of getting students to learn *efficiently*."[106] Bobbitt: "Activity analysis seeks to discover the quite specific types of human activity which men should perform *efficiently*."[107] Bobbitt: "The business of education today is to teach growing individuals . . . to perform *efficiently* those activities which constitute the latest and highest level of civilization."[108]

Second, completed activity analysis results not only in specification of the task to be performed but also in the specification of the method of performing the task. For Bobbitt this means that "When we have discovered the objectives of education in the activities which ought to make up the life-series, we have also discovered the processes of education. . . . The objectives and the pupil activities are identical, and the series is the curriculum."[109] Both "what to do" and "how to do it" are determined during activity analysis.

Third, activity analysis embodies both a theoretical derivation of the curriculum and an empirical testing of the theoretical derivation. Social Efficiency developers believe that there should be constant reference to the empirical world of objective reality in order to check the results of the theoretical derivation. For Gagné this involves checking to see that the deductively derived sequence of progressive objectives is "psychologically" compatible with the action capabilities of children.[110] For Bobbitt, this involved checking to see if the standards for efficient performance of a task were realistic.

Causality

Underlying the process of designing progressive objectives through the use of task analysis are assumptions about causation—assumptions about how the "raw material" is transformed into the "finished product." The basic assumption derives from Newtonian mechanics: causation is conceived of within a context in which cause and effect, action and reaction, or stimulus and response are linked together in a deterministic pattern reducible by analysis to single and simple atomic transferences of energy. Four aspects of this assumption need elaboration.

Causality and Planning for Change

First, planning for change in the human organism is thought of within a cause-effect, action-reaction, or stimulus-response context. Conceiving of human change within this context requires of the Social Efficiency developer that he utilize two types of planning while creating curricula. He must predetermine the relationship between cause and effect, action and reaction, or stimulus and response; and he must plan the causes, actions, or stimuli which in a direct and predictable manner will lead to the desirable effect, reaction, or response. As a result, the changes which are planned for during curriculum creation are only those which fit into a stimulus-response pattern and which are behaviorally observable to be linked together in direct relationship.[111]

Causality and Determinism

Second, this interpretation of causality is deterministic. The curriculum developer conceives of himself as being able to predetermine the changes that will take place in a person's behavior as a result of submitting him to specified stimuli within the curriculum. Changed behavior resulting from exposure to the curriculum is conceived of as being able to be both known before the change takes place and known in its entirety. Free will plays little part within this system—events are entirely determined by previous causes. Bobbitt expressed the spirit underlying the Social Efficiency posture toward determinism when he wrote:

> In the world of economic production, a major secret of success is predetermination. The management predetermined with great exactness the nature of the products to be turned out, and in relation to the other factors, the quality of the output. They standardize and thus predetermine the processes to be employed, the quantity and quality of raw material to be used for each type and unit of product, the character and amount of labor to be employed, and the character of the conditions under which the work should be done. . . .

The business world is institutionalizing foresight and developing an appropriate and effective technique.

There is a growing realization within the educational profession that we must particularize the objectives of education. We, too, must institutionalize foresight, and, so far as conditions of our work will permit, develop a technique of predetermination of the particularized results to be obtained.[112]

Causality and Energy Transferences

Third, change in human behavior is conceived to take place within the context of simple transferences of energy. It takes place as the result of a series of individual stimuli, causes, or actions—each of which is self-contained in nature and unitary in effect—acting directly upon the human organism. Change in human behavior associated with the curriculum does not take place as the result of secondary changes resulting from unspecifiable energy reorganizations within the organism which are set off by a set of complex stimuli outside of the organism. The model is essentially that of the assembly line. The "raw material" is progressively altered by being acted upon by a series of well-defined operators until it is transformed into the "finished product." This model of causation is labeled by philosophers of science as mechanistic.

Causality and Shaping Human Behavior

Fourth, change in human behavior is conceived of as "a shaping process." It is "a shaping process as much as the manufacture of steel rails"[113] is a shaping process. The behavioral engineer aspires to manipulate the human shaping process with the same degree of control as the industrial engineer molds steel rails into the form he desires them to be. Within this context the human being who will undergo the shaping process is treated as though he has about as much to say about what is happening to himself during the shaping as the steel has to say about what is happening to itself during its shaping. As a result, free will and self-determination are treated by the Social Efficiency developer as though they do not exist:

What is abolished is autonomous man—the inner man,

the homunculus, the possessing demon, the man de-
fended by the literature of freedom and dignity.

His abolition has long been overdue. Autonomous
man is a device used to explain what we cannot explain
in any other way. He has been constructed from our
ignorance, and as our understanding increases, the very
stuff of which he is composed vanishes. Science does
not dehumanize man, it dehomunculizes him, and it
must do so if it is to prevent the abolition of the human
species. To man, *qua* man, we readily say good riddance.
Only then can we turn from the inferred to the
observed, from the miraculous to the natural, from the
inaccessible to the manipulable.[114]

DICHOTOMY
Ends and Means

One of the distinctive aspects of curriculum creation within the
Social Efficiency Ideology is the clear dichotomy which exists
between terminal objectives and progressive objectives, between
the social orientation and the methodological orientation, between
the ends of the curriculum and the means of creating the
curriculum. Terminal objectives are associated with the ends of the
curriculum: they are discoverable within society. Progressive
objectives are associated with the means of creating curriculum:
they derive from the methodology of "scientific instrumentalism."
Ends must be clearly specified and their value lies in their ability
to reflect the needs of society. Means must also be clearly
specified and their value lies in their ability to achieve ends
efficiently.

Value

In both cases the criterion of value is independent of the
curriculum. Ends are judged in terms of their ability to reflect the
needs of society and not in terms of anything inherent within
themselves. Means are judged in terms of their efficiency in
meeting ends and not in terms of anything inherent within either
themselves *per se* or ends *per se*.

In both cases, the curriculum developer asks that the value of
his or her work be defined in terms of criteria independent of the

work itself. That criterion is essentially one of efficiency. In the case of ends, efficiency is measured in terms of optimal reflectability of social needs in terminal objectives. In the case of means, efficiency is measured in terms of optimal cost (time, money, natural resources, etc.) in achieving ends. In both cases, ends and means are to be judged as instruments that contribute to the attainment of goals external from themselves, and instrumental values based upon the ethically neutral concept of efficiency are to be used as the criteria for judging them. The developer thus asks that his or her work be judged in terms of the efficiency with which it is completed and not in terms of the nature of the work itself.

As a result, there is no criterion of value for judging "good" or "bad," "just" or "unjust," or "sane" or "insane" ends for the curriculum. Neither is there a criterion of value for judging "kind" or "unkind," "moral" or "immoral," or "responsible" or "irresponsible" means of creating the curriculum. Bobbitt constantly points out the pervasiveness of this system of instrumental values when he writes such things as, "We had not learned that studies are means, not ends. We did not realize that any instrument or experience which is effective . . . is the right instrument and right experience; and that anything that is not effective is wrong."[115] Criteria of value are not internal to the curriculum endeavor for either ends or means: they are external to the curriculum endeavor and based in the ethically neutral concept of efficiency. This can be attributed, to some extent, both to the impulse of Social Efficiency developers to be "scientific" and to their concept of curriculum development as "instrumentalistic."

Dominance

Discussion of this dichotomy has been in terms of two presuppositions. One has been associated with a social orientation, terminal objectives, and the ends of the curriculum. The other has been associated with a methodological orientation, progressive objectives, and the means of creating curriculum. The question arises as to the relationship between these presuppositions: is there a balance among them or is one dominant over the other?

Bobbitt, at times emphasizes the social presupposition:

In this volume we have tried to look at the curriculum

problems from the point of view of social needs; and
thereby to develop, in some measure at least, the social
point of view as regards education.[116]

The social presupposition is assumedly fulfilled by the methodological presupposition:

We greatly needed something to shatter our self-com-
placency and bring us to see education in terms of the
society that was to be educated. We needed *principles of
curriculum making*. We did not know that we should
first determine objectives from a study of social
needs. . . .[117]

But in the end it is the methodological presupposition which is
triumphant and becomes dominant. As Bobbitt says:

At the present stage of developing courses of training it
is more important that our profession agree upon a
method of curriculum-discovery than that we agree
upon the details of curriculum-content. The writer has
been chiefly interested in this volume in suggesting a
method. . . . The main thing at present is that each
[curriculum developer] find scientific principles and
methods of curriculum-formation which he can himself
accept.[118]

In her study of the development of the curriculum field, Mary
Louise Seguel emphasizes the centrality of the methodological
presupposition for early Social Efficiency developers:

The new method went far beyond previous efforts to
improve the process by which content was selected and
organized. . . . The new method represented a shift in
focus, subtle but profound, from the content of the
curriculum to the method of formulating that content.
In this shift, method assumed priority over content. The
whole question of the content of the curriculum became
dependent on the method of curriculum formulation,
rather than the method dependent on the content.[119]

For Social Efficiency developers after 1950, the methodological
presupposition became even more dominant than it was at the
time of Bobbitt. In terms of the curriculum work of a developer
like Gagné, it is more correct to say that the social presupposition
is completely included within the methodological presupposition

than to simply say that the methodological presupposition is the dominant of the two presuppositions. The central aspect of the Social Efficiency Ideology today is its methodological presupposition, the social presupposition being included within it as a subordinate presupposition.

The Social Efficiency Ideology, as discussed herein, is thus defined by the primacy of the methodological presupposition. This is not mandatory. It is possible to have the social presupposition be the dominant one or to have a balance between the two presuppositions. For example, to the many curriculum developers between 1920 and 1950 who looked to the *Cardinal Principles of Secondary Education*[120] for guidance in constructing curricula, it was the social presupposition which was dominant. These developers held up all educational activity, and in particular all school subjects, against the criterion of social utility. Their activity was largely directed towards redirecting school subjects so that they become socially useful. In doing so they judged school subjects by criteria external to the subjects themselves. School mathematics, for example, was to be examined, judged, and redirected so that it was not primarily directed towards knowing mathematics or towards some value inherent in mathematics itself, but so that it was primarily directed towards some socially useful aim external to the nature of mathematics itself—such as producing persons who were competent in measuring everyday things.[121]

HISTORICAL VIEWPOINT

The Social Efficiency Ideology had its origins in four movements which were active during the first two decades of this century:[122] social reform, utilitarian education, behaviorist psychology, and scientific methodology.[123]

Social Reform

"Muckraking" journalism during the first two decades of the twentieth century developed a reform-conscious population which put social needs above all else. Social needs were those aspects of the culture which provided the context within which people lived. Bobbitt expressed the spirit of the times when he exclaimed: "The ideal of social service is rapidly becoming the corner-stone of faith in every department of human affairs—in none certainly more than in the field of education. In this service, *social efficiency* is becoming the chief watchword and the chief aim."[124] "Muckraking" journalism and the accompanying social reform movement influened the Social Efficiency Ideology by inspiring it to place the needs of the society above all else and by causing it to conceive of society as the sanctioning body within which the needs, rights, and functioning of the individual took on meaning.

Utilitarian Education

The movement for utilitarian education during the last quarter of the nineteenth century and the first quarter of the twentieth century emphasized the importance of making schools useful and relevant to the life of the individual and the nation. Utilitarian education was an outgrowth of the peaking of the vocational education movement and the increasingly popular business ideology. It was Bobbitt's "functional education" which trained "man for the performance of the functions or activities which constitute his life."[125] The utilitarian education movement also embodied a reaction to the academic education within the schools, which consisted of generally useless textbook memorizing followed by lesson hearing that prepared man only for life within the university. The revitalization of the National Education Association's Committee on the Culture Element in Education was reflective of the impulse for utilitarian education: in 1912 the Committee changed its name to the Committee on the Economy of Time and set out to revitalize "culture" by relating it to the life of the present day—by making the "cultural subjects" within the schools socially useful.[126]

Behavioral Psychology

Behavioral psychology provided the Social Efficiency Ideology with a psychological context within which to frame its endeavors. The de-emphasis upon the subjective behavior of man, the interpretation of mind as the total behavioral response of man, the emphasis upon the effect which the controllable conditions of learning have upon molding the behavior of man, and the concern with accurate statistical evaluation provided Social Efficiency developers with an ideal tool.[127] Behavioral psychology at first interpreted by John Watson and Edward L. Thorndike as later reinterpreted by B.F. Skinner was rapidly accepted as the psychological base of the Social Efficiency Ideology. For the early Social Efficiency developers, Thorndike's *An Introduction to the Theory of Mental and Social Measurements*, published in 1904, rapidly became popular. Such works as Thorndike's *Handwriting Scale* and Courtis' *Arithmetic Studies* were set up as exemplars.[128] Today the Social Efficiency Ideology is conceived by some practitioners as primarily an application of behavioral psychology to curriculum.[129] Others, however, view behavioral psychology as a tool used within the larger context of the Social Efficiency Ideology. In either case, Social Efficiency developers view psychology as does Gagné, who lists Pavlov, Thorndike, Skinner, Hull, and Tolman as major contributors to his beliefs about education and learning.[130]

Scientific Methodology

"Scientific methodology" became popular in education at the beginning of the twentieth century. It referred to the methodology of technology and connoted a collection of techniques such as statistics, accurate measurement, task analysis, efficiency engineering, and industrial management.[131] Developers working with the Social Efficiency Ideology conceived of their work as being based on "scientific methodology." They adopted "scientific methodology" both as a reaction against the inefficiency of existing curriculum-making techniques and in alliance with the successful use of "scientific techniques" in the business and industrial worlds. Bobbitt's use of "scientific methodology" was modeled after that of "scientific management" in the world of material production.[132] On the other hand, Gagné's approach to "scientific methodology" derived from his training in the use of task analysis as a neo-behaviorist psychologist for the United States Air Force. "Science" has been a magic word for developers with the Social Efficiency Ideology throughout the century. Developers working within this curricular ideology assume that prestige and usefulness are automatically accorded their work if they use "scientific" techniques of curriculum creation.

From Society to Client:
Half a Century of Forgetting

Before proceeding further, it is necessary to place the social orientation utilized by the Social Efficiency developer in historical perspective.

The client for whom the early developers within the Social Efficiency Ideology conceived of themselves as agents was society. Society provided the sustaining context within which education took place; the needs of society were to be fulfilled by the curriculum developer; and the preparation of the individual for a balanced and constructive life within the society was the aim of the curriculum developer. Part of the initial impulse underlying the very development of the Social Efficiency Ideology was reaction against education being a servant of special interest groups within society—in particular against it being a servant to "the dictation of the special predilections of selfish academic interests"[133] which originated within the communities of academic scholars at the universities. Education was not to serve special interest groups within society, but was to serve society as a whole. As such, the aims of the curriculum were to be drawn from society as a whole and not from special interest groups within society.

But as time passed and Social Efficiency developers discovered the difficulty of drawing comprehensive objectives from society, things changed. At the present, the client for whom the Social Efficiency developer works may be any group desiring the services of a curriculum developer. Gagné's first client was the U.S. Air Force: his terminal objectives were given him *a priori,* and his task was to unquestioningly design curricula to accomplish them. A later client of Gagné's was the American Association for the Advancement of Science: he was both to define terminal objectives which would meet the needs of the scientific community of academia, and to construct a learning sequence to accomplish those objectives.

Because the client of Social Efficiency developers may be any group desiring the curriculum developer's service, and because those groups already established tend to perpetuate themselves,[134] the desire of the early Social Efficiency developers to remove "academic special interest" curricula from the schools and substitute curricula based on the needs of society as a whole has not been achieved. Most developers working within the Social Efficiency Ideology today tend to work either within the context of an academic discipline or within the context of some other special interest group. In so doing they design curricula which will fulfill the particular needs of the groups. As such, their original socially-oriented curriculum development system has become a client-oriented curriculum development system.

The major school client of Social Efficiency developers has become the academic disciplines. The evolution of the Social Efficiency Ideology from having a social orientation to having a content orientation can be conceptualized as involving three shifts. The first shift in emphasis involved moving from the developer discovering social needs, selecting those to be installed in the curriculum himself, and then designing curricula to fulfill such social needs to the developer discovering social needs, the school departments selecting which were to be implemented in the curriculum, and the developer designing curricula around such needs.[135] The second shift in emphasis involved moving to the position where the school departments chose the content for curriculum, justified the use of the content upon the criterion of social need and social utility, and then commissioned developers to create curricula.[136] The third shift of emphasis involved the dropping of the social criterion and the acceptance of any special interest group as the client by curriculum developers (by far the most common client remaining the academic disciplines within the schools).[137]

A variety of reasons could be given for this shift. One important reason may have been the lack of a value system intrinsic to the developer's endeavor which made specific the relationship between the ends and means of curriculum development. Another important reason may have been that the major emphasis was placed upon techniques of development which resulted in the de-emphasis upon content, which in turn led to the substitution of traditional subjects, as the most available source of content, in the place of social ends.

Although the initial impulse to base education upon the popular functional aspects of the life of society has largely evaporated from the Social Efficiency Ideology, the conception of the curriculum developer as an instrument responsible to an outside client has remained and deeply affects the manner in which the Social Efficiency developer works. He is to act as an unbiased agent of a task whose vested interests are other than his own. And although the particular orientation of the Social Efficiency Ideology is no longer specifically social, the attributes of a social orientation—such as accountability—still remain in such a manner that it can be said that even though the "content" of the Social Efficiency Ideology has changed, its form, methods, and concerns have remained constant.

Discussion of the Social Efficiency Ideology will now shift from examining the context within which the developer works to examining several concepts which mold the manner in which the developer creates curricula. These concepts have to do with the aims of the developer, knowledge, learning, the child, teaching, and evaluation.

AIMS OF THE CURRICULUM DEVELOPER

The developer working within the Social Efficiency Ideology conceives of his aim in creating curricula to be one of carrying out a task for a client. He conceives of himself as an agent of a client. He acts as an instrument to achieve a given end.

In doing so he sees himself as an educational engineer who shapes the behavior of people in much the same way as the industrial engineer shapes steel into railroad rails. Here the analogy involves the assumptions that the educational engineer and industrial engineer both obtain their tasks from a client; both are evaluated by the ability of their product to fulfill the needs of a client (both are accountable to a client in the final analysis); both use a precise, particularized, and atomized approach to accomplishing their purposes; both plan with a high degree of care and explicitness; both pay rigorous attention to empirical events; both value sophisticated use of scientific technique; and both take a programed approach to transforming their "raw material" into a finished product" in the sense that a methodology of predetermination of sequence of "progressive tasks" is set up that precisely and explicitly defines fixed relationships of action to be performed on the progressively evolving "raw material."

Be the task engaged in by the developer the discovery of

terminal objectives, the design of a learning sequence, or the creation of learning experiences, the aims of the developer are not directly associated with the substance of the curriculum *per se* but rather with the efficient and effective design of the curriculum. The developer's vested interest is not in what is achieved but in *how well* it is achieved. His concerns are with the means of accomplishing ends and not with the ends themselves. Theoretically his client is society. In practice his client may be any group desiring his services.

KNOWLEDGE

That knowledge which is conceived to be of most worth by Social Efficiency developers and which they design their curricula to convey has two characteristics. First, its nature is that of a capability for action which can be taught to learners. And second, its identification and its worth demands the acceptance of the duality between subjective and objective reality. Each of these characteristics will be discussed in turn.

The Nature of Knowledge

The nature of knowledge is that of a capability for action which can be taught to learners. Gagné implies this when he states that " 'knowledge' is that inferred capability which makes possible the successful performance of a class of tasks that could not be performed before the learning was undertaken."[138] Three aspects of this conception of knowledge need elaboration.

First, knowledge is an "inferred" capability. It is a capacity, ready for utilization, which is assumed to exist within the learner. It is defined in terms of things that the student is able to accomplish or in terms of the expected capabilities of students.[139] It refers to something the knower can do in the present or will be able to do at a future time. It does not refer to something he could do in the past.

Second, knowledge is defined in terms of characteristics capable of being embodied within the knower: in terms of things "the student is able to accomplish." It is person-specific and is not defined abstractly without a referent. For example, worthwhile knowledge does not exist in books, it exists only in human beings. For school curriculum the person to whom knowledge refers is the student.

Third, knowledge is an action-oriented capability: it is a capability that can be framed within the context of "to do." It is identifiable as the "successful performance of a class of tasks." It is defined in behavioral terms. This is the crucial characteristic of knowledge. The Social Efficiency developer equates such things as "knowledge," "wisdom," "insight," and "understanding" with behavior. This is partially so because the only tangible evidence we ever have of "knowledge," "wisdom," "insight," or "understanding" is behavioral evidence. It is partially so because the only way to determine whether or not a person "knows" or "is ignorant" of something is to see how he behaves in certain situations. This emphasis upon the behavioral context brings about a corresponding deemphasis upon the informational context. The possession of the correct *behavior* is emphasized over the possession of the correct *information*. There is certainly a relationship between having the necessary information to act and being able to act: between "knowing that" and "knowing how." However, it is the ability to act which is more important than the ability to be informed. Bobbitt speaks of such in comparing the "old education" and the "new functional education" when he writes that according to the old education "the well educated man is to be defined as a walking body of knowledge. The more swollen the bulk of information that he carries about with him, the better educated he is."[140] While within the new functional education "Man is not a mere intellectual reservoir to be filled with knowledge. He is a . . . creature of . . . *action*. His most salient characteristic is not his memory reservoir, whether filled or unfilled, but *action, conduct, behavior*."[141] Gagné expresses his emphasis on the behavioral interpretation over the informational interpretation of knowledge when he writes:

> There are a number of ways of conceiving the meaning of "process" as exemplified in *Science—A Process Approach*. First, perhaps, it should be mentioned that an emphasis on process implies a corresponding deemphasis on specific science "content" . . . the children . . . are not asked to learn and remember particular facts on principles. . . . Rather, they are expected to learn such things as how to observe . . . , how to classify . . . , and how to perform experiments.[142]

The most striking characteristic of these materials is that they are intended to teach children the *processes* of science rather than what may be called science content. That is, they are directed toward developing fundamental skills required in scientific activities.[143]

Some confusion exists about the nature of the behavioral context within which knowledge is defined. The confusing question is whether, for example, the facts of Newtonian mechanics are or are not knowledge. By itself a fact is not knowledge. By itself the possession of a fact by an individual does not mean that he possesses knowledge. However, the ability to state a fact when appropriately stimulated does fall within the behavioral context. The ability to act in accordance with the ability to state a fact falls even more within the behavioral context. The relevant criterion is whether the possessor of a fact is capable of acting upon the knowledge represented by the fact when he is stimulated to so act.

For example, let us take the case of knowledge about "honesty." It is one thing to be able to state what society considers to be "honest behavior," but quite another thing to be able to act in an honest manner. It is the ability to act in the appropriate manner which Social Efficiency developers call knowledge, rather than the ability "to know," "to understand," or "to appreciate" what the appropriate behavior should be. What is "in man's head" is not the important thing. What is important is the ability to translate "what is in man's head" into "the behavior in which man engages."

Several other aspects of the Social Efficiency developer's conception of the nature of knowledge need mention. Two of them are illustrated in his interest in taxonomic analyses of knowledge. *The Taxonomy of Educational Objectives. Handbook I: Cognitive Domain* and *The Taxonomy of Educational Objectives. Handbook II: Affective Domain* are perhaps the most popular educational taxonomies. They present analyses of human behaviors (knowledge) based on a hierarchy of simple to complex action. In contrast, Gagné's *The Conditions of Learning* is a taxonomy of human behavior based on a hierarchy of prerequisite conditions that produce learning, and thus knowledge. These taxonomies illustrate the Social Efficiency assumptions that knowledge can be broken up into specific atomistic behaviors and that the atomistic bits of knowledge can be arranged in a hierarchical ordering based on some sequencing rule (such as simple to complex).

Finally, it is important to note one consequence of the Social Efficiency developer's conception of himself as an instrument to achieve the ends of a client. The developer's concern is primarily with the means of achieving ends rather than with ends; it is primarily with the means of achieving knowledge rather than with knowledge; it is primarily with learning rather than with knowledge. As a result, Social Efficiency developers pay more attention to learning than to knowledge, and in many ways view knowledge from the perspectives of learning or teaching. Thus, Social Efficiency developers are more likely to write about *The Conditions of Learning* than the conditions of knowing, are more likely to produce teaching machines than knowledge machines, and are more likely to speak about the nature of learning than the nature of knowledge.

Knowledge and Objective Reality

Social Efficiency developers accept the duality between the "subjective reality within man's mind" and the "objective reality in the world outside of man." They hold that the objective reality is the more significant of the two realities. Accordingly, they deal with their world as an empirical entity. That which cannot be observed or measured in some way is treated as though it does not exist—more to be ignored than denied. Attention is directed towards those aspects of quantitative reality which can be observed as overt behavior. That which cannot be quantified as overt behavior, such as some of the "spiritual" dimensions of man's being, is simply overlooked, avoided, and not dealt with. There are two consequences of this worthy of mention here.

First, knowledge derives its value from its ability to fulfill needs within the objective world of mankind. Its worth is determined with respect to the consequences that can result from its possession. As such, knowledge which is desirable for inclusion within the curriculum is identified by evaluating the potential results of its possession upon the possessor and the society within which he will function. The important criteria for identifying worthwhile knowledge are not the insights into himself that the possessor derives from its possession or the sources from which the knowledge derives. It is the power it gives the curriculum client to fulfill his needs and the power it gives the possessor to function efficiently and constructively in fulfilling his own needs by fulfilling the needs of the curriculum client. The test for useful knowledge is thus found in the real-world affairs of the curriculum client: if an item furthers the client's aims, it is of worth; if it thwarts and stifles the client's aims, it is not of worth.

Second, knowledge has its origin within objective reality. It has its origin within the objective reality of the developer's client population. It has its origin within the normative aspects of a particular social group and is discoverable by taking a "numerical count" of the needs of the majority of the members of the society. As such, knowledge is interpreted within the context of a pragmatic cultural relativity: the important needs which are to be met and which give rise to knowledge are those of a particular social group within which individuals function.

These views give rise to a congruence theory of knowledge. This implies that knowledge is of worth only by virtue of its close correspondence to things, viewpoints, events, or "bodies" outside of man, and only if it provides man with the minimal possible resistance in functioning within the objective reality about him.

This view of knowledge is represented in Figure 3.4. In this diagram knowledge has its origin within the normative objective reality as represented in the behavior of members of the developer's client population ($\Sigma 0$ where Σ represents the norma-

Figure 3.4

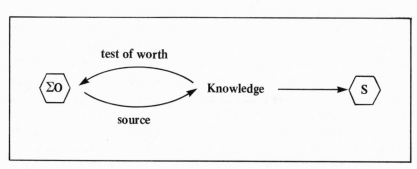

tive aspect of objective reality, 0). The worth of knowledge derived from the client population is tested by determining the consequences which result from its possession within the client population. Once curricular knowledge is determined, it is imparted to the individual (represented by S).

LEARNING
A Behavioral Viewpoint
The learning theory used by curriculum developers working within the Social Efficiency Ideology is essentially that of behavioral psychology. These developers accept a conception of mind as the total behavior response of the human organism. Learning, then, which results in a change in the organization of mind, is synonymous with the change in the behavior of the organism. Gagné expresses this as follows:

> Learning exhibits itself as a change in behavior . . . the inference of learning is made by comparing what behavior was possible before the individual was placed in a "learning situation" and what behavior can be exhibited after such treatment.[144]

> A learning event, then, takes place when the *stimulus situation* affects the learner in such a way that his *performance* changes from a time *before* being in that situation to a time *after* being in it. The *change in performance* is what leads to the conclusion that learning has occurred.[145]

Learning is not viewed in terms of changes in the subjective consciousness of the learner—be such changes ones in cognitive structures, moral philosophy, or insight into oneself—but in terms of changes in the observable behavior of the learner.[146]

The emphasis in the learning theory utilized by the Social Efficiency developer is not on the learner but on (a) the stimuli which cause the learner to change, (b) the responses which indicate that the learner has changed, and (c) the relationships between the stimuli and responses. Learning takes place within a stimulus-response context which includes three components: the stimulus situation, (S), the response of the learner, (R), and the relationship between the stimulus and the response which accounts for the transformation which takes place within the learner

(→). The three components involved in this learning theory are illustrated in Figure 3.5. The stimulus situation (S) is of primary importance because it is what can be controlled and deliberately manipulated by the curriculum developer in order to produce the desired learning in the student. It is what the curriculum developer primarily focuses his attention upon while developing curricula. The behavioral responses, (R), are the specific acts which can be identified as occurring as the result of exposing the learner to the stimulus situation. They are what indicate to the developer whether or not the student is learning and whether his programming of stimuli which impinge upon the student is producing the

Figure 3.5

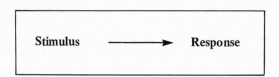

desired results. The relationship between the stimulus and the response, (→), represents the transformation that takes place within the learner. It tells the developer how to get the results he desires. And "The learning change is from stimulus → (nothing) to stimulus → Response."[147] Gagné sums up this view of learning as follows:

> An observer of learning must deal with an input, an output, and a functioning entity in between. The input is a *stimulus situation* (S), which includes the varieties of changes in physical energy that reach the learner through his senses. . . . The stimulus situation is . . . *outside the learner* and can be identified and described in the terms of physical science. . . .
>
> The output, R, is also in a real sense outside the learner. It is a response or a set of responses that produces an identifiable product. The R that is the

focus of interest here is not muscular movements. . . .
Rather, it is the external, observable effect of these
movements . . . [such as] speaking . . . words . . . [or]
writing words. . . .

The nature of the connection between an S and an R
cannot be directly observed. . . . To speculate about
how such mechanisms work . . . is not intended
here. . . . [Our intent is] simply to describe what the
requirements must be in order for an observed transformation between S and R to occur.[148]

There are several assumptions associated with this view of
learning that deserve elaboration.

Learning Within Objective Reality

Within this approach to learning there is no mention of what
occurs "within" the student during learning. This is a "black box"
conception of learning in which the only relevant things are
"external, observable" things outside of the learner: the input to
the learner, (S); the output from the learner, (R); and the mapping
connecting inputs and outputs, $(S_i \rightarrow R_i)$.[149] As the above quote
indicates, no attempt is made to describe what happens "within"
the learner that results in changes in behavior—that is, learning.
There is only mention of what occurs "outside the learner," only
mention of things that "can be identified and described in terms
of physical science."

When and where changes in the learner are spoken of, they are
directly related to the physical conditions inherent in the stimulus
situation which impinges upon the learner's senses. This is because
it is believed that "learning is largely dependent upon events in the
environment with which the individual interacts,"[150] upon
observable environmental conditions that "can be altered and
controlled."[151] In speaking of eight different types of learning
that are of interest to him, Gagné expresses the flavor of the way
in which what occurs "within" the learner is dealt with by
focusing upon events (stimulus conditions) that exist outside of
the learner:

Eight different classes of situation in which human
beings learn have been distinguished, that is, eight sets
of conditions under which changes in capabilities of the

human learner are brought about. The implication is that there are eight corresponding kinds of changes in the nervous system which need to be identified and ultimately accounted for. Each of these may involve different initial states or different structures, or both. From the standpoint of the outside of the human organism, however, they seem to be clearly distinguishable from one another in terms of the conditions that must prevail for each to occur.[152]

The focus here is upon learning from outside and not from inside the learner. It is upon the stimulus conditions that bring about learning and not upon what occurs "within" the individual. It is upon the external objective behavior of man and not the internal subjective behavior of man.

Many Types of Learning

Social Efficiency developers assume that there exist many different types of learning: "that all learning is basically the same . . . is categorically rejected."[153] Taken to its extreme, it is assumed that "there are as many varieties of learning as there are distinguishable conditions for learning,"[154] as many varieties of stimulus-response relationships as there are stimulus situations. For practical purposes, however, all possible learnings are usually grouped into a fairly small number of classes which share certain factors. Gagné, for example, distinguishes eight classes of learning that "produce different learning outcomes in the sense that the learner acquires a different class of capability in each case."[155] They are called signal learning, stimulus-response learning, chaining, verbal association, discrimination learning, concept learning, rule learning, and problem solving.[156] Several assumptions about learning can be associated with the belief in the existence of many types of learning.

There is the assumption that learning is atomistic. This shows up in the developer's concern with devising specific stimulus conditions that will condition the learner to emit specific behavioral responses. Associated with this is the assumption that each learning and its associated stimulus-response relationship is a separate and distinct entity and that the total learning of the child is a summative accumulation of specific learnings.

There is the assumption that not all learning is of the same difficulty. Some types of learning are considered to be higher level skills than others. For example, in *Science: A Process Approach* twenty-three different levels of difficulty in a learning hierarchy are identified.[157] During activity analysis the curriculum developer defines the hierarchical relationships among the specific learnings the learner is to acquire.

There is also the assumption that since there are many different types of learnings, there must also be many different types of learning conditions—one type of learning condition being best for each type of learning that a curriculum might contain. As Gagné phrases it:

> The point of view of this text is that learning must be linked to the design of instruction through consideration of different kinds of capabilities that are being learned. In other words, the external events that are called instruction need to have different characteristics, depending upon the particular class of performance change that is the focus of interest.[158]

Learning Versus Growth

The two major categories of learning that must be identified are those which the human organism naturally develops for genetic and survival reasons and those which are products of cultural evolution and which cannot be attributable to either growth or natural accumulation. Developers working within the Social Efficiency Ideology are not concerned with the former types of learning while creating curricula. The types of learning considered by Freud and Piaget are largely irrelevant to their efforts. These developers are interested in only those learnings which can *not* be attributed to either growth or natural accumulation. They are interested only in those learnings that the student would *not* naturally develop or encounter during his life.[159] As Gagné says, "Learning is a change in human disposition or capability which can be retained and which is not simply ascribable to the process of growth . . . *it must be distinguishable from the kind of change that is attributable to growth*."[160] Developers within the Social Efficiency Ideology are interested in learning and not growth. They are interested in learning which accrues as a result of students encountering "artificially" and "deliberately" contrived environments which stimulate them to respond in certain specified manners. They are interested in learnings that are purposeful in helping learners to achieve what would otherwise not be possible to achieve.

As a result, these developers reject "readiness" arguments based on genetic reasoning. "Readiness" to undertake learning is viewed as a function of the presence or absence of the necessary prerequisite learnings within the learner. As Gagné phrases it: "readiness for learning any particular new intellectual skill is conceived as the presence of certain specifically relevant subordinate intellectual skills."[161] Thus, "At any given age, a child may be unable to perform a particular intellectual task because he has not acquired the specifically relevant intellectual skills as prerequisites to that task."[162] However, "Such learning may be readily accomplished if the learner has acquired, or will undertake to acquire, the intellectual skills prerequisite to the task."[163] In particular, it is assumed that "Children can learn any intellectual thing we want them to learn, provided they have learned the prerequisites."[164] In terms of Figure 3.3, for example, when the learner is competent in c and d, he is by definition ready to learn a. Until he is competent in c and d he is not ready to learn a.

Partitioning learning from growth and conceiving of learning as atomistic in nature raises the question of what the relationship is between the learning required by a curriculum and the self-evolving nature of the child's life. This question is raised in terms of how to unite or mesh the organic life series within the child and the atomistic learning series within the curriculum. Bobbitt recognized the problem and spoke of it in 1924 in "Education as a Social Process." It was not until later, however, that the concepts of transfer and curriculum organization—in terms of integration and continuity—were used to theoretically account for the relationships between the parts of the atomistic curriculum and the organic life of the child. Transfer refers to the issue of how to generalize specific learnings so that they will be useful to the learner in contexts other than the specific situations constructed by the curriculum developer within his curriculum. Two types of transfer are often spoken of: lateral transfer and vertical transfer. Lateral transfer "refers to a kind of generalizing that spreads over a broad set of situations of roughly the same 'level of complexity.' "[165] It roughly corresponds to taking account of integration during curriculum organization, where accounting for integration involves accounting for and compensating for (a) learnings which take place within a curriculum and activities that take place independent of the curriculum within the learner's everyday life, and (b) the coordination of learnings within separate curricula which the learner is running simultaneously. Vertical transfer "refers to the effects that learned capabilities at one level have on the learning of additional ones at higher levels."[166] It roughly corresponds to taking account of continuity during curriculum organization, where accounting for continuity involves accounting for and compensating for (a) the natural flow of learning from activity n to activity n+1 and (b) the revisitation of related learnings within a topic at several different levels of difficulty.

Acquisition of Learnings

The accepted dichotomy between subjective reality and objective reality when combined with the stimulus-response conception of learning raises the problem of how to get something outside of the learner to become part of his repertoire of behavior. That is, it raises the question of how to bridge the gap between subjective and objective reality in order to help the learner acquire skills originating outside of himself. The learner acquires knowledge by observing a behavior he is to acquire and practicing it until he can satisfactorily reproduce it or by experiencing the objective reality outside of himself and repeatedly responding to it until he achieves a satisfactory ability to respond appropriately. Learning is always by observation or experience of realities outside of oneself. Bobbitt constantly uses the phrases "by observation of reality" and "experiential contract with the realities themselves" to describe learning as a process involving an active incorporation of external reality into the internal consciousness.[167]

The words "observation" and "experience" are used with a perceptive interpretation. Observation and experience are always observation and experience of things outside of oneself through the senses. Learning is always getting something outside of oneself into oneself through the medium of physical sensation.

Here the distinction between sensation (a bodily function of receiving stimuli and conveying them to the mind) and perception (the mental function of becoming aware of the bodily stimuli resulting from sensation) raises the question of how to transform "physical stimuli" into "mental stimuli." The problem is one of how to set up communication between the "mind" and the "world" once the body-mind duality is accepted. Developers have not seriously raised this question, for their concern is with the stimuli, the responses, and the mappings between stimuli and responses, and not with what goes on in between. However, they have provided a solution. It is that learning is a process of being "molded" or "shaped." The learner is molded or shaped by the arrangement of stimulus, response, and reinforcement conditions within the objective reality outside of himself, although it is through his own expenditure of internal subjective energy that he molds himself or shapes himself so that his behavior corresponds to the requirements of the world outside of himself. Here the subjective being of the learner is made to conform to the requirements of objective reality through the behavioral impulses of the learner himself that originate within his subjective consciousness. Within this context the Social Efficiency developer designs the requirements for appropriate behavior that reside within the objective reality outside of the learner, although it is the learner's subjective impulses that impel him to condition his behavior so that it conforms to the requirements of the objective world outside of himself. Figuratively speaking, here the curriculum developer designs a mold within objective reality and the learner forces himself into the mold and thus into the necessary shape.

That learning can be a molding or shaping process is based on three assumptions:

(1) The learner must make the response he is to learn. He learns what he does. (2) The responses must be strengthened. Learning progresses as the responses in question are reinforced and increase in probability. (3) The responses should be put under control of particular stimuli; these stimuli will set the occasion for the occurrence of the responses.[168]

The first of these assumptions refers to Bobbitt's functional education within which the learner must practice the behavior he is to acquire or make the response he is to learn—that is, learn to function by functioning in the desired manner. The second of these assumptions refers to Thorndike's law of effects (or Skinner's contingency of reinforcement theory) and pertains to the belief that the way to get a learner to acquire a behavior is to so arrange the conditions within which he learns that he is immediately rewarded or reinforced when he emits the desired behavior. There are three component assumptions making up this belief: first, correct responses are strengthened by being followed by immediate reinforcement; second, incorrect responses are weakened by not being followed by a reward; and third, complex behaviors are built up gradually through the reinforcement of prerequisite behaviors that gradually approximate the desired behavior through trial and error with only successes being rewarded. The last of the above assumptions refers to the belief of Social Efficiency developers that to be efficient a learner's behavior must be so conditioned that he responds virtually "automatically," immediately, and in a predetermined manner to the presence of specific stimuli—without "contemplation," without internal "thought," and without hesitation.

THE CHILD
Lack of Concern

Social Efficiency developers show little concern with the child *per se* while developing curricula. When they do show concern for the child, it is not concern for the child as a person but for the child as a potential adult possessing behavioral capabilities who can provide an energy input into the educational endeavor.

The Attributes of the Child

The child is not viewed as an entity who has meaning unto himself. The child is viewed as an entity who has meaning because of the way in which he can develop into an adult and can serve the world around him. He is first a member of society and capable of fulfilling the needs of society and only second an individual with needs unto himself. He is first a potential adult member of society—"the man within the child"—and only second a child. He is first a bundle of action capabilities and only second a person possessing the ability to act. Perhaps this last distinction shows how the child is viewed during curriculum creation.

If the distinction is made between the *acts* of a person and a *person* acting, it is the former with which Social Efficiency developers are concerned and not the latter. It is the *"actual activities* of mankind"[169] that are focused upon in contrast to the "actual activities *of mankind."* It is the *activity* engaged in by man that is of interest in distinction to *the man* as engaged in activity. Man and the attributes of man are dichotomized in a similar manner to the way in which subjective reality and objective reality are dichotomized. The emphasis is placed upon the attributes of man in contrast to man in a similar manner to the way in which emphasis is placed upon objective reality in contrast to subjective reality.

The Child as a Worker

In the following passage, Bobbitt points out the manner in which the child is viewed as a worker capable of providing an energy input into the educational endeavor:

Looking at a school system as a large organization of individuals for the purpose of turning out certain necessary human products, the pupils are in fact the ultimate workers. They are the rank and file over whom the teachers stand in supervisory capacity. The work is a development of the potential abilities which the pupils carry around within themselves into actual abilities of a given degree. These actual abilities are the educational products. It is the work of the student, not the work of the teacher, that produces these products.[170]

From this perspective, the child is viewed as the one who does the work in school. He provides the energy inputs that work upon himself to transform parts of him into suitable educational products. He knows what work to perform upon himself and the standards up to which he must bring himself because of the supervision he is given by the teacher.

Individualized Programed Instruction

Perhaps the stance of Social Efficiency developers towards individualized programed instruction brings out both of these points. First, individualized programed instruction is designed to help the child achieve a set of standard capabilities. It is designed to teach a *task* rather than a *student*. It deals with a very limited part of the child's total functioning: it is not designed to give the student a "total, well rounded, complete education" but to provide him with a set of particularized capabilities. Second, the instructional materials sit idle until begun by the student. They are activated by the student who provides the primary energy input that takes him through the materials. They educate him at a rate that is a function of his intellectual potential and the amount of energy which he puts into them.

TEACHING
Role of the Teacher

Developers working within the Social Efficiency Ideology make a clear distinction between the endeavors involved in developing curriculum and those involved in teaching. They make a clear distinction between the tasks of the curriculum developer and the work of the teacher. The curriculum developer is to design the sequence of learning experiences that the learner is to have on his journey from incompetence to competence. The teacher is to make sure that the learner appropriately works through the sequence of learning experiences designed by the developer so that the terminal performances are actually obtained. "The teacher is the *manager of the conditions of learning*"[171] who both prepares the learning environment so that learners can work within it and who supervises the activity of learners as they work their way through the sequence of learning experiences. The teacher, if at all possible, is not to engage in the actual design of learning experiences for students.

Part of the teacher's job is to prepare the environment within which the student will learn (do his work upon himself). This consists of doing whatever is necessary to prepare the curriculum for use by the student. Once the student engages the learning environment the teacher's job becomes one of supervising students, much as the manager of an assembly line supervises the workers on the assembly line. As Bobbitt phrases it:

> The teacher is supervisor, director, guide, stimulator, of the rank and file of the workers [students] in order to bring about on the part of the latter the development of these various abilities. The teaching problem is in fact a supervisory problem at the first level.[172]

> In a school system . . . the pupils are the ultimate
> workers . . . [and] the teachers rank as foremen. It is
> their business not to do the work that educates, but to
> get it done by the pupils. In doing this, they must know
> the pupils: know their varying mental capabilities, their
> interests, their aptitudes and abilities, their states of
> health, and their social milieu. They must know how to
> arouse interest; how to motivate them from within; how
> to adjust the conditions of the work to child-nature;
> how to keep up an abundant physical vitality in the
> children; and how to employ community influences for
> vital stimulation of the pupils.[173]

Managing, directing, or supervising the work of students involves
guiding them, motivating them, and assessing them. Guiding
students (as workers) involves indicating to them what they are to
learn (the work they are to do). In guiding a student, the teacher
must be knowledgeable of the student and of the curriculum so
that appropriate help can be given to the student as it is needed.
Motivating students (as workers) involves knowing one's students
and appropriately interacting with them in such a way that they
become persuaded to do the sequence of activities that they must
do in order to obtain the desired competencies (work through the
curriculum). Assessing students involves monitoring each student's
work as he progresses through the curriculum and maintaining
quality control so that he acquires all of the necessary prerequisite
behaviors that lead to the terminal objective. The job of teaching
involves fitting the student to the curriculum and fitting the
curriculum to the student. It involves stimulating students to run
the curriculum and adjusting the curriculum to the capabilities of
students. This involves knowing one's students and closely
supervising them in their idiosyncratic natures as they do their
work. It is thus the teacher's job to take into account the specific
nature of students. This is not the job of the curriculum developer.
As a result, the developer designs curriculum for a standard
student, and the teacher makes adjustments for particular students.

Within this context of the teacher being a manager of the
conditions of learning, it is important to note that "The objective
of this management is to insure that learning will be efficient, that

is, that the greatest change in the student's behavior will occur in the shortest period of time, and that this change will lead progressively to increased self-management of future learning."[174] Teaching is to be evaluated against a criterion of efficiency in getting the student to learn what the curriculum developer provides for him to learn.

Consequences

There are several important consequences of this view of teaching. First, the teacher's role as manager of the conditions of learning—in a manner similar to a foreman's managing of an assembly line in a large factory—removes the teacher from having any input in determining the ends toward which the student's work is being directed or from having any input in determining the particular progressive learning activities in which the student must engage in order to achieve those ends. The teacher is simply to get students to run the curriculum. The teacher is not to question the ends or means of the curriculum, nor is he to try to implement his own ends or the ends of the children within his care. He is a supervisor or manager of children engaging in a preconceived task and not a designer of that task. Thus, although the teacher's function is different from that of the curriculum developer, the teacher is conceived to be an instrument of ends other than his own, in the same way as is the curriculum developer. That is, the teacher is an instrument whose purpose is to implement the curriculum created by the developer; the developer is an instrument who creates a curriculum to fulfill the needs of a client; and, therefore, the teacher is ultimately an instrument to fulfill the needs of a client. Second, since "the objective of this management is to insure that learning will be efficient," it almost automatically follows that the way to evaluate the teacher's management is to see how "efficient"—rather than humane, creative, enlightening, or insightful—it is in getting learning to take place in accordance with the needs of the client. The result is that the teacher's endeavors end up being judged within the context of an instrumental value system based upon efficiency, as are the curriculum developer's endeavors. Third, excluding teachers from extemporaneously designing curricula for the particular needs of their classes has the effect of guaranteeing that "A 'quality control' of the choice of instructional conditions is insured and maintained."[175] That is, having the curriculum developer predesign the curriculum guarantees to the greatest degree possible that the "ultimate product" that results from the educational process will measure up to the "definite qualitative and quantitative standards" that are required to fulfill the needs of the curriculum client by making sure that "Quality does not suffer from variations in teacher's skills."[176] But the result of making sure that "Quality does not suffer from variation in teacher's skills" also produces a standardization of educational products and an inhibition of classroom flexibility.

EVALUATION
Reasons for Evaluation

Curriculum developers working within the Social Efficiency Ideology believe that it is essential to assess both the efficiency of their curricula and the behavior of students running their curricula. Preparing for curriculum evaluation and student evaluation is considered to be an integral part of the activity involved in developing curricula. There are four primary reasons why Social Efficiency developers consider evaluation to be important. One reason relates to the instrumentalistic views of the nature of curriculum development within which the curriculum developer is an agent of a client; another reason relates to the issue of scientific procedure; a third relates to the nature of progressive objectives as representing a sequence of learnings that systematically moves the learner from incompetence to competence; and a fourth reason relates to learning being viewed within a stimulus-response context.

First, the curriculum developer conceives of himself as an instrument whose purpose is to achieve ends other than his own. He conceives of himself as an agent of a client. As such, he holds himself accountable to that client for his actions. In order to demonstrate accountability, the developer must justify his efforts by producing evidence that indicates that he has fulfilled the needs of the curriculum client. In order to do so, the developer evaluates his curriculum to demonstrate that its terminal objectives have been achieved. This then (a) protects the curriculum client from obtaining "faulty products" (insufficiently trained students); (b) protects the student by making sure he has the necessary behaviors to function appropriately; and (c) protects the curriculum developer from adverse comments by proving that he has fulfilled his contract.

Second, developers within the Social Efficiency tradition see their endeavors within the mainstream of science. One aspect of the scientific endeavor is conceived to be the demand for reproducibility, predictability, reliability, and proof. Another aspect of the scientific endeavor is conceived to be the use of evaluation in order to demonstrate reproducibility, predictability, reliability, and proof. As such, curriculum developers working within the Social Efficiency Ideology believe that objective evaluation is necessary in order to scientifically demonstrate the value of their curricula.

Third, Social Efficiency developers see progressive objectives as representing a systematic sequence of learnings that the child must acquire one by one to move from incompetence to competence. To insure that the learner masters each progressive objective in its turn and to insure that the learner does not proceed to successive objectives before mastering previous ones, the learner's performance must be continually monitored through the use of evaluative measures that are built into every progressive objective. Based upon continual monitoring through evaluation decisions about the learner's future can then be accurately made. As Gagné phrases it, a

primary reason for direct measurement of the outcomes of a learning exercise session is to insure that instructional objectives have been met. If a student fails to exhibit the performance required on such a test, he needs to undertake additional learning covering the same ground. It is inefficient, even useless, for him to try to proceed to the learning of advanced topics, in view of the hierarchical nature of knowledge. . . . Whether by "repeating" the same instruction he has been given or by using a more elaborately "guided" form of instruction, the defined objective must somehow be achieved if subsequent learning is to be even minimally efficient for this student.[177]

Fourth, the Social Efficiency developer conceives of learning as taking place within a stimulus-response context. In this context, it is believed that the results of evaluation constitute an important source of feedback to the learner about his behavior, whether positive or negative. The results of evaluation thus become intimately bound up with the learning process itself through the concept of rewards (or reinforcements).

Nature of Evaluation

Social Efficiency evaluation involves comparing either the student or the curriculum to an *a priori* standard through the use of criterion-referenced tests. Such comparisons are made with respect to criteria which are decided upon before evaluation takes place. Evaluation is not made with respect to *a posteriori* comparisons that depend upon norms of a population which are discovered during testing. The criteria with respect to which evaluation takes place are the terminal and progressive objectives of the curriculum. They are not the norms of the student population running the curriculum. As Gagné says, evaluation's "purpose is to compare each student's performance with an external standard representing the defined objective."[178]

The type of data obtained from evaluation is of a "go—no-go" form. It is not a rank-ordering type of data, nor is it in a form that indicates possible curricular improvements. The important thing for student evaluation is whether the student passes or fails his test, and not if he is seventh or eighth from the top. The important thing for summative evaluation of the curriculum is whether the curriculum achieves the standards set for it, and not how well. The important thing for formative evaluation of the curriculum are decisions of the form "more refinement is needed" or "things are fine."

Evaluation takes the form of a comparison of an individual event x_i with an *a priori* standard $\bar{x}_i$ that tells the developer whether $\bar{x}_i - x_i$ is greater or less than zero. If it is on one side of zero, things are acceptable. If it is on the other side of zero, more refinement is needed. It should not concern the developer how large $\bar{x}_i - x_i$ is.

Objectivity, Particularity, and Atomization

Three other characteristics of the nature of evaluation need mention. First, evaluation involves objective unbiased measurement of objective reality rather than subjective testimonials based upon other than rigorous observation or reflection. Gagné indicates: "the outcomes of learning, the achievements of the learner, need to be assessed by an agent 'external' to the student, in order to ensure that they are objective and unbiased."[179] Statistical assessment is the preferred type of evaluation.

Second, evaluation of learning relates to learning achieved with respect to a particular stimulus condition. Evaluation of learning is not evaluation of change in general but evaluation of change as it is tied to a particular action on the part of the curriculum developer. As Gagné expresses it:

> Attention must also be paid to the form of each item that the test contains. The item must be designed to measure the objective specifically, not in a general sense. For example, there must be an item to measure "spelling verb forms that double their terminal consonants when made into a gerund by the addition of 'ing,' as sum, summing"; not just a collection of items that measure "spelling."[180]

Third, evaluation takes place within the context of atomization. The total learning or achievement to be evaluated is partitioned into specific atomic events each of which is evaluated separately. When each of the partitioned events is evaluated it is examined in terms of characteristics that should be inherent in the partitioned element. The question asked is whether or not the partitioned characteristics are present in the child or the curriculum.

Appropriateness of Evaluation

There are at least three characteristics of the Social Efficiency tradition that facilitate evaluation. First, the aims of the curriculum are stated in the form of behavioral objectives that define specific human performances. Behaviors are observable and thus easily measured. As Gagné phrases it:

> When instructional objectives are derived and defined . . . it becomes readily possible to observe the human performances to which they refer. Moreover, it is possible to assess (or measure) the attainment of these objectives. Thus . . . the problems of measuring many of the outcomes of instruction can be approached in a fairly straight-forward manner.[181]

Second, learning is conceived within the context of an identifiable change in behavior resulting from an identifiable stimulus condition. It is a change from the absence of a behavior to the presence of a behavior. Conceptualizing learning as an exhibitable change in behavior of the student facilitates evaluation.

Third, the Social Efficiency conception of causation as a deterministic stimulus-response event facilitates evaluation. Because causes are easily attributable, evaluation of the action of the developer is simple. One must simply show absence of behavior, display the stimulus-response linkage, show the stimulus created by the developer, and show the response of the student in order to illustrate that learning took place as a result of the developer's curriculum efforts. If causation was not so direct and easily analyzable, one would have a more difficult time evaluating.

Notes

[1] Franklin Bobbitt. "Some General Principles of Management Applied to the Problems of City School Systems." In *Twelfth Yearbook of the National Society for the Study of Education: Part I*. Chicago: University of Chicago Press, 1913.

[2] Franklin Bobbitt. *The Curriculum*. Boston: Riverside Press, 1918, pp. 41-42.

[3] *Ibid.*, p. 42.

[4] Ralph W. Tyler. *Basic Principles of Curriculum and Instruction*. Chicago: University of Chicago Press, 1949.

[5] *Ibid.*, p. 1.

[6] *Ibid.*, p. 3.

[7] *Ibid.*, p. 62.

[8] *Ibid.*, p. 3.

[9] *Ibid.*, p. 5.

[10] *Ibid.*, p. 5-6.

[11] *Ibid.*, p. 44.

[12] *Ibid.*, p. 62.

[13] *Ibid.*, p. 44.

[14] *Ibid.*, p. 65. (The italics are mine.)

[15] *Ibid.*, p. 63.

[16] *Ibid.*

[17] *Ibid.*

[18] *Ibid.*, p. 64.

[19] *Ibid.*

[20] *Ibid.*

[21] *Ibid.*, p. 83.

[22] *Ibid.*, p. 85.

[23] *Ibid.*, p. 110.

[24] *Ibid.*, p. 105-106.

[25] *Ibid.*, p. 106.

[26] *Ibid.*

[27] James G. Holland. "Teaching Machines: An Application of Principles from the Laboratory." *Journal of the Experimental Analysis of Behavior.* Vol. 3 (1960), p. 278. Copyright © 1960 by the Society for the Experimental Analysis of Behavior, Inc.

[28] *Ibid.*, p. 275.

[29] *Ibid.*

[30] Teaching machines have existed, in conceptualization if not in actuality, throughout the twentieth century. In 1912, Edward L. Thorndike (Edward L. Thorndike. *Education.* New York: Macmillan, 1912, pp. 164-167.) described the essence of a teaching machine this way: "If by a miracle of mechanical ingenuity, a book could be so arranged that only to

him who had done what was directed on page one would page two become visible, and so on, much that now requires personal instruction could be manged by print. . . . On the whole, the improvement of printed directions, statements of facts, exercise books and the like is as important as the improvement of the powers of teachers themselves to diagnose the conditions of pupils and to guide their activities by personal means. Great economies are possible. . . . A human being should not be wasted in doing what forty sheets of paper or two phonographs can do." Important to note in this description are the conceptual precursors to the modern teaching machine: the "mechanical" device corresponds to the teaching machine itself; the arrangement of learning conditions so that "only to him who had done what was directed on page one would page two become visible" is (a) similar to the way teaching machines continually evaluate learner responses and allow learners to proceed to successive more difficult learnings only after mastering easier prerequisite learnings and (b) similar to the way teaching machines reinforce correct student responses by allowing them to proceed to successive learnings; the improved "printed directions" and each of the "forty sheets of paper" are similar to the single frames of the teaching machines, each of which presents the student with only one item of material at a time; the saving of "great economies" is the forerunner of claims for efficiency by producers of todays teaching machines; and the freeing up of the teacher to "diagnose the conditions of pupils and to guide their activities" is identical to the present day conception of the role of the teacher *vis-a-vis* the teaching machine.

[31] C.M. Lindvall and John O. Bolvin. "Programed Instruction in the Schools: An Application of Programing Principles in 'Individually Prescribed Instruction.' " In *The Sixty-Sixth Yearbook of the National Society for The Study of Education: Part II, Programed Instruction.* Chicago: University of Chicago Press, 1967, p. 231.

[32] *Ibid.*

[33] Robert M. Gagné. *The Conditions of Learning: Second Edition.* New York: Holt, Rinehart, and Winston, 1970, p. 329. Reprinted by permission of Holt, Rinehart, and Winston.

[34] Lindvall, *loc. cit.*, p. 237.

[35] *Ibid.*, p. 231.

[36] *Ibid.*

[37] *Ibid.*, p. 249.

[38] *Ibid.*, p. 231.

[39] *Ibid.*, p. 249.

[40] Bobbitt. "Some General Principles," *loc. cit.*, p. 7.

[41] For early Social Efficiency developers, such as Bobbitt, one of the "scientific tools" was statistics. For later Social Efficiency developers, such as those of the 1960's, one of the "scientific tools" was Operations Research-Systems Analysis. It is to be noticed that the distinction between science and technology is rarely made.

[42] Bobbitt. "Some General Principles," *loc. cit.*

[43] *Ibid.*, p. 11.

[44] *Ibid.*, pp. 12, 33, 34, 35.

[45] *Ibid.*, p. 37.

[46] *Ibid.*, p. 12.

[47] William L. Patty. *A Study of Mechanism in Education: An Examination of the Curriculum-Making Devices of Franklin Bobbitt, W.W. Charters, and C.C. Peters, from the Point of View of Relativistic Pragmatism.* New York: Teachers College Press, 1938, pp. 6-7.

[48] Bobbitt. *The Curriculum, loc. cit.*, p. 282, infers this when he says: "In this volume we have tried to look at the curriculum problems from the point of view of social needs; and thereby to develop, in some measure at least, the social point of view as regards education. . . . The first necessary thing is for our whole educational profession to acquire a social, rather than a merely academic point of view."

[49] Franklin Bobbitt. "Education as a Social Process." *School and Society*. Vol. XXI, No. 538 (Saturday, April 18, 1925), p. 453.

[50] Franklin Bobbitt. *Curriculum Investigations.* Chicago: University of Chicago Press, 1926, p. 1.

[51] Bobbitt. *The Curriculum, loc. cit.*, p. 207.

[52] Bobbitt. *Curriculum Investigations, loc. cit.*, p. 6.

[53] Franklin Bobbitt. "The New Technique of Curriculum Making." *The Elementary School Journal*, Vol. 25, No. 1 (September, 1924), pp. 45, 46, 46-47.

[54] Robert M. Gagné. "Elementary Science: A New Scheme of Instruction." *Science,* Vol. 151 (January, 1966), p. 51. Copyright © by the American Association for the Advancement of Science.

[55] Bobbitt. *The Curriculum, loc. cit.,* p. 207, phrases it this way: "Education is preparation for the affairs of the mature world. This is not to lose sight of the fact that the education of the nine-year-old child is to prepare for the life of the ten-year-old; and this in turn for that of the eleven-year-old. But at the same time and in the same way, education during the formative stages of childhood and youth is to prepare for the long stage of maturity."

[56] Franklin Bobbitt. *How to Make a Curriculum.* Boston: Houghton Mifflin Company, 1924, p. 7.

[57] Bobbitt. "The New Technique," *loc. cit.,* p. 48.

[58] Bobbitt. *How to Make, loc. cit.,* p. 8.

[59] W.W. Charters. *Methods of Teaching.* Chicago: Row, Peterson, and Co., 1909, p. 3.

[60] *Ibid.,* p. 13. See also: Charles C. Peters. *Foundations of Educational Sociology.* New York: Macmillan, 1930, p. 25; and Bobbitt, *Curriculum Investigations, loc. cit.,* pp. 1-6.

[61] Robert Gagné. *The Conditions of Learning* (First Edition). New York: Holt, Rinehart, and Winston, 1965, p. 237. (The italics are mine.)

[62] Bobbitt. *Curriculum Investigations, loc. cit.,* pp. 1-2.

[63] Franklin Bobbitt. "What Understanding of Human Society Should Education Develop?" *The Elementary School Journal,* Vol. 25, No. 4 (December, 1924), pp. 292-293.

[64] Bobbitt. "The New Technique," *loc. cit.,* pp. 47, 49.

[65] Bobbitt. *The Curriculum, loc. cit.,* p. iv.

[66] *Ibid.,* p. 64. Bobbitt continues on page 68 in this way: More and more schools are recognized as agencies of social progress. Where deficiencies are discovered in any aspect of social life, schools are being called upon to overcome and prevent. . . . In such a list of . . . weaknesses we can discover the objectives of . . . education. The purpose is to so train men and women that the weaknesses will not appear."

[67] Bobbitt. *Curriculum Investigations, loc. cit.*, p. 2.

[68] Bobbitt. *How to Make, loc. cit.*, p. 8.

[69] The refusal of society to construct a complete and definitive set of terminal objectives for the school systems to implement is a long standing problem. Curriculum developers have been concerned about it from the time of Bobbitt, in *The Curriculum* (1918), to the time of Goodlad, in *The Changing School Curriculum* (1966).

[70] Bobbitt. "The New Technique," *loc. cit.*, pp. 49-50.

[71] American Association for the Advancement of Science. *Science–A Process Approach: Part C. Description of the Program.* Washington, D.C.: American Association for the Advancement of Science, 1967, p. 3.

[72] One of the consequences is that Bobbitt concentrated primarily on his Principle I while Gagné concentrated primarily on Principle II. The results are that although the two men develop curricula while working within the Social Efficiency Ideology, the nature of their curricula are very different. Bobbitt delivers the teacher objectives to be aimed at. Gagné delivers the teacher elaborate protocols to follow in accomplishing the desired objectives.

[73] Peters, *loc. cit.*, p. 433.

[74] Bobbitt. *How to Make, loc. cit.*, p. 4.

[75] In constructing the masterlist of terminal objectives by "going out into the field" in order to collect data about objective reality the Social Efficiency developer must remember to take account of the nature of the society about which he is collecting data. This had led Social Efficiency developers to assume in theory an attitude of cultural relativity. They see the need to determine terminal objectives with respect to the nature of the particular culture or subculture that they are examining. Bobbitt indicates the origin of his belief in cultural relativity in *The Curriculum, loc. cit.*, pp. 283, 284. A more widespread and well formulated belief in cultural relativity came about later in the century. This is observable in Tyler and Taba spending considerable energy in clarifying the idea in *Basic Principles of Curriculum and Instruction* and *Curriculum Development: Theory and Practice.*

[76] Bobbitt. *Curriculum Investigations, loc. cit.*, p. 20.

[77] Bobbitt. *The Curriculum, loc. cit.*, p. 41. Here Bobbitt phrases the Social Efficiency reaction against vague and general objectives this way: "The technique of curriculum-making along scientific lines has been but little developed. The controlling purposes of education have not been sufficiently

particularized. We have aimed at a vague culture, an ill defined discipline, a nebulous harmonious development of the individual, an indefinite moral character-building, an unparticularized social efficiency.... So long as objectives are but vague guesses, or not even that, there can be no demand for anything but vague guesses as to means and procedure. But the era of contentment with large undefined purposes is rapidly passing. An age of science is demanding exactness and particularity."

[78] Bobbitt. *The Curriculum, loc. cit.*, p. 117.

[79] *Ibid.*, p. 5.

[80] Bobbitt. *How to Make, loc. cit.*, pp. 8, 9, 10.

[81] Peters, *loc. cit.*, p. 184.

[82] There are a variety of reasons for the reordering and a variety of manners to execute the reordering. Charters discusses both his rationale and his reordering algorithms in W.W. Charters. *Curriculum Construction*. New York: Macmillan, 1923. Seguel discusses the rationale and algorithms used by Charters in Mary Louise Seguel. *The Curriculum Field: Its Formative Years*. New York: Teachers College Press, 1966, pp. 98, 99. Craig provides an informative and neatly executed description of both the initial collection of objectives for a masterlist and the reordering of the objectives in his doctoral thesis at Teachers College. The finished masterlist was used to create a curriculum for elementary school science which Ginn published for nearly forty years. The thesis is published in part in Gerald Spellman Craig. *Certain Techniques Used in Developing a Course of Study in Science for the Horace Mann Elementary School*. New York: Teachers College Press, 1927. Bobbitt discusses the need for the reordering in *The Curriculum*, while discussing how to determine the nature of the ideal man. He indicates the reason for the need on page seven of *Curriculum Investigations* in discussing his eleven thousand item survey of *The Readers Guide to Periodical Literature*.

[83] Bobbitt. *The Curriculum, loc. cit.*, p. 42.

[84] There is a serious question as to whether it is possible to discover the ends of education using "scientific" means (that is, means in accordance with instrumentalism, mechanism, and atomism). Developers within the Social Efficiency Ideology insist that terminal objectives of all necessary sorts are discoverable through the use of "scientific" techniques. I believe it fair to seriously raise the question of whether the type of "science" used by the Social Efficiency developer is capable of dealing with certain types of non-normative issues such as values. Can value systems be justifiably dealt with in an atomistic, instrumentalistic, statistical context, or is there something about the very nature of values that defies attempts to partition

the action from the context within which it takes place (a form of atomism), that defies attempts to separate ends from means (a necessary aspect of instrumentalism), and that defies attempts to evaluate in a normative manner (an aspect of the statistical context). Perhaps the universe of discoverable verifiable objectives contains two types of elements: those that can be "scientifically" discovered and those which must be "intuitively" or "personally" discovered.

[85] Robert F. Mager. *Preparing Instructional Objectives.* First Edition. Palo Alto: Fearon Publishers, 1962, p. 1. Copyright © 1962 by Fearon Publishers, Inc. Reprinted by permission of Fearon Publishers, Inc.

[86] American Association for the Advancement of Science, Commission on Science Education. *Science—A Process Approach: An Evaluation Model and Its Application, Second Report.* Washington, D.C.: AAAS Miscellaneous Publication 68-4, 1968.

[87] Gagné. *The Conditions of Learning: Second Edition, loc. cit.,* pp. 326, 327.

[88] Bobbitt. "Some General Principles," *loc. cit.,* p. 11.

[89] See, for example, Harold Rugg. "The Foundations and Techniques of Curriculum Construction." In *The Twenty-Sixth Yearbook for the National Society for the Study of Education: Volumes I and II.* Bloomington, Illinois: Public School Publishing Co., 1926; Raymond E. Callahan. *Education and the Cult of Efficiency.* Chicago: University of Chicago Press, 1962; or Robert F. Mager and Kenneth M. Beach. *Developing Vocational Instruction.* Palo Alto: Fearon Publishers, 1967.

[90] For a more complete description of Bobbitt's form of activity analysis, see: Bobbitt, "Some General Principles," *loc. cit.;* Bobbitt, *How to Make, loc. cit.;* Charters, *Methods of Teaching, loc. cit.;* Charles C. Peters, *Objectives and Procedures in Civic Education.* New York: Longmans, Green, and Co., 1930; Patty, *loc. cit.;* or W.W. Charters, *Teaching of Ideals.* New York: Macmillan, 1927.

[91] Robert M. Gagné. "Learning and Proficiency in Mathematics." *The Mathematics Teacher,* Vol. LVI, No. 8 (December, 1963), p. 622.

[92] For a full blown and well worked out hierarchy chart, see *Process Hierarchy Chart for Science—A Process Approach, Parts A-D.* New York: Xerox Education Division, 1967.

[93] For a more detailed analysis of Gagné's form of activity analysis see: Gagné, *Conditions, loc. cit.;* AAAS. *Evaluation Model, loc. cit.:* AAAS

Commission on Science Education. *The Psychological Bases of Science—A Process Approach.* Washington, D.C.: AAAS, 1965; Robert M. Gagné. "Curriculum Research and the Promotion of Learning." In *American Educational Research Association Monograph Series on Curriculum Evaluation No. 1: Perspectives on Curriculum Evaluation.* Chicago: Rand McNally, 1967; Robert M. Gagné. "The Analysis of Instructional Objectives for the Design of Instruction." In Robert Glaser (Ed.). *Teaching Machines and Programmed Learning II: Data and Directions.* Washington, D.C.: NEA, 1965; or Robert M. Gagné, *et al.* "Factors in Acquiring Knowledge of Mathematical Tasks." *Psychological Monographs,* No. 76 (1962).

[94] Bobbitt. *The Curriculum, loc. cit.,* p. 42. (The italics are mine.)

[95] Bobbitt. *Curriculum Investigations, loc. cit.,* p. 5. (The italics are mine.)

[96] American Association for the Advancement of Science. *Science—A Process Approach: Part C. Description of the Program, loc. cit.,* p. 10. (The italics are mine.)

[97] Sequence, as conceived by Gagné, but not all developers working within the Social Efficiency Ideology, has two significant characteristics: first, it has a hierarchical nature with some elements of the sequence being innately prerequisite to others and of a lower order than others (there is a value judgment here), and second, while creating curricula sequence is defined as a recursive function of decreasing order where the nth element in the sequence is derived as a function of the $n+1^{th}$ element of the sequence.

[98] Gagné. *The Conditions of Learning: Second Edition, loc. cit.,* pp. 26-27.

[99] See, for example: Jerome Bruner. *The Process of Education.* Cambridge: Harvard University Press, 1960; or Jerome Bruner. *Toward a Theory of Instruction.* Cambridge: Belknap Press, 1966.

[100] Gagné. *The Conditions of Learning: Second Edition, loc. cit.,* Chapter 10, Readiness for Learning, presents this view quite explicitly.

[101] Charters. *Curriculum Construction, loc. cit.,* p. 94.

[102] Bobbitt. "The New Technique," *loc. cit.,* p. 50.

[103] Bobbitt. *How to Make, loc. cit.,* p. 30.

[104] Gagné. *The Conditions of Learning: Second Edition, loc. cit.,* p. 245.

[105] *Ibid.*, p. 331. (The italics are mine.)

[106] *Ibid.*, p. 24. (The italics are mine.)

[107] Bobbitt. "The New Technique," *loc. cit.*, p. 49. (The italics are mine.)

[108] Bobbitt. *Curriculum Investigations, loc. cit.*, p. 1. (The italics are mine.)

[109] *Ibid.;* p. 3.

[110] American Association for the Advancement of Science. *Science—A Process Approach: An Evaluation Model, loc. cit.*

[111] American Association for the Advancement of Science. *Guide for Inservice Instruction: Science—A Process Approach.* Washington, D.C.: AAAS Miscellaneous Publication 67-9, 1967, p. 32.

[112] Franklin Bobbitt. "The Objectives of Secondary Education." *The School Review*, Vol. 28, No. 10 (December, 1920), p. 738.

[113] Bobbitt. "Some General Principles," *loc. cit.*, p. 12.

[114] B.F. Skinner. *Beyond Freedom and Dignity.* New York: Alfred A. Knopf, 1972, p. 201.

[115] Bobbitt. *The Curriculum, loc. cit.*, p. 283.

[116] *Ibid.*, p. 282.

[117] *Ibid.*, p. 283.

[118] *Ibid.*, p. 285.

[119] Seguel, *loc. cit.*, p. 103.

[120] Commission on the Reorganization of Secondary Education. *Cardinal Principles of Secondary Education.* Washington, D.C.: U.S. Bureau of Education Bulletin No. 35, 1918.

[121] A source for exploring some of the facets of this offshoot of the early Social Efficiency Ideology is: Edward A. Krug. *The Shaping of the American High School 1880-1920.* Madison: University of Wisconsin Press, 1969, Chapter 15: "Mr. Kingsley's Report." See also: Herbert M. Kliebard. "The Curriculum Field in Retrospect." In Paul Witt (Ed.). *Technology and the Curriculum.* New York: Teachers College Press, 1968.

[122]Three different interpretations of the origins of the Social Efficiency tradition in education can be found: Raymond E. Callahan. *Education and the Cult of Efficiency*. Chicago: University of Chicago Press, 1962; Charles J. Brauner. *American Educational Theory*. Englewood Cliffs: Prentice-Hall, 1964; and Mary Louise Seguel. *The Curriculum Field: Its Formative Years*. New York: Teachers College Press, 1966. All sources leave quite a bit to be desired. Callahan's concern is school administration, Brauner's concern is teacher training, and Seguel's concern is curriculum. Callahan is by far the most interesting source.

[123]Franklin Bobbitt and W.W. Charters, two leading curriculum developers of that time, were perhaps most responsible for pulling from these movements the unifying themes of the Social Efficiency Ideology. Charters pulled the themes together from the perspective of improving teaching, while Bobbitt pulled them together from the perspective of improving the management of education. For two very different interpretations of the central role which Bobbitt and Charters played see Seguel, *loc. cit.*, and Patty, *loc. cit.*

[124]Bobbitt. "Some General Principles," *loc. cit.*, p. 50.

[125]Bobbitt. "The New Technique," *loc. cit.*, p. 45.

[126]Sequel, *loc. cit.*, pp. 71-73.

[127]Phil C. Lange (Ed.) *The Sixty-Sixth Yearbook of the National Society for The Study of Education, Part II: Programed Instruction*. Chicago: University of Chicago Press, 1967.

[128]See, for example, the way in which Bobbitt praises these studies in "Some General Principles of Management Applied to the Problems of City School Systems" and in *The Curriculum*.

[129]James G. Holland, Carol Solomon, Judith Doran, Daniel A. Frezza. *The Analysis of Behavior in Planning Instruction*. Reading, Mass.: Addison-Wesley Publishing Company, 1976.

[130]Gagné. "The Analysis of Instructional Objectives," *loc. cit.* In this article Gagné traces his technique of curriculum creation to three sources: U.S. Air Force Task Analysis (pp. 35-37), behavioral psychology (pp. 37-39), and educators (pp. 39-41). He speaks of influences that behavioral psychology has had on him in greater detail in Chapter 1 of *The Conditions of Learning*.

[131]The following book was influential in popularizing the "scientific method" as it was used in industry: F.W. Taylor. *Principles of Scientific*

Management. New York: Harper and Brothers, 1911. The book was also published as a series of three articles in *American Magazine*, beginning March, 1911. From the educational viewpoint see: Paul Monroe and E.L. Thorndike. "Research Within the Field of Education: Its Organization and Encouragement." *The School Review Monographs: No. 1*. Chicago: University of Chicago Press, 1911; and Chester S. Parker. "The Present Status of Education as a Science." *The School Review Monographs: No. II*. Chicago: University of Chicago Press, 1912.

[132] Bobbitt. "Some General Principles," *loc. cit.*, p. 7.

[133] Bobbitt. "The New Technique," *loc. cit.*, p. 49.

[134] Reasons are considerably more complex than this. However, these are two major contributing reasons for the decline in influence of the social orientation.

[135] Bobbitt. *How to Make, loc. cit.*, p. 43.

[136] Kliebard, *loc. cit.*, pp. 75-76.

[137] The discussion of these shifts rest not upon historical interpretation but are, rather, theoretical constructs to explain the transformation in thought. Developers have existed at each stage of these shifts simultaneously in time and the shifts have not necessarily followed upon each other sequentially.

[138] Robert M. Gagné. "The Acquisition of Knowledge." *Psychological Review*, Vol. 69, No. 4 (July, 1962), p. 355.

[139] Gagné. "Curriculum Research," *loc. cit.*, p. 21.

[140] Bobbitt. "The New Technique," *loc. cit.*, p. 45.

[141] *Ibid.*, p. 46.

[142] *Science–A Process Approach: Purposes, Accomplishments, Expectations*. Washington, D.C.: AAAS Miscellaneous Publication 67-12, 1967, p. 3. Copyright © 1967 by the American Association for the Advancement of Science.

[143] Robert M. Gagné. "Elementary Science: A New Scheme of Instruction." *Science*, No. 151 (January, 1966), p. 49.

[144] Gagné. *The Conditions of Learning: Second Edition, loc. cit.*, p. 3.

[145] *Ibid.*, p. 5.

[146] John Watson. "Psychology as the Behaviorist Views It." *Psychological Review*, Vol. 20 (1913), pp. 158, 163, 176. Here he says: "Psychology as the behaviorist views it is a purely objective experimental branch of natural science. Its theoretical goal is the prediction and control of behavior. Introspection forms no essential part of its methods, nor is the scientific value of its data dependent upon the readiness with which they lend themselves to interpretation in terms of consciousness. . . . The time seems to have come when psychology must discard all reference to consciousness; when it need no longer delude itself into thinking that it is making mental states the object of observation. . . . What we need to do is to start work upon psychology, making behavior, not consciousness, the objective point of our attack."

[147] Gagné. *The Conditions of Learning: Second Edition, loc. cit.*, p. 6.

[148] *Ibid.*, pp. 33-34, 34, 34-35.

[149] A variety of reasons are presently given for the advantage of a "black box" conception of learning. The most sensible one is perhaps that the human mind is so complex that we can not at present understand its working and that the curriculum developer should at this time be doing other things than trying to understand how and why it works.

[150] Gagné. *The Conditions of Learning: Second Edition, loc. cit.*, p. 2.

[151] *Ibid.*

[152] *Ibid.*, p. 62.

[153] *Ibid.*, p. 65.

[154] *Ibid.*, p. 24.

[155] *Ibid.*, p. 70.

[156] *Ibid.*, ch. 2.

[157] Science—A Process Approach. "Hierarchy Chart." New York: Xerox Educational Division, no date.

[158] Gagné. *The Conditions of Learning: Second Edition, loc. cit.*, p. v.

[159] In *The Curriculum*, Bobbitt continually distinguishes between learnings resulting from "work" and learnings resulting from "play." He says that education as carried on in the schools is deliberately designed to teach only the former, although in so doing it makes use of the latter.

[160] Gagné. *The Conditions of Learning: Second Edition, loc. cit.*, p. 3. (The italics are mine.)

[161] *Ibid.*, p. 291.

[162] *Ibid.*, p. 290.

[163] *Ibid.*

[164] *Ibid.*, p. 300.

[165] *Ibid.*, p. 335.

[166] *Ibid.*

[167] *Ibid.*, p. 94.

[168] Robert E. Silverman. "Using the S-R Reinforcement Model." *Educational Technology, 8* (March 15, 1968), pp. 3-4.

[169] Bobbitt. *How to Make, loc. cit.*, p. 9.

[170] Bobbitt. "Some General Principles," *loc. cit.*, p. 32.

[171] Gagné. *The Conditions of Learning: Second Edition, loc. cit.*, p. 324.

[172] Bobbitt. "Some General Principles," *loc. cit.*, p. 32.

[173] Bobbitt. *The Curriculum, loc. cit.*, pp. 84-85.

[174] Gagné. *The Conditions of Learning: Second Edition, loc. cit.*, p. 325.

[175] *Ibid.*, p. 332.

[176] *Ibid.*

[177] *Ibid.*, pp. 342-343.

[178] *Ibid.*, p. 342.

[179] *Ibid.*, pp. 27-28.

[180] *Ibid.*, p. 341.

[181] *Ibid*, pp. 327-328.

4.
Child Study Ideology

THE IDEAL SCHOOL
The Ideal School as Different

Underlying the thoughts and endeavors of curriculum developers using the Child Study Ideology is an image or vision of an ideal school: a *School of Tomorrow*, as John Dewey wrote about it in 1915.[1] To the uninitiated visitor, the ideal school of the Child Study developer would look nothing like a traditional school. This is the way Harold Rugg described it in 1928:

> Is this a schoolhouse. . . . These cheerful rooms—walls colorful with children's paintings, floors spotted with bright rugs, light, movable tables and comfortable chairs. . . .
>
> Here is a group of six and seven year olds. They dance; they sing; they play house and build villages; they keep store and take care of pets; they model in clay and sand; they draw and paint, read and write, make up stories and dramatize them; they work in the garden; they churn, and weave, and cook.
>
> A group is inventing dances, which, we are told, are for a pageant. In a darkened room films are being shown. A high school class is teaching the seventh grade how to use the library. . . . A primary class is getting ready for an excursion . . . to a bakery. . . . At the end of the hall is a toy shop where industrious members . . . ply lathe and saw, pattern and paint, in fashioning marvelous trucks and horses. . . . Here is a

nature-study laboratory with green things growing. A breathless group is stocking a new aquarium to be sent to the third grade; while over in the corner white rabbits, mice, and guinea pigs—even a turtle—loll in well-attended ease.

... we come across a shop where.... Over all the walls are blueprints, maps, and posters and models of things made and in the making—ships, steam engines, cars, airplanes, submarines, sets for scenes, and even the swords and bucklers of medieval armor.[2]

What a contrast this picture of the ideal school presents when compared to the Child Study developer's view of the traditional school:

Think of children sitting with arms folded, eyes front, putting up a hand for a begrudged permission to move, chanting lessons in unison.... There *memorize, recite, pay attention* are the keynotes. Not "What do you think?" but "What does the book say?" directs the educative process.[3]

In that pattern children are pigeonholed in long rows of desks, filed in stereotyped classrooms ... children must sit quietly, study their lessons silently, obey the teachers promptly and unquestioningly.... The listening school is a place where the chief weapons of education are chalk-talk on a dismal blackboard, a few intensely dull required texts, and a teacher's tired voice.[4]

Although this particular contrast between the ideal school and the traditional school may sound oversimplified, the act of making such a clear distinction is central to the Child Study Ideology. Child Study developers see this sharp distinction between the type of school they are attempting to bring into existence and the type of school they see other educators supporting. An important dimension of the Child Study developer's vision of his ideal school is that he perceives it to be dramatically different from the traditional school. It is "different in atmosphere, housing, furniture; different in its basic philosophy and psychology; different in the role that it assigns to pupil and teacher initiative."[5] The Child Study concept of education is viewed as presenting such a dramatic alternative to traditional education that it challenges the viability of the traditional model of education, "the practices associated with it, and the fundamental assumptions upon which those practices are based."[6] Not only does the Child Study developer's ideal school challenge the traditional model of education, it also challenges variations on the traditional model. This is because the Child Study developer's ideal school "is not a refinement of or tinkering with the traditional model, as are programmed instruction, team teaching, nongrading, and most of today's 'educational innovations', but rather rests on significantly different assumptions about children, learning, and knowledge ... [that] give rise to significantly different kinds of educational practices and institutions."[7]

Historical Context

Ideal schools, such as those envisioned by the Child Study developer, have existed in the past and exist today. They have been a reality for a few children and Child Study developers believe that they should become the *Schools of Tomorrow*, as Dewey phrased it, for all children. The most famous of the ideal schools developed between 1890 and 1950 grew out of the Progressive Education Movement. They included the Dewey School,[8] founded by John Dewey at the University of Chicago in 1896, and the Organic School,[9] founded by Marietta Johnson in Fairhope, Alabama, in 1907. The most famous of the ideal schools developed since 1950 were associated with the Open Education Movement. They were often referred to as the integrated day school, the developmental school, the informal school, or the open classroom school.

The ideal school envisioned by the Child Study developer is different from the traditional school because it is a "child-centered school," because it is an "activity (or experience) school," because it is an "organic (or developmental) school," and because it is an "integrated school." Let us look at each of these different aspects of the ideal school separately, one by one.

The Child-Centered School

The ideal school of the Child Study developer is different from the traditional school because it is based on "Nothing less than the reorientation of the entire school around the child."[10] Within the child-centered school the needs and interests of the child determine the school program, rather than the needs of teachers and principals, the interests underlying the school subjects, or the expectations of parents.

Firstly, child-centered schools are "child-centered institutions in contrast to the teacher-centered and principal-centered schools of the conventional order."[11] They are child-centered rather than teacher or principal-centered because the interests, needs, wishes, and desires of the child dictate the nature of the school program, the content of the school curriculum, and (to as large a degree as possible) the governance of the classroom and school, rather than the needs and interests of teachers and principals. As Rugg puts it, "These schools believe that boys and girls should share in their own government, in the planning of the program, in the administering of the curriculum, in conducting the life of the school."[12] Within the child-centered school "The routine needs of the school, as well as the lesson assignments, the planning of excursions and exhibits, and the criticism of reports are taken over by the pupils."[13] This is very different, say Child Study developers, from the traditional school, where the interests of teachers and principals dictate all aspects of the child's education and where the child must obey the every wish of the teacher and principal promptly and unquestioningly.

Secondly, the child-centered school is organized around the needs and interests of the child rather than the demands of the school subjects. Harold Rugg writes in *The Child-Centered School*:

> In the formal schools . . . the program of the child's education is organized about school subjects. Not so in the new schools. . . .
>
> There is a . . . new article of faith—child interest as the orienting center of the school program. . . .
>
> The new school is setting up a program of work which has a personal connection with the immediate life of the child. It starts from his needs and interests. The units of the new program approximate as nearly as possible what to children are real-life situations. Hence the new school organizes its program around the centers of interest rather than around academic subjects.[14]

In the child-centered school, centers of interest such as clay boats, worms, care of a flock of chickens, musical instruments, or building and using a radio dominate the school curriculum. In contrast, within the traditional school, academic subjects such as arithmetic, reading, spelling, grammar, or history dominate the school program.

Thirdly, the child-centered school orients itself around the needs and interests of children rather than around parental expectations for their children. This is difficult for many parents to accept, for as Marietta Johnson says of the parent who sends his child to her Organic School:

> He is afraid that the desired amount of "subject matter" will not be acquired. To think of growth in other terms than reading, writing, arithmetic, science, history, and geography is impossible for him. . . . The idea that education is a preparation for something in the future has such a strong hold upon the imagination that few parents can believe that if the need of the present is met fully, the future is assured.[15]

Just the same, the child-centered school must concentrate on meeting the needs, interests, and desires of the child and must insist that "children should not be conscious of [or subjected to] adult expectancy. [For] This is a source of self-consciousness and waste in childhood."[16]

The Activity School

The ideal school envisioned by the Child Study developer is a school full of activity, a school where experience is the medium through which children grow and learn, a school where "Experience [is considered to be] the keynote of the new education!"[17] It is a school where it is believed ". . . that knowledge comes . . . through the interaction of an individual with the surrounding world, both inanimate and social,"[18] and a school where it is believed that ". . . children naturally *think* through experience—through activity."[19] In this activity school, or experience school, it is proclaimed that "I would have a child say not, 'I know,' but 'I have experienced.' "[20] The "I know" is taken to be the slogan of the traditional school whose program is based on reading and silence, on sitting and reciting, on listening and acquisition of facts. In contrast, the "I have experienced" is taken to be the slogan of the activity school, whose program is based on direct firsthand experience with reality, on experience involving physical materials, on experience involving movement and physical activity, and on experience involving activity both outside and inside of the classroom. Each of these four aspects of the program of the activity school needs elaboration.

The program of the activity school provides children with direct firsthand experiences with reality. It avoids the practice of the traditional school of providing the child with only secondhand experiences acquired through reading, listening, and viewing. The Child Study developers of Elementary Science Study write:

> It is part of the ESS approach to avoid introducing the formal names of things and concepts before the reality is understood. . . . We feel it is necessary for the student to confront the real world and its physical materials directly, rather than through intermediaries such as textbooks.[21]

In the activity school:

> One mandate is imperative for our style of work: there must be personal involvement. The child must work with his own hands, mind, and heart. It is not enough for him to watch the teacher demonstrate or stand in line to take a hurried glimpse of the reflection of his own eyelashes in the microscope eyepiece. It is not enough for him to watch the skillful classmate at work, not enough to follow the TV screen. He needs his own apparatus, simple, workable.[22]
>
> The child must discover the fact for himself in his own time. He will do this if the relevant material is available to him in sufficient quantity and variety, if he is given many opportunities of handling it and trying it out.[23]

In the activity school a great emphasis is placed on children having direct firsthand experiences with reality because it is believed that growth, learning, knowledge—in essence, education—come through personal interaction of the child with his world.

Since the child must personally experience reality firsthand in order to grow—and thus become educated—it becomes necessary for the activity school to provide the child with the "reality" he is to experience. It does this by having a program that provides the child with a multitude of experiences involving physical materials and social encounters. Physical materials of both animate and inanimate form are particularly prominent in the activity school. Children experience the growing of plants firsthand in the activity school, in contrast to reading about them in the traditional school. Children care for and personally handle animals in the activity school, in contrast to looking at pictures of them in the traditional school. Children personally make things such as airplanes, boats, trains, and swords using hammers, nails, saws, and soft wood in the activity school, in contrast to listening to lectures about the making of such things in the traditional school. And children experience the weighing and measuring of sand, water, wood, people, and rocks in the activity school, in contrast to writing answers about weighing and measuring in workbooks in the traditional school. In the activity school, "manipulative materials are supplied in great diversity and range with little replication,"[24] for it is believed that in order to grow, learn, and become educated, children must personally interact with a wide range of physical materials. For example, in activity schools one finds materials such as plants to grow, animals to handle and care for, tape recorders to tell stories into, stoves for cooking, a kiln for baking pottery, a Polaroid camera for taking pictures of interesting occurrences or projects just finished, record players that create music to dance to, a play store from which things can be bought and sold, old clothes in which one can dress up and play "make believe," a stage to act upon, a multitude of books to be read, hammers, nails, sandpaper and wood to build with, bottle caps, spools, seashells, peas, buttons, string, wire, rope, ribbon, rulers, scales and balances with which to weigh and measure, paper and pencils with which to write, and magic markers, crayons, and paints with which to create pictures.[25] As a result, the traditional school, with its desks, its chairs, and its standardized books neatly arranged, is very different in appearance from the activity school, with its multitude of physical materials:

> To go into this room, even without the children, was to
> be dazzled by a riot of colors, shapes, and textures.
> Drums, pots, mobiles dangling from the ceilings, masks,

painting, printing gear, a small electric kiln—all the disorder of a dozen simultaneous workshops was pent up in this small room. But there was discernible a pattern, or perhaps a series of patterns, the kind of pattern which children can feel at home in, where the organization is sometimes the minimal amount necessary for efficient working and sometimes the exaggerated arranging lavished on a sacred object or a sacred process. It was a room of shrines cohabitating with the muddle which is incidental to utter absorption in a task, a room through long experience immediately submissive to every change or mood imposed upon it by its masters.[26]

The program of the activity school is designed in such a way that the ideal school of the Child Study developer is, in essence, a school full of activity: a school full of physical, verbal, social, and emotional activity. It is a school that radiates the belief that healthy intellectual, social, and emotion growth must be accompanied by physical and verbal activity.[27] It is a school where "children move freely about the room without asking permission."[28] It is a school where "talking among children is encouraged."[29] It is a school where "many different activities go on simultaneously."[30] It is a school where one finds that "There is a large amount of actual physical exertion, of overt bodily movement, of a wide variety of sensory contracts, of the type of energy-release which is ordinarily designated as play."[31] In the activity school it is believed that one must "Free the legs, the arms, the larynx of a child" in order to "take the first step towards freeing his mind and spirit" to grow and learn.[32] This is because adherents of the Child Study Ideology believe that perhaps the "most deep-seated tendency in human life is movement, impulse, activity . . . [and] therefore, are experimenting vigorously with the fundamental psychological law—that the basis of all learning is . . . action."[33] As a result, the activity school is very different from the traditional school, which encourages stillness and quiet: ". . . where the school maintained . . . silence as the ideal classroom atmosphere, the new [activity school] removes the ban from speech, [and] encourages communication as a vehicle for social understanding and personal development."[34]

In the activity school, for example, one might find children acting out Greek and Roman myths through improvisational drama rather than just studying classics from a textbook; one might find children telling each other stories and acting out fantasies rather than just writing language arts essays; one might find children dancing old English folk dances and singing old English ballads rather than just reading English literature; one might find children discussing railroading while building a model railroad, rather than just reading about and filling in a worksheet on the history of railroads; one might find children exploring and mapping gullies, streams, and bays near the school rather than just listening to a lecture about physical geography; one might find children talking mathematics while measuring each other's weights or the height of their school building rather than just writing in an arithmetic workbook; one might find children playing a dictionary dominoes game rather than taking a vocabulary quiz; and one might find children discussing surface tension as they "play" with water rather than just watching the teacher perform a physics demonstration.[35] In the activity school one might find all of these activities occurring simultaneously, in contrast to the traditional school, where one thing happens at a time.

Finally, the program of the activity school is designed to provide children with experiences that occur outside of the classroom as well as experiences that occur within the classroom. Those running the activity school are to:

> *Whenever possible, encourage and permit children to explore the real world outside of the classroom and outside of the school. . . .* In this way, a whole world of possibilities opens up, and the entire environment becomes the locus of the child's learning. The countryside offers a study of nature, creatures of every kind, plants, and streams; the suburbs offer opportunities to explore various forms of transportation (buses, trains, trucks, boats, cars); cities offer opportunities to view construction of roads, bridges, and skyscrapers. All give access to weather, food, buildings, movement, change, pattern, and excitement. Whenever there is a school, there is a community which is rich in potential learning experiences.[36]

Because the activity school provides children with educational experiences outside of the classroom—within the halls of the school, within the schoolyard, and within the neighborhood of the school—it is strikingly different from the traditional school in which learning is conceived as taking place only at the child's desk within the classroom:

> While in the traditional classroom the child learns at his desk, in the open school *the locus of learning is where something of particular interest to the child happens to be.* With this confidence, the teacher accepts and respects what each child chooses to do and where he chooses to do it.[37]

The Organic School

The ideal school invisioned by the Child Study developer is an organic or developmental school. It is a school designed to further the natural growth of the developing human organism—hence the term organic. It is a school founded on the belief that ". . . life—growth—education—are synonymous . . ."[38] and with the ". . . idea that education is growth and that the school program must minister to growth. . . ."[39] It is a school organized to ". . . respect the inner movement of growth . . ."[40] of children and to provide children with educational experiences compatible with their stage of social, emotional, and intellectual development. As a result, the organic school is viewed by the Child Study developer as different from the traditional school in a number of ways.

The organic school is different from the traditional school because its curriculum is based upon the natural growth of the developing human organism, rather than upon any demands external to the child. As Marietta Johnson says of her Organic School, "Our school has always been an effort to work with children from the point of view of meeting their needs rather than getting them to meet the demands of any system."[41] Particularly important to the organic school is that it does not pressure the child to acquire academic skills and knowledges before the child is developmentally ready for them. The differing approaches taken to teaching children to read and write by the organic and traditional school provide an example of this. In the organic school, care is taken not to force children to learn to read or write before their bodies and minds are ready to voluntarily engage in the activities inherent in reading and writing. In the traditional school, children are encouraged, or required, to read and write as soon as they can be made to do so.[42] At issue here is the difference between training and growing:

> "Training" and "growing" are quite different. In training, we often dominate or force in order to accomplish certain definite external results. In growing, we provide the right conditions and the end is human and immediate—included in the process—and the moving power is within . . . the child.[43]

It is the task of the organic school to provide the medium for growth—a rich variety of materials for the student to experience and a teacher who facilitates the child's interaction with the materials—and it is the task of the child to do the growing in the way that is natural to him. In contrast, Child Study developers conceive of the task of the traditional school to be one of training students by imposing knowledge and skills upon them.

The organic school is different from the traditional school because it views the child as different from the adult, treats the child differently, and bases its curriculum upon the nature of the child "as a child" rather than "as a potential adult." The organic school views the child as an evolving organism that undergoes growth from infancy to adulthood by passing through a series of stages of growth. Each stage of growth that the child evolves through is viewed as qualitatively different from all the others, including adulthood. What the organic school endeavors to do is to deal with the child in the manner most appropriate to the stage of development at which he finds himself. This involves attempting to minister directly to the nature of the child *as the child experiences his nature* at a particular stage of growth. By doing this the organic school cherishes childhood and "stresses the present, not the future; living, not preparing for life; learning now, not anticipating the future"[44] under the belief that to live life fully "as a child is the best preparation for adulthood."[45] What is at stake here, and what differentiates the organic school's approach to childhood from the traditional school's approach, is how the child is treated and the types of activity that are viewed as appropriate for the child to engage in. The organic school treats the child "as a child" and provides the child with "child-like" activities that are designed to be in congruence with, to nurture, and to elaborate upon the particular stage of development at which the child finds himself. In contrast, the traditional school treats the child "as a potential adult" and provides the child with "adult-like" activities that are designed to prepare the child for adulthood and speed the child on his way to adulthood. For example, the organic school provides the child with activities that might be classified as having the essence of "play" under the belief that

> if the need of the present is met fully, the future is assured. Growth has no external end. The end and the process are one. If the child is happily engaged in wholesome activity, he is growing, he is being educated.[46]

In contrast, the traditional school provides the child with activities that might be classified as having the essence of "work" under the assumption that

> anything which is productive for children in school is difficult and often painful. If it hurts, there must be something beneficial about it. Conversely, it has been assumed that those things which are fun and pleasurable are unproductive and usually take place in "free time" or out of school.[47]

What is important to note here is that within the organic school "Play is not distinguished from work as the predominant mode of learning."[48] In fact, within the organic school the distinction between work and play is an inappropriate one. It is more appropriate to distinguish between "involvement in an activity" and "lack of involvement in an activity," since it is believed that "If a child is fully involved in and having fun with an activity, learning is taking place."[49] As a result, the atmosphere of the organic school is viewed by the Child Study developer to be one in which children are actively involved in experiences. In contrast, the atmosphere of the traditional school is viewed as one in which children are forced to partake in tedious work.

The organic school is also different from the traditional school because it is believed that individual "children learn and grow intellectually," socially, and emotionally "at their own rate, and in their own style"[50] rather than in a uniform manner. This belief dictates that the organic school be organized and conducted in such a way that it supports the natural organic differences among individual children in all their qualitative richness. As a result, the organic school has an individualized instruction program quite different from that of the traditional school. In the organic school "Many different activities go on simultaneously"[51] from which children can make choices of what they are going to do based upon their personal needs and interests. In contrast, in the traditional school only one activity usually takes place at any one time and all children must participate in that activity independent of their personal needs or interests. In the organic school "activities do not arise from predetermined curricula"[52] for "The teacher plans instruction individually and pragmatically, based upon reflective evaluation of each child's particular needs and interests."[53] In the traditional school, a predetermined curriculum determines what will occur in the classroom independent of the needs, interests, abilities, or styles of learning of individual children in the classroom. In the organic school, "Children have the right to direct their own learning, to make important decisions regarding their own educational experience"[54] based upon their own felt needs, interests, abilities, and styles of learning. Children exercise this right by deciding which activities they will become involved in, how long a period of time they will spend involved in the activity, whether they will work alone or in a group on the activity, and if they work in a group who will be the members of the group. In contrast, within the traditional school the teacher—not the child—decides what activities the child will engage in, how long he will work on them, whether he will work alone or with others, and if he works with others those with whom he will work. Since the organic school is conducted with the belief that "There is no set body of knowledge which must be transmitted to all"[55] children and that "The structure of knowledge is personal and idiosyncratic, and a function of the synthesis of each individual's experience with the world,"[56] what the child personally learns within the organic school is viewed as a function of his own organic nature at his particular stage of development. In contrast, within traditional schools the knowledge the child is to learn is clearly predetermined before the child encounters it and is independent of the organic nature of any individual child. In essence, the organic school is organized and conducted in such a way as to support the multitude of differences that naturally exist among young human organisms— differences of interest, style of learning, rate of learning, and meaning acquired from previous instruction. In contrast, the traditional school is viewed as suppressing individual differences and attempting to establish uniformity in learning among children.

The Integrated School

The ideal school invisioned by the Child Study developer is an integrated school. It is a school that takes a unified rather than a segmented approach to the education of the child. It is integrated in many ways.

First, it is integrated because it treats the child as an integrated organism possessing an integrity as a complete organism *per se*. The child is dealt with as an inseparable conglomerate of intellectual, social, emotional, and physical components rather than as a creature whose attributes can be partitioned and dealt with separately. The integrated school takes "a holistic view of personality"[57] that requires that one "must look at the whole child"[58] and simultaneously "deal with all the attributes of people—intellect, emotion, and sensation"[59] Unlike the traditional school, the integrated school "does not see 'skill development' as a separate activity which can be isolated, studied, and improved independent of the rest of the child, like one step in a chemical synthesis . . . intellectual growth cannot take place without growth and development of the whole personality of the child."[60] As Rugg phrases it, while pointing out how the diversity of materials in the activity school supports the attempt of the integrated school to simultaneously educate all aspects of the child:

> The whole child is to be educated. Hence the materials
> of education are as broad and interrelated as life itself.
> For experience is not only an intellectual matter, it is
> physical, rhythmic, emotional. Thus the vocabulary of
> the new school has coursing through it a unitary,
> integrating theme.[61]

Second, the ideal school is integrated because it integrates the knowledge of the many disciplines within the curriculum rather than considering them separately. It does this by taking an interdisciplinary approach to knowledge in which the separate "school subjects are rejected in favor of broader and more integrated centers of work."[62] It does this by encouraging the child not to identify the learnings he is encountering in terms of the separate academic disciplines. Integrated schools "prefer to let the learner integrate knowledge of the many disciplines in his own mind, or rather never to let him disintegrate knowledge"[63] for:

> When a child is given freedom to explore materials in his own way, he is likely to be oblivious to categories in which adults have placed them. If a child is building a boat for the neighboring stream, neither he nor the teacher distinguishes among his activities when he measures, studies a picture in a book, paints the sails, or notices that the current in the river changes after a rainfall, although a traditional teacher might label them "mathematics," "history," "art," and "science."[64]

Third, the ideal school is integrated because it integrates the way time is used during the school day. It does this by having "very few fixed time periods"[65] during the day when particular events occur. In the traditional school, time is broken up into segments for specific purposes under the belief "that children's intellectual development can be made to follow the convenience of arbitrary adult-made timetables."[66] Not so in the integrated school, where it is believed that "until adults know more about how children think and learn, the child is a better judge of his needs with respect to time than is the adult."[67] As a result, there is a fluidity of use of time within the integrated school, during which children begin activities, finish their involvement in each activity, and move on to new activities when such feels proper and natural to them. As Brown and Precious interpret it, "Subject barriers and division of time do not and could not exist in this school with such a dynamic atmosphere. The children's interests and needs are the determining factor, not the timetable and subjects."[68]

Fourth, the ideal school is integrated because within it "many different activities go on simultaneously."[69] This is in sharp contrast to the practice in the traditional school of partitioning the day in such a way that only one activity takes place at a time. The effect upon the ideal school is that activities naturally become integrated into each other in the following two ways. Activities simultaneously taking place in different parts of the room merge together, as when, for example, several children's involvement with mice merges with other children's involvement with building blocks to result in mice running through the structures built out of blocks to perhaps become a study of animal behavior in mazes. And activities taking place at one point of time naturally flow into later activities, as when, for example, work with plants leads to a search for information in the classroom library that in turn leads to involvement in reading.

Fifth, the ideal school is integrated because it attempts to integrate the child's school life and home life. Within the integrated school, "The boundaries most American children carefully draw between 'school' and 'home' are blurred. Children, like teachers, take things and ideas of interest home to ponder, just as they bring things and ideas of interest from home to school. The result is a more fully 'integrated day.' "[70] The result is that the integrated school, unlike the traditional school, fosters in children a sense that the world is not fragmented into isolated places of "home" and "work."

It is important to note that these five aspects of integration are not viewed in isolation from each other. The simultaneity of activities within an undifferentiated classroom time schedule that supports the continuity between home and school life while cutting across subject areas is directed towards supporting to the fullest extent possible all aspects of the growth of the child.

CHILDREN
The Child as Central Focus

Curriculum developers working within the Child Study Ideology see the world through the eyes of children. They focus directly upon the child as the central concern underlying their endeavors. In 1894 Francis Parker affirmed: "The centre of all movement in education is *the child*."[71] In 1967 the opening sentences of the Plowden Report declared: "At the heart of the educational process lies the child. No advances in policy, no acquisitions of new equipment have their desired effect unless they are in harmony with the nature of the child, unless they are fundamentally acceptable to him."[72] The very aim and end of the Child Study developer's endeavors is to "meet the needs of the growing" child.[73] As Bussis and Chittenden say of Education Development Center, a major curriculum development agency housing some Child Study developers:

> Perhaps one of the most distinguishing assumptions of the EDC approach is that children constitute the basic resources of the educational process. In contrast to those educational theories which "assume" the presence of a child during instruction, an EDC approach "requires" the presence of a child to define instruction. Teaching begins with the assumption that the children coming into a classroom come with capabilities and experiences—shared and unique—and it is the teacher's job to see that those resources give a direction and meaning to learning.[74]

In focusing directly upon the child, Child Study developers focus upon the "all 'round" growth of the whole child: his intellectual growth, his affective growth, his psycho-social growth, his physical growth, his moral growth.

Focus Directly upon the Child

The Child Study approach to curriculum creation involves an effort to create curriculum in such a way that the child's organic nature, "the child's own needs" and "His immediate interests are to furnish the starting point of education."[75] The concern is with children rather than with theories about children, with sensitivity and responsiveness to children rather than with scholarly rigor in the study of children, and with the facilitation of those learnings of immediate concern to the child rather than with teaching the child what he "needs" to know. The Child Study developer begins not with the needs of society or the academic disciplines but with the needs and concerns of the individual child as perceived by the developer himself. This involves an effort, while creating curricula, to "apply to the education of children the lessons learned from the study of children themselves."[76]

The Child as Curricular Ends and Means

The child is viewed as the source of content for the curriculum; his ends and his means are viewed to be the appropriate ends and means for the curriculum. The first consideration of the Child Study developer while creating curricula is given to the child's needs as the child himself feels them, for "Education is the process of meeting the needs of children."[77] Lillian Weber describes the centrality of the child to the Child Study developer's mode of creating curricula in this way:

> Central to the conversations [of Child Study advocates] was always a child: What does he need? What is he interested in? What is he ready for? What are his purposes? How does he follow them? What are his questions? What is he playing? These questions about children seemed to be uppermost in developing plans for the classroom, for plans were made not from the vantage point of a syllabus of demand which a child had to meet, but with relevance to children in the most immediate way. A plan fitted itself to a child. It was developed in response to the pace and internal pattern of his own growth and in support of his own purposes. It was developed through watching a child, studying him at his moments of deepest involvement in play.[78]

It is the needs of the child as felt by the child that are considered by the Child Study developer to be one's best guide in opening the doors of learning for the child.[79] This means that whatever knowledge the developer possesses about children is to be used to help the child further his own ends. Knowledge of the child is *not* to be used to manipulate the child to learn content not inherently deriving from his nature, to maneuver the child to endure modes of learning not natural to him, or to further ends other than those of the child himself. The curriculum is to organize itself around the child's intention to learn, rather than the curriculum developer's intention to teach him. And, as Marietta Johnson so aptly states, "Our constant thought is not what do children learn or do, but what are the 'learning' and the 'doing' doing to them."[80] The concern is not with "what do you know" but with "what do you need"; and the answer is to be found by looking to the very nature of childhood itself.[81]

The Nature of the Child

The Child Study Ideology sees the child as imbued with natural goodness: it

> professes belief in the natural, inherent goodness of man. It believes that a child's natural tendency is to grow into a happy, healthy, well-functioning adult. Further, it believes that the capacity for self-fulfillment is good, that the ability of humans to command their own educational destinies is good, that a child's search toward fuller understanding is normal, natural, and good.[82]

"Childhood is a good and a natural stage of life"[83] and the child's natural modes of growth and impulses for action are constructive *if* they are not inhibited or distorted. The child is also conceptualized as a self-activated maker of meaning: he is viewed as an actively self-propelled agent of his own growth and not as a passive organism to be filled or acted upon. The child is viewed

> not as a passive vessel waiting to be filled nor as an amorphous lump of clay awaiting some form-giving artist but as a self-activated maker of meaning, an active agent in his own learning process. He is not one to whom things merely happen: he is one who by his own volition causes things to happen. Learning is seen as the result of his own self-initiated interaction with the world. The child's understanding grows during a constant interplay between something outside himself—the general environment, a pendulum, a person—and something inside himself—his concept-forming mechanism, his mind.[84]

Thus, the child is not considered to be an empty organism to which things merely happen—rather he is viewed as having inherent capabilities for growth which are activated by his own activity, for "personality evolves from within. It . . . develops only through growth in the power of self-propulsion."[85]

As a result, education is seen as an enterprise involving the "drawing out" of the inherent capabilities of the child. It is a facilitator of the natural growth of the child. And it will result in healthy, virtuous, and beneficial learnings if what is "drawn out" is allowed to "come out" naturally.

THE GROWING CHILD
Growth

This conception of the child as (a) containing his own capabilities for growth, (b) being the agent who must actualize those capabilities, and (c) being basically good in nature, leads developers within the Child Study Ideology to have as the central theme of their endeavors the concept of "growth." They dramatically proclaim "Not 'what do they know' but 'how do they grow' is our slogan."[86] They steadfastly swear that "The idea that education is growth and that the school program must minister to growth so fully possessed me that I have always been most grateful for the privilege of working at it."[87] What underlies the Child Study developer's devotion to growth is the belief that ". . . life—growth—education—are synonymous . . ."[88] and, thus, since the child is at the center of their attention, that "ministering to growth, meeting the needs of the organism, is the sole function of the educational process."[89] Growth of the child in terms of his unfolding in "conformity to the law of his being" becomes the objective of the Child Study developer.[90] "The doctrine of growth"[91] demands that education of each child be in harmonious resonance with the inner "being" of that child: that "education . . . is obliged to respect the inner movement of growth"[92] of the child, that education should be "organic education," that learning should be in vibration with the "rhythms of life," and that growth should be through creative self-expression. This perspective emphasizes the development of the individual and his individuality, for it is assumed that each child has a unique "being" and must grow in accordance with that unique "being."

Freedom and Individualism

Developers within the Child Study Ideology insist upon the individual's "freedom to develop naturally, to be spontaneous, unaffected, and unselfconscious."[93] In the "freedom versus control" debate, the Child Study developer insists upon freedom: freedom of the individual child to determine the directions which his education will take; and, as a result, freedom of the individual child to develop into the unique person that corresponds to his own inner "being." The crux of the issue surrounding the "freedom versus control" debate concerns which agent will decide the nature of the child's education: the child, the society, the academic subjects, the teacher, the parents—in other words, the child or someone else. The Child Study developer answers with a resounding declaration that the child must be the agent of his own learning, growth, education, and life. The medium through which the child determines the direction that his education will take is by responding to his own innate nature, felt needs, and organic impulses. The intention is to let the child grow naturally into the person he will become. This involves insisting that society, parents, school subjects, and teachers must not attempt to control the growth of the child and must not attempt to mold the child to conform to their expectations. Rather, they should allow the child the freedom to determine his own directions for growth, his own education, and his own life. Harold Rugg indicates this when he writes that for Child Study developers "it is the creative spirit from within [the child] that is encouraged, rather than conformity to a pattern imposed from without,"[94] a pattern of "social adjustment, adaptation to the existing order . . . [or] compliance with social demands."[95] Insisting that the child be the prime agent in his own education—"a self-reliant, independent, self-actualizing individual who is capable, on his own, of"[96] directing his own growth—leads the Child Study developer to a belief in individualism. The belief in individualism asserts that children are different, that their own unique inner impulses motivate them to grow in different manners, and that as a result education must be individualized. Not only does it lead them to a position of accepting individualism among children, but it also leads them to a position where they "not only acknowledge but deliberately attempt to foster individual differences among children."[97] The individualization in learning, growth, and education that is provided for by the Child Study developer, as a result, "goes well beyond any simple notion of 'each according to his own speed' "[98] or each according to his own learning style, for it "sees a fundamental independence of each learner from all others, from all would-be assistants, such as teachers or parents, and from all codified knowledge as it exists in universities or texts."[99] The necessity of building curriculum that will nurture individual differences by allowing each child to be the agent (or director) of his own growth raises a potential problem for the curriculum developer, since education demands a social setting. As Harold Rugg puts it:

> The leaders of our schools are confronted by a no more important and overwhelming problem than that of providing an environment by which each child can learn to live with others and yet retain his personal identity. To live with others, learn how to adjust himself to them, and yet grow in the confident knowledge that he, like each of them, is a unique individuality, a rare personality . . . a distinct personality, an individualist. . . .[100]

The beauty of the Child Study Ideology is that this potential problem is handled by the very nature of the developer's ideal school where children have the freedom to choose what activity they will become involved in and how they will pursue that activity within an environment containing many different activities that occur simultaneously.

Autonomy

Inherent in the Child Study developer's belief in freedom and individualism is a belief in the autonomy that must be accorded to children who have "both the competence and the right to make significant decisions concerning their own learning."[101] "Viewing the child as an autonomous agent who directs much of his own learning"[102] means that "What he does and who he becomes are his to decide."[103] In the final analysis this means that

> at that point when the child firmly decides against doing what the teacher thinks is best, the teacher often will make the decision to honor the child's position and give up, for the time being, this particular opportunity to extend his understanding of geography or whatever. To many this appears to be rank permissiveness; to advocates of open education, however, it expresses an important priority, namely, that it is more important for a child to have the experience of receiving someone else's *respect* for him and for his wishes than to have the experience of *submitting* to someone else's notion of "what's good for him."[104]

This belief that it is important for the "child to have the

experience of receiving someone else's respect for him" is an important aspect of the Child Study developer's view of the autonomy of the child. The experience of the child of actually *recognizing* and *feeling* that he is treated with "courtesy, kindness and respect"[105] and valued "as a human being whose rights are no less valid than those of an adult"[106] is just as important as the actual treating of the child in this way. As Rathbone phrases it:

> Most essential in this psychological climate is the condition of autonomy—not only the fact of it but the child's appreciation of and belief in that fact. Being expected to behave as an independent agent and living in an environment that assumes that every child has the innate capacity and urge to make sense of the world and to make meaningful decisions concerning his own activities in that world—these expectations do have their effects on the child. They teach him to accept himself as a maker of meaning and as someone whose choices count. They teach, however obliquely, a self-respect and self-esteem—and again, a view of himself as an agent.[107]

This view of the autonomy of the child is a delicate one to handle, for on one hand it is believed that the needs and desires of the child as expressed by the child should guide the developer while creating curricula (rather than the needs and desires of the academic disciplines, the parents of the child, the society sponsoring the school, or the teacher responsible for the child's growth), while on the other hand the Child Study developer actually has definite goals in mind for the child—such as competence in reading, writing, and arithmetic (which are usually drawn from the needs and desires of the academic disciplines, the parents of the child, the society sponsoring the school, and the teacher responsible for the child's growth). The problem in dealing with this dilemma of child autonomy versus developer objectives is really one of priorities. The developer must have his objectives, but he must imbed them in his curriculum in such a way that the needs and desires of the child always take priority over his objectives whenever the two come into conflict. In addition, the developer must imbed his objectives in his curriculum in such a way that the child is given real choices where he can exercise his autonomy while encountering the curriculum—choices of alternative directions to proceed along within the curriculum, choices of a rich array of alternative learnings that can be generated from within the curriculum, and choices from a rich array of alternative styles and rates of proceeding within the curriculum. As Rathbone phrases it, "The ideal . . . school begins, therefore, neither with societal requirements nor with the organization of knowledge but with the needs and concerns of the individual child"[108] but:

> That does not mean to say that the . . . school has no goals in mind for the child; it most certainly does. But in certain rather basic situations traditional academic objectives are not considered to be the *first* order of priority. For example, though a teacher may believe strongly in the importance of a child's learning to do sums, when this belief is weighed against the teacher's unwillingness to be coercive, the sums are postponed.[109]

The Child Study developer handles the issue of the autonomy of the child in such a way that his objectives can be implemented *when they correspond with the needs and desires of the child*. The developer's objectives are implemented more frequently than might be expected, for the developer proceeds under the assumption that the curriculum he designs, and thus what the teacher makes available to the child in the classroom, has an extremely powerful effect upon what the child becomes involved in and thus what the child learns and how the child grows. As Barth indicates:

> Many open educators eschew any attempt whatsoever to control or manipulate children's behavior. However, in the act of selecting materials for the classroom, the adult does in fact exercise a large measure of control over the direction of the child's learning and exploration. Ideas and concepts emerge out of activity with materials. Control of materials, then, implies control of experience, which in turn implies control of ideas and concepts. By bringing books into the classroom the teacher makes it more likely that children will want to learn to read. If there were no written words available, perhaps they wouldn't. By bringing a telescope into the classroom the teacher increases the likelihood that children will become interested in the stars and planets. . . .

The success of the open classroom would seem to depend not on adults' giving up of control to children but on a deliberate and conscious sharing of responsibility for learning on the part of both child and teacher. The adult, to a large extent, determines the nature of the school environment; the child decides with which of these materials he will work, to which problems he will address himself, for how long, and with whom.[110]

As a result, both the autonomy of the child is preserved and the Child Study developer can create curricula which have inherent in them directions for child growth and objectives for child learning.

The Child in the Present Tense

The Child Study developer orients himself around the theme, "growth of the child." He commits himself to childhood, he orients himself to the growth of the child in the present moment, he focuses upon the child "as a child" rather than upon the child "as a potential adult," and he refuses to sacrifice the "here and now" of childhood to the requirements of the future. The developer views the child as qualitatively different from the adult and focuses his endeavors upon enhancing the life of the child "as a child" undergoing growth "as a child" in the moment during which he is undergoing the growth. His assumption is that "Each day's activity is important and enough in itself"[111] and that "If the child is wholesomely, happily, intelligently employed, he *is* being educated!"[112] While creating curriculum, the Child Study developer attempts to design materials and activities that stress the present in the child's life and not the future, living life and not preparing for the future, growing now and not worrying about how one should be growing in order to reach some predetermined end in the future. As a result, the ends and means of education are telescoped into each other for the Child Study developer. The aims of the developer tend not to be long-range ends but immediate ends realizable through the means he uses to stimulate the growth of the child in the present moment.

Developmental Viewpoint

Two major assumptions underlying the work of Child Study developers are the beliefs that children grow through distinctly different stages of development and that there is an immense difference between the thought world of children at different stages of development.[113] Whether the stages of development through which the child grows are psycho-social in nature—as those described by Erikson and Freud[114]—cognitive in nature—as those described by Piaget[115]—or moral in nature—as those described by Kohlberg[116]—the child is viewed as an organism that evolves through a sequence of qualitatively and quantitatively different stages of development from infancy to maturity. Each stage of development that the child passes through is believed to be distinctly different from all others; and, as a result, children at different stages of growth are thought of as perceiving, understanding, and reacting to their world in very different ways. Thus, children of eight years of age who are undergoing the cognitive stage of development labeled by Piaget as "concrete operational" are viewed and treated as being very different from children of fourteen years of age who are undergoing the cognitive stage of development labeled by Piaget as "formal operational." What is important to the curriculum developer is that he design his curriculum so that it "respect the inner movement of growth"[117] of the child and complements the stage of development of the child for which it is designed. Since children are basically different at the different stages of growth, this means that curricula designed for children at different stages of growth will also be basically different in nature. As a result, the curriculum developer must be particularly knowledgeable about and sensitive to the way in which the human organism grows so that he can design his curriculum to appropriately match the needs and nature of the children for which it is being designed. To help him ascertain the nature of the stages of growth that children experience so that he can design his curricula to conform to such, the Child Study developer looks to developmental learning theories. As Marietta Johnson says, "The main work of the child is to grow. To be able to recognize the signs of growth in children at any age is a great art! One must study the results of the experts—must respect the findings of authorities—and then one must study at first hand the reaction of children."[118] What is of particular import in this statement is that after studying "the results of the experts" that "then one must study at first hand the reaction of children." A necessary component of a Child Study developer's work in creating a curriculum and in judging its appropriateness for a group of children at a particular stage of growth consists of the developer himself making firsthand observations of children and their interactions with his curriculum.

For the Child Study developer the significance of viewing the growth of the child from a developmental viewpoint goes beyond just making sure that the activities inherent in a curriculum are congruent with the intellectual, social, and psychological abilities of the child who will experience it. The developmental viewpoint indicates that the evolution of the child from infancy to maturity takes time. The Child Study developer interprets this to mean that the child is not to be hurried from stage to stage, but that he is to be allowed to evolve at his own rate from one stage to the next. Curricula are to be created so as to allow each child to evolve naturally: "each in his own way, and at his own rate, and in his own time."[119] Curricula are to be designed not to efficiently accelerate the child's progress through the stages of growth, but to better adapt the environment within which the child learns to the immediate needs of the child as reflected by the stage of growth within which he is engaged. From the Child Study developer's point of view, curricula are to enrich the child's growth within a developmental stage and not to speed his growth through that stage.

In addition, the developmental viewpoint is taken to imply that the particular thoughts of the child and the thinking processes of the child evolve along a sequence from concrete to abstract. As a result, the Child Study developer assumes that real, concrete, personal experiences within one's environment form the roots out of which thoughts and thinking processes grow. This means that within curricula designed by Child Study developers that "Verbal abstractions should follow direct experience with objects and ideas, not precede them or substitute for them."[120]

George Hein sums up the developmental viewpoint of the Child Study developer when he writes that:

A major foundation for open education programs is the belief in developmental learning theory. . . . Although many have contributed to it . . . the overpowering influence at this time is Jean Piaget. . . . His view of learning

as an interactive process between the child and the
environment, his recognition of stages of development,
and his acceptance of each stage in the child's own
development for itself rather than in terms of adult
standards have brought about profound changes in
educational views. Piaget stresses that . . . the process of
intelligence is changed through interaction with the
environment. Thus there is a stress on experience,
materials, "stuff" of the world, as well as concern that
children have time and opportunity to assimilate these
experiences, to "work" on them internally so that they
increase their capacity to learn, to reason, to think.[121]

THE LEARNING CHILD
Learning: The Child in an Environment

The potential for growth lies within the child. However, the
child grows, his thoughts develop, and his thinking processes
evolve through stimulation that results from interacting with his
environment. This is a crucial assumption underlying the Child
Study Ideology. Child Study developers believe not only in the
weaker assumption that "active exploration in a rich environment,
offering a wide array of manipulative materials, *facilitates* children's learning,"[122] but they also insist upon acceptance of the
stronger assumption that "Learning *depends* upon direct interaction with materials and one's social and physical environment."[123] The underlying belief is that "all children naturally
think through experience"[124] and as a result "Learning is seen as
a *consequence* of the interaction between the child and the real
world—be it an idea, a person, a gerbil, a book, or a can of paint
and a brush."[125]

Learning is thus a function of the interaction between a child
and his environment: it takes place when a receptive, inquiring
child engages a stimulating environment. The child is not a passive
agent in this interaction; he is an active agent of his own learning.
Learning is not something transferred from the environment *to* the
child but something created *by* the child in response to the
environment. Learning is the child's "creative self-expression" that
results from his active exploration of and response to his
environment. It is generated by the child for himself through his

own endeavors of making sense out of his personal interactions with his world.

Work and Play

Curriculum developers working within the Child Study Ideology often speak of the equivalence of work and play while speaking of learning. Learning, they say, results from work-play. Or "learning is a necessary consequence of active exploration in a rich environment"[126] which is "play" to the adult but "work" to the child. In either case, learning is viewed as an activity of business: as a serious endeavor where serious learning is expected to result. Further—and of crucial importance—"real" learning requires that the child experience the involvement and engrossment connected with "whole-hearted," "all-involving" play. Learning does not result from passivity or lack of involvement. It results from the child's engrossing involvement with his environment that comes from his innate impulse to understand, to master, and to make sense out of his active interactions with that environment.

Learning Leads to Knowledge

Child Study developers are much less interested in knowledge than they are in growth or learning. This is because they are interested, first, in facilitating the growth of the child, by second, providing him with learning experiences through which he can make meaning for himself. Knowledge enters the scene because it is an inevitable by-product of learning, and thus of growth. It results from a child making meaning out of his experiences. From the Child Study developer's point of view, the process by which a child learns—learning—yields the product of learning—knowledge. As such, "knowledge is seen as an integral part of learning rather than a separate entity"[127] unto itself which the child must go out of his way to acquire. Put another way, learning leads naturally to knowledge, and knowledge is not viewed as something special for which learning must take place in order for the child to acquire it. It is not that knowledge is of no importance at all to the Child Study developer, but rather that it is considerably less important than growth or learning. It is not seen as an end of education—as is growth—but rather as a vehicle through which the ends are reached. For the Child Study developer, knowledge is viewed as the secondary consequent of growth; and it derives from learning, which is viewed as the primary consequent of growth. As Rathbone phrases it:

> Open education's belief about *how* a child comes to understand is linked to its understanding of *what* he learns. The model advanced for explaining the *process* of a child's learning clearly implies that the product of his learning results from the particular interactions he and he alone has experienced. This further implies that what a child learns is not only his *but may well be his alone*, even though it closely resembles the learning of someone else.[128]

Two important assumptions follow from the Child Study developer's belief that learning leads to knowledge. First, there is the assumption that knowledge is a personal creation of the child who engages in learning through interacting with his environment. Second, there is the assumption that the knowledge which the "child learns is not only his but may well be his alone" since learning—and thus the result of learning, knowledge—is something personal that "results from" the child's "particular interactions" with his environment that "he and he alone has experienced." The crucial belief deriving from these assumptions is "that forming a conception of the way things are is an individual act based on experiences that can never be identical to anyone else's."[129] As a result, "one must admit not only the possibility but the inevitability of individual differences of conceptualization"[130] and thus that the particular knowledge an individual possesses is a personal creation that is unique to him and him alone.

Nature of Knowledge

Several important consequences follow from the belief that the knowledge an individual possesses is a personal creation that is unique to him and him alone.

First, knowledge is not viewed as a universal, abstract, impersonal quantity. It is unique to the person who has created it for himself and "does not exist outside of individual knowers."[131] Knowledge is not a thing apart from the individual who possesses it but a unique possession of that individual. "The data that goes into books and into the Library of Congress is not the same as the knowledge people know. Though it can be mouthed and memorized, abstract knowledge needs a more personal referent before it becomes 'real' "[132] to the knower. This does not mean that people cannot simulate situations which allow them somewhat imprecisely to share their knowledge with others through such media as languages, books, records, and film. But one must not confuse the construction of a medium or environment by an individual which facilitates the creation of knowledge by another individual with the direct transmission of knowledge itself.

Second, knowledge is assumed to be "idiosyncratically formed, individually conceived, fundamentally individualistic."[133] It is the result of an individual's personal "creative self-expression" resulting from his personal interaction with his environment. It is "personal and idiosyncratic, and a function of a synthesis of each individual's experience with the world."[134] Theoretically, it is assumed that "no two people's knowledge can be the same, unless their experience is identical."[135] This means that what a child learns is not only a personal possession of his own, but that it may well be his alone, even though it closely resembles the learning of another child. This does not mean that the conceptions of different people of "house" or "justice" or "red" will be so different as to exclude communication at the level of ordinary conversation, but only that there are inevitable differences in conceptualization and that the knowledge of no two people is identical.

Third, the particular objectives of education are not expressed in terms of knowledge—since such is unique to the individual who creates it—but in terms of the experiences the developer desires the child to have. One cannot give knowledge to another in a nice neat package, although one can provide experiences for another out of which he may generate knowledge. The Child Study developer is not a giver of knowledge, but rather a giver of experience out of which the child will—with some degree of unpredictability—create knowledge for himself by drawing personal meaning out of his interactions with the experiences he encounters. Knowledge is thus rarely spoken of in terms of "to know" but often in terms of "to experience." As Rugg says, "I would have a child say not, 'I know,' but, 'I have experienced.' "[136]

Fourth, since "knowledge is a function of one's personal integration of experience" it "therefore does not fall neatly into separate categories or 'disciplines.' "[137] Although it may be useful to the Child Study developer to think of certain materials or experiences as associated with specific disciplines, such thinking is employed (a) more for the purpose of enabling himself to know how to organize materials and experiences into curriculum "than as attempts to categorize experience and knowledge for children,"[138] and (b) more for the purpose of helping teachers to know how to organize their classrooms so that they "will know where to put things and students will know where to find them, [rather] than as attempts to categorize experience and knowledge for children."[139] There is the strong belief that "knowledge is not inherently ordered or structured, nor does it automatically subdivide into academic 'disciplines.' "[140]

Fifth, education of the child is thought of in terms of growth, in terms of change over time. As a result, the knowledge possessed by the child is thought of as changing over time. Both the nature of the child's "knowledge" and his "way of knowing" are assumed to evolve as the child grows. Piaget's "genetic epistemology," which views the child's knowledge as evolving rather than eternally static, is used to support this hypothesis.

Sources of Learning Theory

The sources of the Child Study developer's learning theory are many and varied. They range from Piaget's genetic epistemology, which postulates the evolution of knowledge within the child, to Freud's and Erikson's psycho-social epigenetic approach, which emphasizes the interaction of the child with his environment in forming an identity, to Tolman's gestalt theory, which emphasizes the primacy of the totality of perception and experience. Child Study developers categorically reject the behavioristic position and the "conveyor belt direct transference of knowledge" position with respect to learning theory. The position of Child Study developers with respect to learning and knowledge derives from their conception of the centrality of child growth, with learning being the first derivative of growth and knowledge the second derivative.

Teaching

Within this context, teaching is viewed as a process of facilitating learning. Since the teacher "cannot program or determine the learning style or that which is learned for another,"[141] the teacher's job is viewed as one of presenting opportunities for experience to the child and as one of intervening between the child and those opportunities for experience in order to facilitate the child's learning. In neither case does the Child Study developer view the teacher as a person who imposes something upon the child from without, but rather as one who presents possibilities to the child and then helps to draw out the capabilities within the child. As Rathbone phrases it:

Traditionally teaching has been viewed as a vertical phenomenon, an activity wherein some higher, older, and wiser person (the teacher) passes down certain facts, skills, or concepts to a younger, inferior, less-wise person (the student). Open education sees teaching more as a lateral interchange, a transmission not *from* superior to inferior, but rather *between* two persons of nearly equal status, one of whom happens to have a special need for something possessed by the other. To this way of thinking, it is the student who is most often the initiator, not the teacher, the student who makes demands on the teacher, not vice versa. . . .

What this means in terms of actual classroom performance is that open education de-emphasizes the view of teacher as instructor, possessor of special knowledge, transmitter of answers, filter or mediator between materials and learner, determiner of curriculum, orchestrator of large groups of children, evaluator, standard setter; it emphasizes, on the other hand, teacher as trained observer, diagnostician of individual needs, presenter of environments, consultant, collaborator, flexible resource, psychological supporter, general facilitator of the learning requirements of an independent agent. This means that in open education the teacher is mainly *assistant to* not *director of* the child's activity.[142]

One aspect of the teacher's job is thus to "provide the

conditions which will make the child's active exploration of the real world both likely and fruitful."[143] These conditions include physical, personal, social, and intellectual components. The other aspect of the teacher's job is to be an assistant to the child engaging in activity. As an assistant to the child in his learning, the teacher intervenes between the child and his environment in order to do such things as present the child with appropriate materials which will extend his exploration, or help the child consolidate his experience by helping him verbalize his experience through language. The interventions of the teacher are to be made after careful observation and diagnosis of the child, and are to be based upon those observations and that diagnosis rather than some motive exterior to the child. This means that the teacher must be a careful "student of the child, an observer of his progressive learning, an anticipator of his learning needs."[144]

THE CURRICULUM

The endeavors of the Child Study developer are directed toward creating curricula. Central to his endeavors is the issue of "How shall the activities and materials of instruction be organized to guarantee maximum child growth?"[145]

Unit of Work Versus School Subject

Curriculum is not thought of as subject-matter-set-out-to-be-learned but rather as contexts, environments, or units within which children can make knowledge for themselves. Curricula are often associated with Kilpatrick's *The Project Method*,[146] with physical materials, or with centers of child interest. However, this type of association does not really lay bare the prime character-istics of the Child Study developer's view of curriculum. Child Study developers often contrast their type of curricula—here called the unit of work—with the so-called traditional curricula—here called the school subject.

Scope

The first differentiation between the unit of work and the school subject is one of scope. The school subject is thought of as a relatively narrow and logically arranged body of predetermined knowledge associated with established conventions (be they academic, social, or otherwise). The unit of work is thought of in much broader terms, assembling for study material often found in several subjects. Compare, for instance, the names given the two types of curricula: the units of work display such titles as "Peas and Particles," "Boats," "Batteries and Bulbs," and "Water," while the school subjects display such titles as arithmetic, history, geography, or grammar. The school subject is thought of as unidimensional subject-matter-set-out-to-be-learned, whereas the unit of work is thought of as a multidimensional area of investigation within which the child can explore different directions and make choices among the things he will learn. Either type of curricula could be developed by a mathematician hoping that the child would learn, for example, graphing. The developer creating a school subject would proceed (a) by delineating all the things the student must know, and (b) then laying them out to be learned [here the (a) and (b) are sequential]. The developer creating the unit of work would proceed by (a) delineating all the things that *might* be learned about graphing, and (b) creating activities from which children *might* learn such [here the (a) and (b) are not necessarily sequential]. As a result, a curriculum as designed by a Child Study developer and as experienced by a child are different: for the child it is the sum of the particular growth experiences he encounters; for the developer it is the range of activities which might bring about growth within the child.

Sequence

A second differentiation between the unit of work and the school subject is one of internal organization: sequence, integration, and continuity. The school subjects are thought to be organized by the curriculum developer with the assumption that the developer's organization will be preserved in the child's head. The unit of work is not organized for learning but for presentation by the developer: the organization for learning is the job of the student. The unit of work is thought of as being incorporated into the child by the child, integrated into the child by the child, and organized within the child by the child with respect to the child's own personality structure. For the unit of work there is no one correct means of organization and it is thought of as the job of the child and not the developer to meaningfully organize that which is learned.

Flexibility

A third differentiation between the unit of work and the school subject is what might be called flexibility. The school subject is thought of as content rigidly laid out in scope and organization, ready to be learned by the child. The unit of work is designed for spontaneous activity and maximum flexibility based upon the interests and needs of the child: it is designed for student initiated directions within a teacher prepared context. Within the school subject, room for choice by the student is not allowed. Within the unit of work the opportunity for choice and decision making by the student based upon his needs and interests is deliberately built into the curriculum.

The Whole Child Curriculum

A fourth differentiation between the school subject and the unit of work is what might be identified as the range of child capacities affected by the curriculum. The school subject is thought of as designed to affect only a narrow range of student capabilities: usually only the cognitive (and generally intradisciplinary), although the purely physical is dealt with in physical education. The unit of work shows concern for the whole child and is designed to affect cognitive, affective, and psychomotor aspects of growth. It is designed to help the child grow socially, emotionally, physically, and intellectually; to help him develop "a fine body, an intelligent mind, and a sweet spirit."[147] The unit of work is designed so as to avoid isolating the child's mental self from his other selves, under the assumption that learning must go on in a thoroughly integrated environment in which all the child's capacities and tendencies for growth have full play.

Concrete to Abstract

A fifth differentiation between the school subject and the unit of work is the range of types of knowing permitted the child. The school subjects present the child with only the abstractions of experience and emphasize only the learning of symbolic concepts. The unit of work emphasizes the necessity to move from the personal, concrete, and physical experience in learning to the abstract, verbal, and intellectual conceptualization. It often incorporates graphic experiences designed to physically involve the student. The unit of work is thus associated with (a) a respect for physical activity and material objects as the stimuli and center from which learning initiates, and (b) a concern that "verbal abstractions should follow direct experience with objects and ideas, not precede them or substitute for them."[148] Curricula developed by Child Study developers, however, need not necessarily make use of physical materials.

Responsibility

A final and crucial differentiation between the school subject and the unit of work involves the question "Who is responsible for what is learned within the curriculum?" Within the school subject, the curriculum developer makes all the decisions as to the content of the curriculum and bears full responsibility for what is or is not learned by the student. Within the unit of work, responsibility for what is learned within the curriculum is borne jointly among the curriculum developer, the teacher, and the child. The curriculum developer is responsible for designing the activities from which the child will learn. The teacher is responsible for intervening between the activity and the child so as to act as an aid to the child in his learning. The child is responsible for providing the initiative, decision making, and capabilities which shape the substance and content of the curriculum. Both the adult and the child thus have responsibility for the child's education: the adult through the selection and construction of activities and the child through his individual response to the activities. Curriculum thus has "the quality both of adult initiation and uniformity and of student initiation and diversity."[149]

The concern throughout is less with whether a child has a particular experience than with the quality and meaning to the child of the experiences he has. The measure of worth of a unit of work thus depends upon the extent to which it branches out into the total life experience of the child in bringing about maximum child growth.

THE AIMS OF THE CURRICULUM DEVELOPER

The aim of the curriculum developer working within the Child Study Ideology is (a) to stimulate growth in students, (b) to stimulate growth in teachers, and (c) to stimulate personal growth in the developer himself. This growth is to be based squarely upon child study. The aim is to help all engaged in the growth of the child to create meaning for themselves. One creates meaning for oneself by engaging in stimulating experiences. The means of bringing about growth in the child, teacher, and developer is by preparing a stimulating curriculum for children to engage in, by helping teachers to participate in that curriculum as learners, and by preparing that curriculum by engaging in growth along with students and teachers. The doctrine of growth provides both the ends and the means for the Child Study developer, and it involves within it all those participating in the education of the child.

The creation of the educational context within which the child and teacher grow is the responsibility of the curriculum developer. Both the child and teacher have responsibilities also. They must engage the educational context prepared by the curriculum developer, initiate the directions of their growth, and make meaning for themselves through understanding the nature of their personal involvement in the educational environment. This does not mean that the developer presents the child and teacher with opportunities for experience without certain expectations. He creates his curricula based upon careful child study and teacher study, and in so doing develops quite definite expectations as to what might or might not occur when child and teacher engage the curriculum. These expectations are furthered by the careful inclusion and omission of curricular activities, the structuring of the curriculum, and the suggestion of possible directions for growth within the curriculum.

THE CHILD
The Child as an Integrated Person

Curriculum developers working within the Child Study Ideology focus upon the child as a "person." They view him as an integrated organism possessing an integrity as a complete organism *per se*. As an integrated organism, the child is viewed within the context of the "whole child": he is seen as an inseparable conglomerate of intellectual, social, psychological, and physical components. Child Study developers believe that in creating curriculum one must "take a holistic view of personality; one must look at the whole child, one must deal with all the attributes of people—intellect, emotion, and sensation—and consider them all as related to personality and of importance."[150] They believe, for example, that one cannot treat " 'skill development' as a separate activity which can be isolated, studied, and improved independent of the rest of the child."[151]

The Child Study developer values the child because of the unique person he is as an existing organism in the present tense. The developer does not value the child, in contrast, because of the behaviors or attributes he possesses or because of what he might be at some future time. The child is valued as a unique individual; it is his uniqueness with which the Child Study developer is concerned, rather than his ability to conform to standardized norms. As a unique person, the child is valued because he is believed to be naturally good; his innate nature is one of goodness, and his impulses for growth and capabilities for growth will mature constructively if they are not hampered or distorted by "corrupting outside forces."

The Child as a Meaning Making Organism

These curriculum developers view the child as a meaning making organism. They see the child as an organism who naturally creates meaning—and thus knowledge—for himself as a result of interacting with his environment. They assume that the child contains within himself his own capabilities for growth and that the child is the one who activates those capabilities through his own efforts: "the assumption [is] that children are innately curious and predisposed toward exploration and are not dependent upon adults, for either the initiation or perpetuation of learning."[152] The child is not considered to be an empty organism to which things merely happen. He is viewed as having inherent within him his own capabilities for growth which are activated by his own endeavors. He is not viewed as an organism to which meaningful things merely happen, but as an organism who by his own activity causes meaningful things to happen to himself. As Rugg says, "Now personality evolves from within. It cannot be imposed from without. Individuality develops only through growth in the power of self-propulsion."[153] The child's capacity to grow, the child's motivation to learn, and the child's making of meaning occurs because of innate capabilities and exploratory behaviors within the child. From the Child Study developer's point of view, it is crucial that the adult "trust in the innate abilities of children, in their capacity to energize and direct their own exploration, and in their wanting to explore and learn"[154] for it is believed that "the child will display natural exploratory behavior if he is not threatened"[155] by the adult and will learn and grow in ways that are best for him if he is not pressured by the adult.

The Child and His Subjective Being

One of the languages used by the Child Study developer while speaking about the child refers to processes and states of being internal to the child. These internal processes and states form the subjective reality of the child. They make up what Child Study developers consider to be the most significant aspects of the child's being.

Using conceptualizations such as those of Freud, Erikson, and Piaget to aid in the study of the child, the developer speaks of the child as if one could look within him to see the inner workings of his mind. It is not the behaviors of the child resulting from certain stimuli which are of interest to these developers, but rather what goes on between the stimulation and the response. It is not the "what the child knows" or "what the child can do" that is important to these developers, but what is behind the knowing and doing or what structures internal to the child support that knowing and doing.

As a result, the developer's primary interests are with parameters such as the state of the child's "mental health," "self-esteem," "self-concept," "self-confidence," "creative-spirit" or "dignity" rather than with the knowledges and skills the child possesses.[156] As Rugg expresses it: "Witness the little girl of five . . . who said of her painting, 'It looks the way you feel inside.' It's the feel inside [that] . . . the new education seeks to evoke and to build upon."[157] How the child feels about himself is viewed as crucial by these developers. As Barth bluntly puts it: "the ultimate goals of education [are] self-esteem, dignity, and control over himself and his world,"[158] for "a strong self-concept on the part of the child is the *sine qua non* of open education; if, and only if, the child respects himself will he be able to be responsible for his own learning,"[159] his own growth, his own education, and his own life. For these developers, whether the child is smart, dull, fast, or slow is not as important as the state of the child's subjective reality as reflected in parameters such as the child's self-concept.

LEARNING
Learning as Natural

Learning is the activity in which man engages while making meaning out of his interaction with his world. It is the "undergoing" phase of man's growth. It is natural to mankind: both the impulse to learn and the ability to learn are innate characteristics of the human species. Learning needs no justification. It should be enjoyed in and of itself.

Natural learning takes place spontaneously and is congruent with the child's inner nature. It takes place as a natural response of the child to his environment and is in rhythm with the organic personality of the individual child. Learning is not viewed as an artificial construction of an agent other than the child. It is viewed as a natural function of living, as a function of the present tense and not the future tense, and as innate in the child's response to experience and not artificially forced upon him.

The Mechanics of Learning

Learning takes place when the child interacts with the world around him and makes meaning for himself out of that interaction. It takes place when a receptive, inquiring child engages a stimulating environment. Three things are required for learning to take place: a child, an environment, and the act of the child involving himself with that environment through direct experience. The learning itself is the process of the child making meaning for himself out of his experiences with his environment—it is the process of "making meaning" that is important here, for learning is not viewed as a process of discovering, memorizing, or in any way absorbing "meanings" that already exist outside of and independent of the child. Figure 4.1 portrays the nature of learning. Stimuli from an environment, the dotted arrows, impinge upon the child. In response to the stimulation, the child actively engages the stimuli, the solid arrow, and makes meaning out of the interaction based upon his own personality structure. It should be

Figure 4.1

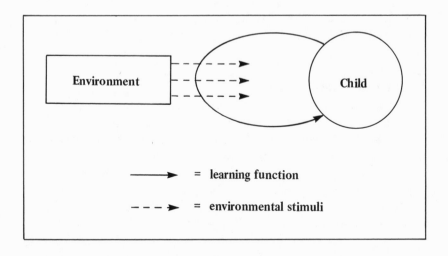

noted that the learning arrow, the solid arrow, is unique to the child as learning agent. It originates within the child, engages the environment which stimulates the child, and returns to the child. It is unique to the child because the capacities for learning lie within the child, because learning results from the student actively engaging his environment, and because what the child learns is the result of his creative self-expression to himself of his experiences.

Learning is a function of the unique interaction of the individual child with his environment. The more "active" and "personally engaging" the exploration of the child, the greater the potential for learning; and the "richer" the environment in which the exploration takes place, the greater the potential for learning. Although both the "child" and the "environment" are important during learning, each has a different significance. In terms of what is happening to the child, it is the "active" and "personally engaging" behavior of the child in making meaning out of his experiences for himself that is the crucial variable during learning. This is because the learning considered to be of most worth by Child Study developers has its origins and consequences within the child's subjective consciousness rather than within the child's objective experiences. For the curriculum developer and the teacher, however, it is the "environment" within which the child makes meaning for himself that is of crucial importance, for it is the environment within which the child learns that they can control. The developer and the teacher help the child learn by arranging the environment within which the child learns in such a way as to stimulate desired learnings. The developer and teacher proceed in helping the child to learn by arranging his environment, because it is not viewed as appropriate to manipulate the inner nature of the child, to program the child through indoctrination, or to inject experience into the child.

The question of just exactly how the child makes meaning for himself is one to which Child Study developers do not give a definitive answer. That the child "learns from essentially private experiences between himself and objects in his real world,"[160] that the learning takes place as the result of the child being "a self-activated maker of meaning,"[161] and that the learning takes place "inside himself—his concept forming mechanism, his mind"[162] —are readily agreed upon. But *how* the child's "mind" "actively" "makes meaning" is an issue to which a definitive answer is, perhaps appropriately, neither given nor agreed upon.

Stages of Learning

While growing, the child is viewed as developing through an epigenetic sequence of learning stages. These stages can be viewed as psycho-social, epistemic, or perhaps even as having to do with the development of moral judgment. What is important is that the manner in which the child learns and the meaning to the child of that which is learned are different within each stage of growth. Further, the developer's emphasis is upon enriching the learning of the child within a stage of growth, rather than stimulating the child to move on to more advanced stages of growth. The emphasis is upon meeting the child where he is, based upon the child's expressed needs and interests.

In addition, the distinction is made between concrete and abstract learning. The developer assumes that the child's healthiest learning proceeds from concrete to abstract; that "verbal abstractions should follow direct experience with objects and ideas, not precede them or substitute for them."[163] He also assumes that concept formation resulting from movement from concrete to abstract proceeds very slowly. As a result, learning is viewed in a leisurely manner, much in the spirit expressed by Hawkins and Featherstone:

> all of us must cross the line between ignorance and insight many times before we truly understand. Little facts, "discoveries" without the growth of insights are *not* what we should seek to harvest.[164]

> Learning takes place over time . . . involving what often looks to an adult like mere play or mindless repetitions.[165]

Since the manner in which children learn is a function of their individual personality structures, a variety of styles or modes of learning are encouraged and curricula are designed to be receptive to varying styles of learning.

TEACHING

Teaching as a Derivative Concept

Curriculum developers working within the Child Study Ideology derive the functions of the teacher and teaching from their concepts of the nature of the child, growth, and learning. Teaching is not a self-contained function. It is viewed as that aspect of the instructional system which facilitates learning and growth of the child. While speaking about teaching, the developer's attention constantly shifts from concern with methods of teaching to methods of learning, and from concern with that which is taught to that which is learned.[166]

The Nature of Teaching

A comprehensive study of teaching from the perspective of the Child Study Ideology has been produced by Walberg and Thomas.[167] In their study, they identify eight themes helpful in conceptualizing the nature of teaching, the role of the teacher, the pedagogical style of the teacher, and the assumptions of teachers. They then go on to define the eight themes by delineating the particular characteristics of teaching and teachers inherent in each theme. The eight themes and their characteristics are described and listed in Tables 4.1 to 4.8.[168] Several of the assumptions inherent in these themes deserve elaboration.

Table 4.1

Provisioning for Learning

Provisioning for Learning. The teacher provides a rich and responsive physical and emotional environment.

Manipulative materials are supplied in great diversity and range with little replication; i.e., not class sets.

Books are supplied in diversity and profusion.

The environment presents a balance of commercially prepared materials and materials brought in or developed by teacher and students.

Common environmental materials (plant life, rocks, sand, water, pets, egg cartons, plastic bottles, etc.) are used.

Materials are readily accessible to children.

The teacher constantly modifies the content and arrangement of the classroom based upon continuing diagnosis and reflective evaluation of the children.

Children work directly with the manipulative materials.

The teacher permits and encourages constructive unplanned use of materials.

Space is divided into activity areas.

Students do not have their own individually assigned desks.

Activity areas are attractive and inviting.

Activity areas provide for a variety of potential usage and allow for a range of ability levels.

Spatial arrangements are flexible.

Children are able to make use of other areas of the building and schoolyard for educational purposes.

Children move freely about the room without asking permission.

Many different activities go on simultaneously.

Talking among children is encouraged.

Children help one another.

There are very few fixed time periods.

Determination of each child's routine each day is largely the child's choice.

Children generally work individually and in small groups.

Children generally group and regroup themselves through their own choices.

The teacher does not group children by ability according to tests or norms.

Formal class lessons are not conducted.

The teacher sometimes gathers the whole group for such activities as story or discussion.

The class is heterogeneous with regard to age.

The class is heterogeneous with regard to ability.

There is an overall purposefulness and a sense that the children value their work and their learning.

There is an overall sense of community, of mutual respect and cooperation.

Table 4.2

Instruction—Guidance and Extension of Learning

Instruction—Guidance and Extension of Learning. The teacher acts primarily as a resource person who, in a variety of ways, encourages and influences the direction and growth of learning.

The basis for a child's instruction at the primary level is his interaction with materials.

The teacher becomes involved with the child diagnostically before suggesting any change, extension, or redirection of activity.

The teacher plans instruction individually and pragmatically, based upon reflective evaluation of each child's particular needs and interests.

The teacher becomes "actively involved in the work of each child . . . as one who seeks to help him realize his goals and potential."

The teacher tends to give individual children small concentrated amounts of his time rather than giving his general attention to the children as a class all day.

Instead of giving assignments, the teacher amplifies and extends the possibilities of activities children have chosen, through individualized conversation, introduction of related materials.

The teacher refrains from direct correction and from making judgmental statements.

The teacher encourages children's independence and exercise of real choice.

The teacher keeps in mind long-term goals for his children which inform his guidance and extension of a child's involvement in his chosen activity.

The teacher provides direct instruction and assignments when warranted.

The approach to learning is interdisciplinary; e.g., the child does not generally confine himself to a single subject, such as mathematics, when learning.

Activities do not arise from predetermined curricula.

Table 4.3

Humaneness—Respect, Openness, and Warmth

Humaneness—Respect, Openness, and Warmth. The teacher promotes an atmosphere of warmth, openness, and respect for one another.

The teacher respects each child's personal style of operating—thinking and acting.

The teacher rarely commands or reprimands.

The teacher values the children's activities and products as legitimate expressions of their interests, not simply as reflections of their development.

The teacher respects the children's ideas.

The teacher respects the children's individuality by rejecting ability grouping, group norms, homogenization.

The teacher takes children's feelings seriously.

The teacher recognizes and does not hide his own emotional responses.

Children generally do not try to suppress emotions.

The teacher strives to recognize emotions differentially and to act as a stabilizer upon whom children can depend when the going is difficult.

Conflict is recognized and worked out within the context of the group, not simply forbidden or handled by the teacher alone through punishment or exclusion.

There is no abdication of adult authority and responsibility.

The class operates within clear guidelines, made explicit.

The teacher promotes openness and trust among children and in his relationship with each child.

In general, relationships are characterized by warmth and affection.

The teacher recognizes and admits his limitations when he feels unable to give a child the help he needs.

In evaluating children's work, the teacher responds honestly, based upon a real examination of the product and a sensitive judgment about the particular child and circumstances.

The climate is unthreatening; fear of failure is absent.

Table 4.4

Diagnosis of Learning Events

Diagnosis of Learning Events. The teacher views the work children do in school as opportunities for him to assess what the children are learning, as much as opportunities for children to learn.

To obtain diagnostic information, the teacher takes an *involved* interest in what the child is doing.

Diagnosis is based upon attention to the child's thought processes more than to his solutions.

Errors are seen as desirable, as a necessary part of the learning process, because they provide information valuable to further learning.

Fantasy is valued; it is another way of knowing about the child and a means the child may use for learning.

Children do not always depend on teacher judgment; they also diagnose their progress through the materials they are working with.

Table 4.5

Reflective Evaluation of Diagnostic Information

Reflective Evaluation of Diagnostic Information. The teacher subjects his diagnostic observations to reflective evaluation in order to structure the learning environment adequately.

Evidence of learning is assessed through direct observation of what the child does and says and produces.

Predetermined yardsticks of performance are not used for evaluating children's work.

The teacher avoids traditional testing procedures and tests.

Evaluation of the effect of a child's school experience covers a long range of time; the teacher preferably has each child more than one year.

The teacher's record-keeping consists of individual histories chronicling the child's development.

The teacher keeps a collection of each child's work and makes use of it as the appropriate measure of his evaluation.

The teacher uses evaluation to provide information he will use in seeking better ways of encouraging and providing for children's development.

Table 4.6

Self-Perception of the Teacher

Self-Perception. The teacher is a secure person and a continuing learner.

The teacher views himself as an active experimenter in the process of creating and adapting ideas and materials.

The teacher sees himself as a continual learner who explores new ideas and possibilities both inside and outside the classroom.

The teacher values Open Education as an opportunity for his own personal and professional growth and change.

The teacher feels comfortable with children taking the initiative in learning, making choices, and being independent of him.

The teacher is able to recognize his own needs (e.g., for importance, recognition) and restrain himself from intervening in children's activities based on these needs rather than the children's.

The teacher accepts the legitimacy in the classroom of his own feelings.

The teacher trusts children's ability to operate effectively and learn in a framework not structured by him and not centered on him.

The teacher sees himself as one of many sources of knowledge and attention in the classroom.

The teacher feels comfortable working without predetermined lesson plans, set curricula, or fixed time periods.

The teacher trusts himself as one who generally can respond sensitively and effectively moment by moment in the classroom.

Table 4.7

Seeking Opportunity to Promote Growth

Seeking Opportunity to Promote Growth. The teacher seeks activities outside the classroom to promote personal and professional growth.

The teacher seeks further information about the community and its physical and cultural resources.
The teacher seeks information about new materials.
The teacher experiments himself with materials.
The teacher makes use of help from someone who acts in a supportive advisory capacity.
The teacher enjoys ongoing communication with other teachers about children and learning.
The teacher attempts to know more about his children by getting to know their parents or relatives and their neighborhood.

Table 4.8

*Assumptions—Ideas About Children and
the Process of Learning*

Assumptions—Ideas About Children and the Process of Learning. The teacher's assumptions about children, the process of learning, and the goals of education are generally humanistic and holistic. Teachers are aware of and respect the child's individuality and his capacity to direct his own learning.

Children's innate curiosity and self-perpetuating exploratory behavior should form the basis of their learning in school; they should have the opportunity to pursue interests as deeply and as long as they find the pursuit satisfying.
Providing for sustained involvement requires a flexible and individualized organization of time.

Table 4.8 (Continued)

Children are capable of making intelligent decisions in significant areas of their own learning.

Learning depends upon direct interaction with materials and one's social and physical environment.

Premature conceptualization based upon inadequate direct experience leads to the child depending on others for his own leadership.

Individual children often learn in unpredictable ways, at their own rate, and according to their own style.

Work and play are not distinguishable in the learning process of children.

Knowledge is a personal synthesis of one's own experience, and learning of "skills" and "subjects" proceeds along many intersecting paths simultaneously.

There is no set body of knowledge which must be transmitted to all.

Measures of performance may have a negative effect on learning and do not necessarily get at those qualities of learning which are most important.

Sensitive observation over a long period of time is the preferable means of evaluation of a child's intellectual, social, and emotional development.

Children have the *right* to direct their own learning, to make important decisions regarding their own educational experience.

The child must be valued as a human being, and treated with courtesy, kindness, and respect.

The child's life in school should not be viewed as preparation for the future; to live as a child is the best preparation for adulthood.

Under consistent, reasonable, and explicit restrictions, children are able to be more free and productive.

An accepting and warm emotional climate is an essential element in children's learning; learning is facilitated by relationships of openness, trust, and mutual respect.

Competition does not contribute effectively to learning.

Fear of making mistakes or of not doing well impedes a child's progress in learning.

Objectives of education should go beyond literacy, dissemination of knowledge, and concept acquisition.

The function of school is to help children learn to learn, to acquire both the ability and the willingness to extend their intellectual and emotional resources, and to bring them to bear in making decisions, organizing experience and utilizing knowledge.

Teacher as the Provider
of the Environment for Learning

One of the functions of the teacher is to provide the instructional environment within which learning takes place. This environment is to be designed with personal, social, material, psychological, and intellectual considerations in mind, so as "to provide conditions which will encourage children to learn for themselves and to fulfill themselves, personally, socially, and intellectually."[169] The teacher must select curricula and position them within the classroom in such physical, emotional, and temporal contexts that they become maximally available to student engagement.[170] Because the teacher cannot directly provide the child with learning, the construction of the instructional environment within which the child learns is crucial. It is one of the ways in which the teacher influences the learning that takes place under his supervision, for the selection of the materials which the child will encounter influences the direction of the child's explorations and hence his learning. As Barth phrases it:

> A teacher cannot directly provide a child the exploratory experiences which lead to learning; he can, however, provide materials which will engage the child's innate curiosity and involve him in the learning process. . . .
>
> For the teachers . . . the problem is one of selection, for through the selection of materials the teacher influences the direction of the child's exploration, and hence his learning.[171]

Decisions about which materials to place in front of the child and when to place them there are to be based upon observation of and diagnosis of the child's stage of development, needs, and interests. It is believed that the teacher must become "involved with the child diagnostically before suggesting any change, extension, or redirection of activity"[172] in which the child is engaged; that in order to select materials to be made available to a child tomorrow, the teacher must know the child's needs, interests, and directions of growth today, so such can be extended and built upon by placing the appropriate materials in front of the child tomorrow. In arranging the environment within which the child will learn, and in placing specific materials in front of the child, the teacher must act in such a way as to not "diminish the child's feeling that he is engaged in *his* own exploration and is pursuing it in *his* own way and toward *his* own ends,"[173] even though the child knows that the teacher is supplying alternatives and arranging the environment.

Teacher as Facilitator of Learning

Another function of the teacher is to be a facilitator, aid, advisor, and consultant to the child during his learning. As an assistant to the child in his learning, the teacher intervenes between the child and the environment he is exploring. Figure 4.2 illustrates the nature of the intervention. Based upon diagnosis of the needs, interests, and nature of the child, and diagnosis of the nature and potentials of the unit of work within which the child is engaged (slashed arrows), the teacher can intervene within the child-environment interaction (curly arrow) to facilitate the learning of the child. One example of the way a teacher can intervene between the child and his environment to aid the child in his learning is by helping the child verbalize the meaning to

Figure 4.2

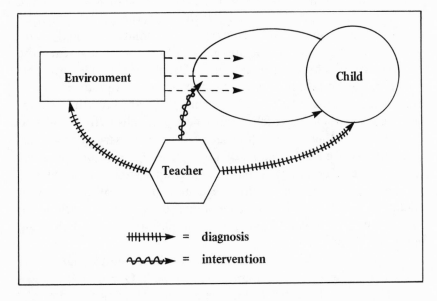

himself of some of the experiences he is having. By so intervening, the teacher can perhaps help the student make sense out of his experiences, acting as an evaluator who reflects back to the student what he is engaged in doing, or helping the student to move from more concrete learning towards more abstract learning.

The teacher also acts as a resource or consultant to the child during his learning. In this role, the teacher is consulted by the child on how to reach some particular objective. Acting in this capacity, the teacher "is, in a sense, a *travel agent*. He helps the child go where the child wants to go. He counsels on the best way of getting there."[174] Whether the teacher acts within the role of intervener or consultant, his behavior is to be based upon careful observation of the nature of the child and diagnosis of his needs and interests.

Characteristics of the Teacher

The Child Study developer views the teacher's main roles to be those of constructing the instructional environment within which children learn and facilitating the growth of children by aiding their functioning within that environment. There are several characteristics of adults that Child Study developers believe aid teachers in carrying out these roles. First, it is believed that the teacher must be able to be an "*ad hoc* responder." He must be available, accessible, and capable of responding quickly and appropriately to children at all times as "He constantly scans the horizon of children's interactions, with materials and with one another, for situations when a response, an appropriate intervention, will contribute to a child's learning"[175] and growth. Second, it is believed that the teacher must be a generalist with respect to knowledge, rather than a specialist: it is necessary that he has "facility with many domains of knowledge, has one or two areas of particular interest, experience, and competence, and is capable of growing in *any* area as the need and interest of the children dictate."[176] Third, the teacher must be a person within the classroom rather than a paragon, examplar, or ideal representing inhuman virtues: teachers are

> encouraged to be themselves: to be honest, angry, loving, upset, tired, happy—to be real. One does not play the role of teacher at the expense of being oneself;

one *is* oneself and *thereby* a teacher. Of equal importance is the fact that from the teacher's honest
expression of feeling, children learn to respect, expect,
and handle the wide range of behavior which they find
in others, and to acknowledge and accept it in themselves.[177]

Fourth, the teacher must be a diagnostician of the child's
behavior. The teacher must take "an *involved* interest in what the
child is doing,"[178] so that he can comprehend how the child is
thinking, what the child is interested in and involved in, what type
of growth the child is undergoing, and where the child needs help
with his work. This diagnostic information is collected both for
the purpose of providing the child with non-judgmental feedback
about his successes and difficulties and for the purpose of
collecting data valuable in providing further learning experiences
to the child. As Brown and Precious phrase it:

One important facet of the teacher's role is her diagnosis
of the children's difficulties and the giving of appropriate help. These difficulties may occur on any front:
social, emotional, or intellectual. It is important that the
teacher observes any wrong interpretations which the
children make. She must discover and help with any
difficulties in learning a new skill or in the development
of concepts or in any problems on a social or emotional
level.[179]

In his role as diagnostician "the teacher avoids traditional testing
procedures and tests"[180] and "predetermined yardsticks of
performance"[181] and assesses the child's growth "through direct
observation of what the child does and says and produces."[182]
This diagnosis through direct observation is easier in the Child
Study developer's ideal school than in the traditional school
because most children

in a classroom full of materials . . . are behaving *overtly*;
the trained eye can "see" what they are doing and can
make inferences about what they are thinking. The
teacher in such a situation has the unique opportunity
to observe children as persons, and as investigators, in
context—interacting with materials. . . . [And] these
children, through their overt behavior, are supplying

information which helps the teacher appraise their learning.[183]

KNOWLEDGE
Knowledge as a Derivative Concept

Curriculum developers working within the Child Study Ideology have considerably less concern with knowledge than with learning or growth. Their emphasis "is on *how* one comes to know and that one *can* come to know, rather than on *what* is to be known and knowing it."[184] They assume that knowledge is an integral part of learning rather than a separate entity to be learned: that the process by which a child learns—learning—implies the nature of the product of learning—knowledge. As such, knowledge originates when a child makes meaning out of experience: it results from the interaction of a child with his environment and is created through the "meaning making" response of the child to the particular environment which he and he alone experiences. Because the particular interaction of the child with his environment—learning—is unique to the child experiencing that interaction it is assumed that the result of learning—knowledge—is also unique to the child. The consequences of this assumption have already been discussed. In summary: (a) knowledge is not a universal, abstract, impersonal quantity, but is unique to the individual knower; (b) the goals of education are not expressed in terms of knowledge, since one has little control over the idiosyncratic meaning a child will generate as a result of encountering an experience, but in terms of the personal qualities the child is to develop (such as a healthy self-concept and an ability to initiate and benefit from new growth experiences); (c) because the child is viewed within the context of growth, it is assumed that the nature of both the child's "knowledge" and "ways of knowing" evolve as the child grows; and (d) it is believed that there is no one way of organizing or categorizing knowledge for learning (such as into academic disciplines), because it is the child who must organize meaning in correspondence with his unique personality structure.

Knowledge and Reality

Child Study developers either make a distinction between subjective and objective reality or deny any distinction between subjective and objective reality. If the distinction is assumed, knowledge is viewed to be person-centered and not object-centered—to be within the province of the child's subjective reality and not within the province of objective reality. It is assumed that the locus of meaning and knowledge lies within the individual's subjective consciousness and neither within the correspondence between subjective consciousness and objective reality nor within objective reality. Knowledge exists only within the individual knower—it is not a thing apart from this individual knower. It is personal and not objective. In terms of Figure 4.3, knowledge resides within S, within the child and his subjective view of reality—even though the generation of that knowledge is dependent upon stimulation by 0, the objective environment outside of the individual.

Figure 4.3

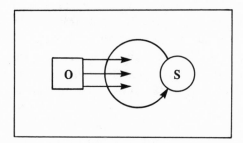

If the distinction between subjective and objective reality is denied, the developer ends up with the same conclusions as to the importance of "knowledge as one knows it." It is simply that reality other than that which one *knows* (and here available language is blatantly inadequate) is either irrelevant or does not exist.

A corollary to Child Study assumptions about knowledge and reality is clarified by Barth when he says that "The quality of being is more important than the quality of knowing; knowledge is a means of education, not its end. The final test of an education is what a man *is*, not what he *knows*."[185] The emphasis of the Child

Study developer is upon the child and not knowledge; upon the quality of the individual's subjective reality rather than upon the knowledge he possesses of objective reality or the manner in which objective reality views the individual as functioning within it.

When the question arises as to how the knowledge one possesses can be tested or verified, the answer seems to be that the truth or "value" of knowledge can only be tested in terms of an individual's internal awareness of the "rightness" or "wrongness" of it. There seems to be an intuitive, subjective approach to verification, in contrast to an empirical or logical approach.

EVALUATION
Evaluation for the Evaluee

In discussing the Child Study developer's concept of evaluation, two cases must be distinguished: evaluation of the child and evaluation of the curriculum. When the child is being evaluated, developers assume that the "evaluation is primarily for the benefit of the learner, and only secondarily for the convenience and benefit of parent, teacher, or administrator,"[186] or curriculum developer. When the object of evaluation is the curriculum, it is assumed that the evaluation is primarily for the benefit of the developer and not for the benefit of teachers or administrators. Evaluation is assumed to take on a reflective quality so as to be of use to the evaluee. It is assumed to reflect back to the evaluee the consequences of his behavior or products so that he may improve them. Evaluation is not looked upon at all favorably when it is designed to inform someone other than the evaluee as to the nature of the evaluee. Evaluation is not to be used for the purpose of comparing evaluees but for the purpose of facilitating the growth of the evaluee.

Characteristics of Evaluation

Several characteristics of Child Study evaluation deserve mention. First, Child Study developers desire to take the moral loading out of evaluation. They want to remove the connotations of good or bad from the actions of the evaluee in order to help the evaluee make use of his mistakes as well as his successes in serving to direct his future learning. In particular, they believe that "Errors are necessarily a part of learning,"[187] just as are the successes, and that "they are to be expected and even desired, for they contain information essential for further learning"[188] and growth.

Second, since subjective reality is held to be more meaningful to a learner than objective reality, it is assumed that subjective intuitive evaluation is more meaningful (and thus more useful? more reliable?) than objective evaluation. Objective evaluation is generally avoided, for it is believed that "evidence of learning is best assessed intuitively, by direct observation"[189] of the person doing the evaluating.

Third, the focus of the Child Study Ideology upon the individual in contrast to the group is sufficiently strong to make repugnant to developers the idea of comparing the individual to an objective standard. Comparisons among individuals are not viewed favorably. The individual is to be evaluated with respect to his own capabilities. He is not to be judged with respect to objective standards. The curriculum, similarly, is not to be evaluated with respect to objective standards.[190]

Fourth, curriculum developers tend to want to view the child and the curriculum as wholes—they want to take a gestalt approach to evaluation. The idea of partitioning either a child or a curriculum into component parts in order to atomistically evaluate each part, under the assumption that the sum of the atomistic evaluations is a sufficient evaluation of the whole, is repulsive to these developers. Evaluation must take place over time and consider the evaluee, whether child or curriculum, in its wholeness.

Student Evaluation

Objective evaluation of the child is avoided. Reasons given vary. One reason is that "knowledge resides with the knower, not in its public expression,"[191] and thus an individual may "possess knowledge of a phenomenon and yet be unable to display it publicly."[192] Another reason is that "those qualities of a person's learning which can be carefully measured are not necessarily the most important."[193] The important things, like a child's self-concept, curiosity, and initiative, are difficult to measure and are in fact seldom measured in most schools, while trivial things like when Columbus discovered America tend to be repeatedly measured because they are easy to measure. A third reason is that "objective measures of performance may have a negative affect upon learning"[194]—letter grades, for example, are often viewed as having such an effect.

All student evaluation, however, is not to be avoided. Diagnosis of the nature, needs, and growth of the child is crucial to both the curriculum developer and the teacher. Diagnosis of the nature of the child is crucial to the curriculum developer because he must design his curriculum around the innate needs and inherent nature of the human organism at a particular stage of development. Diagnosis of the child, his growth, and his learning is crucial to the teacher in order to facilitate the growth of the child by adjusting the instructional environment and the instructional processes to his nature, needs, and interests. In both cases, such evaluation tends to be "based upon attention to the child's thought processes more than to his solutions."[195] This relieves the pressure on the adult from insisting that all projects the child starts must be finished and the pressure on the adult from attending to the *results* of the child's growth—his displayable knowledge—rather than the child's *growth* through involvement in an activity. As Barth phrases it, "To the extent the adult can recognize and share the child's cognitive and emotional investment in his work, *in progress*, he will worry less about incomplete or imperfect products."[196] In addition, student diagnostic evaluation tends to be subjective evaluation of the child while he is engaged in learning. It also tends to be relative to the child's capacities for growth as those capacities are displayed in his every day involvement in activities.

The other type of student evaluation that the Child Study developer encourages is what might be called record-keeping. It is believed that the teacher should not use "a common, predetermined yardstick of academic and personal behavior against"[197] which children are compared for the purpose of "rewarding those who measure up and punishing those who do not."[198] Rather, the teacher should keep "detailed records that chronicle children's efforts."[199] These records consist of both "folders of children's work"[200] and a "journal or anecdotal record of each child, containing comments and observations such as his relationship with peers, his preferences, his family relationships, . . . his physical demeanor"[201] and his cognitive growth in different areas of endeavor. These records of the child's endeavors are then used to apprise "the child, his parents, and [the teacher] himself of the child's progress."[202] The record the teacher keeps of a child's growth is important because it "removes the teacher from attempting to make categorical and arbitrary judgments about a child's performance"[203] and allows the person examining the record—whether child, parent, or teacher—to "make his own judgments"[204] actually based upon *what* the child has done as an individual rather than upon *how* the child has done in comparison to others. It is believed that this record is important to the child and parent, as well as the teacher, because "It is vital to the child and his parents that there is something to show for the child's many hours spent in school."[205]

One of the central issues emphasized by Child Study developers is the necessity for the child to learn how to evaluate his own learning, as well as to learn when it is or is not possible for him to do so. It is assumed that, whenever possible, "appraisal of the child's work is best mediated not by external authorities, be they adults or repositories of knowledge, but rather by the materials themselves"[206] with which the child is involved. It is believed that "The preferred source of verification for a child's solution to a problem comes through the materials he is working with"[207] because they "enable a child to pursue problems ... [and] also provide information *back* to the child—information that lets him know if and to what extent he has answered his question."[208] What is important is that "it is the materials, the world around him, which have verified (or failed to verify) his hypothesis,"[209] and which in the long run provide the basis for the evaluation of the child's endeavors. The Child Study developer's approach to student evaluation has three important components. First, he believes that "The best measure of a child's work is his work"[210] itself. Second, he has "a profound trust in the human being, in the capacity of one to judge intuitively the performance of another."[211] Third, for the Child Study developer student "evaluation is not distinguished from teaching or learning. There is no special time set aside for it because it is going on all the time"[212] within the instructional environment.

Curricular Evaluation

Child Study developers tend to have little interest in summative curricular evaluation. When such is compiled it tends to be in the form of testimonials, and it tends to measure the degree of student involvement in the curriculum and the degree of student enthusiasm about the curriculum. Subjective formative evaluation of the curriculum, in contrast, is undertaken with enthusiasm, for it leads to improvement in the curriculum as it is being developed. Such evaluation is usually based upon measures such as the degree to which students get involved within the curriculum, is usually intuitively conducted through developer observation, and is usually based upon criteria such as the extent to which the curriculum is believed to be in the best interests of the child as dictated by the child's nature, needs, and interests. The nature of the child is, in fact, the standard to which the curriculum must conform in order to be viewed as constructive in facilitating growth. As a result, the questions asked during formative evaluation are of the form "to what degree are the needs and interest of the child met?" The following statements by Child Study developers about their involvement in curriculum evaluation express the spirit with which they undertake it:

> In Leicestershire, evaluation of innovations was seldom attempted. We were content to judge subjectively, to decide by the "feel" of the situation whether or not it was in the best interest of children.[213]

> The most satisfying form of evaluation reported to us is a subtle one. Teachers tell us of children's excitement at what they are learning and of their enthusiasm for the ways in which they are learning. . . . To us, an interested class is a successful one.[214]

Notes

[1] John Dewey and Evelyn Dewey. *Schools of Tomorrow*. New York: E.P. Dutton and Co., 1915.

[2] Harold Rugg and Ann Shumaker. *The Child-Centered School*. New York: World Book Co., 1928, pp. 2, 3-4.

[3] *Ibid.*, pp. 3-4.

[4] *Ibid.*, pp. 2-3.

[5] *Ibid.*, p. 2.

[6] Roland S. Barth. *Open Education and the American School.* New York: Schocken Books and Agathon Press, 1972, pp. 62-63.

[7] *Ibid.*, p. 63.

[8] K.C. Mayhew and A.C. Edwards. *The Dewey School.* New York: Atherton Press, 1966.

[9] Marietta Johnson. *Thirty Years with an Idea: The Story of Organic Education.* University, Alabama: University of Alabama Press, 1974.

[10] Rugg, *loc. cit.*, p. 56.

[11] *Ibid.*

[12] *Ibid.*, p. 57.

[13] *Ibid.*

[14] *Ibid.*, pp. 60-61.

[15] Johnson. *Thirty Years, loc. cit.*, pp. 17, 25-26.

[16] *Ibid.*, p. 25.

[17] Rugg, *loc. cit.*, p. 5.

[18] George E. Hein. *Open Education: An Overview.* Newton, Mass.: Education Development Center, 1975, p. 2.

[19] Johnson. *Thirty Years, loc. cit.*, p. 10.

[20] Rugg, *loc. cit.*, p. 60.

[21] *Introduction to the Elementary Science Study.* Newton, Mass.: Education Development Center, 1966, p. 3.

[22] Philip Morrison. "The Curricular Triangle and Its Style." *ESI Quarterly Report* (Summer-Fall, 1964). Reprinted in *The ESS Reader.* Newton, Mass.: Education Development Center, 1970, p. 111.

[23] John Blackie. *Inside the Primary School*. New York: Schocken Books, 1971, p. 87. Reprinted by permission of Schocken Books, Inc. Crown Copyright © 1967.

[24] Herbert J. Walberg and Susan Christie Thomas. *Characteristics of Open Education: Toward an Operational Definition*. Newton, Mass.: Educational Development Center, 1971, p. 90.

[25] This selection of materials was selected from *Instructional Aids, Materials, and Supplies—Guidelines*. Newton, Mass.: Education Development Center, 1972.

[26] Elwyn Richardson. *In the Early World*. New York: Random House, 1964, p. viii.

[27] Susan Isaacs. *The Children We Teach*. London: University of London Press, 1967, pp. 65-70.

[28] Walberg and Thomas, *loc. cit.*, p. 90.

[29] *Ibid.*

[30] *Ibid.*

[31] Rugg, *loc. cit.*, p. 58.

[32] *Ibid.*, p. 55.

[33] *Ibid.*, p. 59.

[34] *Ibid.*, p. 66.

[35] Many of these activities are discussed in chapters 4, 5, and 6 of *Thirty Years with an Idea* by Marietta Johnson.

[36] Barth, *loc. cit.*, p. 78.

[37] *Ibid.*, p. 75.

[38] Johnson. *Thirty Years, loc. cit.*, p. 18.

[39] *Ibid.*, p. 37.

[40] *Ibid.*, p. 22.

[41] *Ibid.*, p. 15.

[42] In *Thirty Years with an Idea*, Marietta Johnson discusses this at great length in Chapters 1 and 2.

[43] Johnson. *Thirty Years, loc. cit.*, pp. 8-9.

[44] Barth, *loc. cit.*, p. 97.

[45] Walberg and Thomas, *loc. cit.*, p. 85.

[46] Johnson. *Thirty Years, loc. cit.*, pp. 25-26.

[47] Barth, *loc. cit.*, p. 26.

[48] *Ibid.*, p. 24.

[49] *Ibid.*, p. 26.

[50] *Ibid.*, p. 32.

[51] Walberg and Thomas, *loc. cit.*, p. 90.

[52] *Ibid.*, p. 91.

[53] *Ibid.*

[54] *Ibid.*, p. 93.

[55] *Ibid.*

[56] Barth, *loc. cit.*, p. 45.

[57] George E. Hein. *Open Education: An Overview.* Newton, Mass.: Education Development Center, 1975, p. 2.

[58] *Ibid.*

[59] *Ibid.*

[60] *Ibid.*

[61] Rugg, *loc. cit.*, p. 5.

[62] *Ibid.*, p. 61.

[63] Barth, *loc. cit.*, p. 68.

[64] *Ibid.*, p. 75.

[65] Walberg and Thomas, *loc. cit.*, p. 90.

[66] Barth, *loc. cit.*, p. 34.

[67] *Ibid.*, p. 35.

[68] Mary Brown and Norman Precious. *The Integrated Day in the Primary School.* New York: Agathon Press, 1969, p. 57.

[69] Walberg and Thomas, *loc. cit.*, p. 90.

[70] Barth, *loc. cit.*, p. 75.

[71] Francis W. Parker. *Talks on Pedagogics.* New York: E.L. Kellogg and Co., 1894, p. 383.

[72] Lady Bridget Plowden *et al. Children and Their Primary Schools: A Report of the Central Advisory Council for Education.* London: H.M.S.O., 1967, paragraph 9.

[73] Johnson. *Thirty Years, loc. cit.*, p. 52.

[74] Anne Bussis and Edward Chittenden. *Analysis of an Approach to Open Education.* Princeton, N.J.: Educational Testing Service, 1970, pp. 14-15.

[75] Rugg, *loc. cit.*, p. 58.

[76] Arthur T. Jersild. *et al. Child Development and the Curriculum.* New York: Teachers College Press, 1946, p. 1.

[77] Johnson. *Thirty Years, loc. cit.*, p. 55.

[78] Lillian Weber. *The English Infant School and Informal Education.* Englewood Cliffs, New Jersey: Prentice-Hall, Inc., 1971, pp. 169-170. Copyright © 1971. Reprinted by permission of Prentice-Hall, Inc., Englewood Cliffs, New Jersey.

[79] The Provincial Committee on Aims and Objectives of Education in the Schools of Ontario. *Living and Learning.* Toronto: Ontario Department of Education, 1968, p. 55.

[80] Marietta Johnson. "The Educational Principles of the School of Organic Education, Fairhope, Alabama." *Twenty-Sixth Yearbook of the National Society for the Study of Education.* Bloomington: Public School Publishing Company, 1926, p. 350.

[81] *Ibid.*, p. 351.

[82] Charles H. Rathbone. "The Implicit Rationale of the Open Education Classroom." In Charles H. Rathbone (Ed.) *Open Education: The Informal Classroom*. New York: Citation Press, 1971, p. 113. Reprinted by permission of Citation Press. Copyright © 1971 by Scholastic Magazines, Inc.

[83] *Ibid.*

[84] *Ibid.*, p. 100.

[85] Rugg, *loc. cit.*, p. 5.

[86] Johnson. *Thirty Years, loc. cit.*, p. 15.

[87] *Ibid.*, p. 37.

[88] *Ibid.*, p. 18.

[89] *Ibid.*, p. 52.

[90] Parker, *loc. cit.*, p. 383.

[91] Rugg, *loc. cit.*, p. 34.

[92] Johnson. *Thirty Years, loc. cit.*, p. 23.

[93] Rugg, *loc. cit.*, p. 56.

[94] Rugg, *loc. cit.*, p. 63.

[95] *Ibid.*, pp. 62-63.

[96] Rathbone, *loc. cit.*, p. 104.

[97] Barth, *loc. cit.*, p. 72.

[98] Rathbone, *loc. cit.*, p. 103.

[99] *Ibid.*

[100] Rugg, *loc. cit.*, pp. 64, 65.

[101] Barth, *loc. cit.*, p. 26.

[102] Rathbone, *loc. cit.*, p. 114.

[103] *Ibid.*

[104] *Ibid.*, p. 112.

[105] *Ibid.*

[106] *Ibid.*

[107] *Ibid.*, p. 111.

[108] *Ibid.*, p. 105.

[109] *Ibid.*

[110] Barth, *loc. cit.*, pp. 27, 28.

[111] Johnson. *Thirty Years, loc. cit.*, p. 26.

[112] *Ibid.*, p. 9.

[113] Child Study developers have long considered the development of the individual child as non-uniform. In the 1890's the emphasis was upon different rates of growth and styles of learning. Such were interpreted as linear functions with differential slopes. In the 1960's, however, child growth was viewed as approximating a non-linear function. Rather than rates of growth, *stages* of growth were spoken of. Each stage was viewed as qualitatively different from the others. In comparing different stages to each other, one is not believed to be viewing different parts of the same function but entirely different functions. In the 1890's, development was viewed as a continuous function; in the 1960's, it was viewed as a discontinuous function with quantum jumps at the points of discontinuity.

[114] Erik H. Erikson. *Childhood and Society*. New York: W.W. Norton, 1963; or Sigmund Freud. *The Standard Edition of the Complete Psychological Works of Sigmund Freud*. London: Hogarth, 1964.

[115] J.H. Flavell. *The Developmental Psychology of Jean Piaget*. New York: D. Van Nostrand, 1963; Hans G. Furth. *Piaget and Knowledge*. Englewood Cliffs: Prentice-Hall, 1969; and entries in the bibliography of these books.

[116] Lawrence Kohlberg. "Moral Education in the School: A Developmental View." *School Review*, Vol. 74, No. 1 (September, 1966); and Lawrence Kohlberg. "The Child as Moral Philosopher." *Psychology Today*, Vol. 2, No. 4 (September, 1968).

[117] Johnson. *Thirty Years, loc. cit.*, p. 23.

[118] *Ibid.*, p. 10.

[119] Barth, *loc. cit.*, p. 32.

[120] *Ibid.*, p. 33.

[121] Hein, *loc. cit.*, p. 1.

[122] Barth, *loc. cit.*, p. 23. (The italics are mine.)

[123] Walberg and Thomas, *loc. cit.*, p. 93. (The italics are mine.)

[124] Johnson. *Thirty Years, loc. cit.*, p. 10.

[125] Barth, *loc. cit.*, p. 63. (The italics are mine.)

[126] *Ibid.*, p. 83.

[127] *Ibid.*, p. 47.

[128] Rathbone, *loc. cit.*, p. 101.

[129] *Ibid.*, p. 102.

[130] *Ibid.*

[131] *Ibid.*

[132] *Ibid.*

[133] *Ibid.*

[134] Barth, *loc. cit.*, p. 45.

[135] Rathbone, *loc. cit.*, p. 102.

[136] Rugg, *loc. cit.*, p. 62.

[137] Barth, *loc. cit.*, p. 45.

[138] *Ibid.*, p. 75.

[139] *Ibid.*

[140] Rathbone, *loc. cit.*, p. 102.

[141] Barth, *loc. cit.*, p. 49.

[142] Rathbone, *loc. cit.*, pp. 106-107.

[143] Barth, *loc. cit.*, p. 63.

[144] Rathbone, *loc. cit.*, p. 107.

[145] Rugg, *loc. cit.*, p. 68.

[146] William H. Kilpatrick. *The Project Method*. New York: Teachers College Press, 1918.

[147] Johnson. *Thirty Years, loc. cit.*, p. 30.

[148] Barth, *loc. cit.*, p. 33.

[149] *Ibid.*, p. 50.

[150] Hein, *loc. cit.*, p. 2.

[151] *Ibid.*

[152] Barth, *loc. cit.*, p. 20.

[153] Rugg, *loc. cit.*, p. 5.

[154] Barth, *loc. cit.*, p. 20.

[155] *Ibid.*, p. 21.

[156] For example, see Barth, *loc. cit.*, pp. 21, 44; or Rugg, *loc. cit.*, p. 63.

[157] Rugg, *loc. cit.*, p. 6.

[158] Barth, *loc. cit.*, p. 44.

[159] *Ibid.*, pp. 21-22.

[160] *Ibid.*, p. 84.

[161] Rathbone, *loc. cit.*, p. 100.

[162] *Ibid.*

[163] Barth, *loc. cit.*, p. 33.

[164]David Hawkins. "Messing About in Science." *Science and Children.* Vol. 2, No. 5 (February, 1965).

[165]Joseph Featherstone. "A New Kind of Schooling." *The New Republic,* Vol. 158, No. 9 (March, 1968).

[166]W.H. Burnham. "Education from the Genetic Point of View." *Proceedings of the National Education Association* (1905), p. 727.

[167]Walberg and Thomas, *loc. cit.*

[168]*Ibid.*, pp. 90-94 are where the tables are found. Tables reprinted with permission.

[169]Barth, *loc. cit.*, p. 106.

[170]The curriculum developer aids the teacher in the preparation of this environment by making available materials, strategies, and classroom designs—his curricula—from which the teacher can select what he believes appropriate to the needs of his students. Traditionally the curriculum developer's major contribution has been to make available physical materials and strategies for using them to the teacher. In recent years, some developers have made their roles more inclusive. The Advisorates of Leistershire, England, and the learning centers in Philadelphia have laid considerable stress upon the personal environment for learning as well as the physical environment.

[171]Barth, *loc. cit.*, p. 76.

[172]Walberg and Thomas, *loc. cit.*, p. 91.

[173]Barth, *loc. cit.*, p. 93.

[174]Allan Leitman. "Travel Agent." In *Housing for Early Childhood Education,* Bulletin No. 22-A. Washington, D.C.: Association for Childhood Education International, 1968. Reprinted by permission of Allan Leitman and the Association for Childhood Education International, 3615 Wisconsin Avenue, N.W., Washington, D.C. Copyright © 1968 by The Association.

[175]Barth, *loc. cit.*, p. 107.

[176]*Ibid.*, p. 68.

[177]*Ibid.*, p. 65.

[178]Walberg and Thomas, *loc. cit.*, p. 91.

[179] Brown. *The Integrated Day in the Primary School, loc. cit.*, p. 33.

[180] Walberg and Thomas, *loc. cit.*, p. 91.

[181] *Ibid.*

[182] *Ibid.*

[183] Barth, *loc. cit.*, pp. 102-103.

[184] *Ibid.*, p. 66.

[185] *Ibid.*, pp. 44-45.

[186] *Ibid.*, p. 101.

[187] *Ibid.*, p. 38.

[188] *Ibid.*

[189] *Ibid.*, p. 41.

[190] The Child Study developer certainly makes use of subjective standards in designing curricula and diagnosing children—but these standards are used to aid the growth of the individual and not to compare the individual to another.

[191] Barth, *loc. cit.*, p. 47.

[192] *Ibid.*

[193] *Ibid.*, p. 39.

[194] *Ibid.*, p. 40.

[195] Walberg and Thomas, *loc. cit.*, p. 91.

[196] Barth, *loc. cit.*, p. 103.

[197] *Ibid.*, p. 101.

[198] *Ibid.*

[199] *Ibid.*

[200] *Ibid.*, p. 102.

[201] *Ibid.*

[202] *Ibid.*, pp. 101-102.

[203] *Ibid.*, p. 102.

[204] *Ibid.*

[205] *Ibid.*

[206] *Ibid.*, p. 38.

[207] *Ibid.*, p. 37.

[208] *Ibid.*, p. 38.

[209] *Ibid.*

[210] *Ibid.*, p. 41.

[211] *Ibid.*, p. 43.

[212] *Ibid.*

[213] L.G.W. Sealey. "Looking Back on Leicestershire." *ESI Quarterly Report* (Spring-Summer, 1966). Newton, Mass.: Education Development Center, 1966, p. 40.

[214] *Introduction to Elementary Science Study, loc. cit.*, p. 8.

5.
Social Reconstruction Ideology

Curriculum developers working within the Social Reconstruction Ideology view curriculum creation from a social perspective. First, they assume that society is unhealthy. Its very survival is believed to be threatened. This is because the traditional mechanisms developed by the society to contend with social situations are obsolete and incapable of dealing with the problems and conflicts arising within society. Second, it is assumed that something can be done to keep society from destroying itself. This necessitates the development of a vision of a society better than the existing one, within which the problems and conflicts of the present society are resolved, and action directed toward reconstructing society based upon the vision of the new society. Finally, Social Reconstruction developers assume that education provides the means through which society is to be reconstructed. These developers have a supreme faith in the ability of education—through the medium of curriculum—to educate "the masses of humanity" to understand the ills of their society, develop a vision of a better world, and act so as to bring that vision into existence.

Social Reconstruction developers begin with the assumption that "the survival of our society is threatened by an increasing number of unprecedented and, to date, insoluble problems."[1] These problems include, among others, the racism problem, the war problem, the sexism problem, the poverty problem, the environmental pollution problem, the worker exploitation problem, the crime problem, the mental illness problem, the child abuse problem, the political corruption problem, the population explosion problem, the megalopolis problem, the energy shortage problem, the Bomb problem, the illiteracy problem, the health care problem, the unemployment problem, and the breakdown-of-the-family problem. If these problems continue on their rampage, and are not resolved, it is believed that the very survival of our society will be threatened.

However, all is not lost. Social Reconstruction developers assume "that something can be done to improve the situation"[2] and save society. As George Counts phrases it:

> But the point should be emphasized, that the present situation is full of promise, as well as menace. Our age is literally pregnant with possibilities. There lies within our grasp the most humane and majestic civilization ever fashioned by any people. At last men have achieved such a mastery over the forces of nature that wage slavery can follow chattel slavery and take its place among the relics of the past. No longer are there any grounds for the contention that the finer fruits of human culture must be nurtured upon the exploitation of the masses. The limits set by nature have been so extended that for all practical purposes we may say that we are bound merely by our own ideals, by our power of self-discipline, and by our ability to devise social arrangements suited to an industrial age. . . . In other words, we hold within our hands the power to usher in an age of plenty, to make secure the lives of all and to banish poverty forever from the land.[3]

To save society from self-destruction, we must develop a vision of a society better than the existing one, a vision of "the most humane and majestic civilization ever fashioned by any people" within which the problems and conflicts of our present society do not exist. We must act to reconstruct our present society so as to transform it into the envisioned new better society.

For Social Reconstruction developers, it is education that provides the means by which society is to be reconstructed. As Counts says:

> Today, as social institutions crumble and society is shaken by deep convulsions that threaten its very existence, many persons are proclaiming that education

> provides the only true road to safety. They are even
> saying that it should be brought into the service of
> building a new social order.[4]

Social Reconstruction developers assume that education, *if it is
revitalized along the lines they recommend*, has the power to
educate "the masses" of humanity that make up society to
understand their problems, envision a world in which those
problems do not exist, and act so as to bring that vision into
existence.

Social Reconstruction developers hold diverse sets of beliefs
about society, the conflicts within society, and a vision of the
future society. Because of the diversity, the particular beliefs of
developers will not be specified herein. Rather, the *context within
which the beliefs are held* will be discussed. Whether the
curriculum is designed around the oppression of poverty or
illiteracy, the destructiveness of war or environmental pollution,
the social injustice of racism or sexism, the economic problems of
worker exploitation or political corruption, or the social problems
of crime or mental illness, the particular issues and the particular
visions will not be our concern. The concern will be with the
assumptions that underlie the developer's views. To give the
assumptions meaning, however, one example of a school operating
within the context of the Social Reconstruction Ideology will be
described.

HIGHLANDER

The Highlander Folk School, founded by Myles Horton in 1932
on Monteagle Mountain in Tennessee, provides an example of the
work of a Social Reconstruction curriculum developer. The school
was founded to stop what Horton perceived to be an impending
social crisis arising out of the industrial revolution: rich industrial-
ists and land owners were economically exploiting and oppressing
poor factory, farm, and mine workers to such an extent that
democracy as Americans had known it was threatened. Horton
founded the Highlander Folk School to provide an educational
"means by which all suppressed people in America could challenge
their oppressors."[5] The school's purpose was "educating for a
revolution that would basically alter economic and political power
relationships to the advantage of the poor and powerless."[6] To

accomplish this, Horton invited potential labor organizers to the Highlander Folk School, helped them understand the nature of the oppression under which the workers of America were suffering, inspired them with a vision of an ideal society within which laborers were not oppressed, helped them formulate strategies for organizing oppressed laborers, and then sent them to their factories, farms, and mines to organize the masses of oppressed workers to rise up and strike for better living and working conditions and thus begin the establishment of a new social order. For Horton, "The Highlander Folk School's most important contribution will be to help the workers envision their [new] role in society and in so doing, make the labor movement the basis for a fundamental social change."[7] Note that Horton assumed the existence of a social crisis that could be overcome: the economic exploitation of the working class. To overcome the social crisis he used educational means: he educated labor leaders who in turn educated the working class both (a) to envision a new society lacking economic exploitation, and (b) to act in ways that would transform the existing society into the envisioned new society. Crucial to Horton's educational program was his curriculum, which was used to educate labor leaders at the Highlander Folk School and used by the newly educated labor leaders when they returned to their factories, farms, and mines to educate the masses of oppressed laborers.

The essence of Horton's curriculum consisted of labor workshops that lasted for six weeks within which about twenty-five potential labor leaders socially interacted under the careful guidance of the Highlander staff. The labor workshops progressed through three loosely structured but carefully guided stages of discussion. During the first stage of the workshops, participants "state and analyze their problems"[8] in terms of their actual experiences and collectively paint a picture of a society within which such problems do not exist. On the one hand, a feeling of commonality is established among strangers as they share their personal experiences with each other while developing an *understanding* of the social crisis. On the other hand, a feeling of shared hope is developed as participants develop a *vision* of an ideal society that they might bring about in order to eradicate the problems of the existing society. At this stage, an understanding of society both "as it is" and "as it ought to be" is generated as the Highlander staff help the workshop participants reflect on their firsthand experiences with labor problems. For workshop participants, this means that they are required to have had firsthand experiences with labor problems so that they can both contribute to the discussion from their own pool of experiences and personally understand what others have to say in terms of their own experiences. Persons without the required experience are first sent to participate in labor strikes and to live along-side exploited workers before they are allowed to join one of the Highlander workshops.

During the second stage of the workshops, participants discuss alternate strategies that might be used to eradicate the problems of the existing society and bring into existence the new society. On the one hand, this involves guiding participants to engage in "a lot of criticism, a lot of informal discussion . . . about how they've failed"[9] and about "their inability to achieve what they want to achieve"[10] in light of their vision of the ideal society. This self-criticism allows for discussion of unsuccessful change strategies, gives workshop participants insight into their shortcomings as leaders, and frees workshop participants from guilt for past failures. On the other hand, this discussion of alternate strategies involves having participants discuss each other's successes in working to overcome the oppression of laborers, and involves having participants discuss possible new ways of acting as social groups to bring into existence the envisioned new society—ways such as massive strikes and sit-ins. Within this stage of the workshop, the Highlander "staff will deliberately reinforce talk in the group that points to united social action"[11] —versus individual action; will deliberately draw solutions to social problems out of the experiences and thoughts of the workshop participants themselves—versus elaborating upon those of outside experts; and will deliberately examine alternate solutions to social problems in terms of the experiences of the workshop participants themselves—rather than in abstract isolation from their firsthand experiences. What is important here is both that solutions come from the people and relate to the people and that "the search for solutions becomes, itself, a group process. Without saying so, Highlander provides an experience in group problem-solving. The group stretches the imagination of every individual in it and becomes the vehicle for introducing the concept of collective power."[1][2] (Here the social medium of group process complements the social message of collective power—or as Marshall McLuhan might say, "the medium is the message.")

During the third stage of the labor workshops, the participants are led to synthesize what they have learned and to commit themselves to action directed towards transforming the existing crisis ridden society into the future *good society*. Commitment to action, strengthened through vows taken openly in front of one's colleagues, is central to this stage of the workshop. Participants are encouraged to openly commit themselves to what they will do when they get back home: both in terms of educating their fellow workers in the same way they themselves were educated at Highlander, and in terms of the types of action they will lead their fellow workers to take in order to overcome their oppression and bring into existence the envisioned new society. It is thus through the workshop participants' going home to act that Horton disseminates his curriculum and uses it to educate "the masses" of workers who made up society to reconstruct their society.

Three things occurring at all stages of the labor workshops deserve mention. First, the Highlander staff act more as catalysts for and companions to the workshop participants than as teachers or authorities. They communicate *with* them rather than lecturing *at* them or *about* them. Next, at no time does Horton present "a clearly defined program of action" for those coming to Highlander to mindlessly learn and then follow when they return home. He does not intend to teach a clearly defined program, for he believes that men must solve their problems within the context in which they arise. What Horton does provide is a value-laden vision of a new society that allows people to see their problems, to plan ways of overcoming them, and to act to overcome them. Crucial here is that the particular action people must take depends upon the specific time, place, and situation in which they find themselves— the value-laden vision *guides* their action but does not *dictate* their action. Finally, within all three stages of the labor workshops, the Highlander staff make heavy use of social media such as group singing, story telling, and drama. They use such media as a means to bind people together into social groups, to lead them to see their problems clearly, to help them envision a new society, and to inspire them to action directed towards building a new social order. Scores of labor plays and songs, including "We Shall Overcome," were written at Highlander in its attempt "to develop feelings and will more than memory and logic."[13] Education at the Highlander Folk School was thus thoroughly social in nature. It used the social means of human interaction during discussion and song to educate and motivate. It promoted social rather than individual ways of acting, advocating massive strikes and sit-ins. And it educated people to improve society as a whole rather than themselves as isolated individuals.

What is important to note is that what Myles Horton did as a Social Reconstruction curriculum developer in the 1930's and 1940's for the labor movement could be done at other times and in other places with different social crises. For example, during the 1950's and 1960's Horton devoted his efforts to the civil rights movement. The Citizenship Schools that sprang up throughout the South and the sit-ins of the Student Nonviolent Coordinating Committee (SNCC) were programs created at the Highlander Folk School. Although the issues and times were different, the method, vision, and purpose were the same: Horton was still using interactional workshops as a social means of "educating for a revolution that would basically alter economic and political power relationships to the advantage of the poor and powerless."

Similarly, other curriculum developers have struggled with other social crises, from environmental pollution to war. No matter what the social crisis, however, there have been similarities in approach. Social Reconstruction curriculum developers have consistently attempted to educate students and through them educate "the masses" of society to understand a social problem, develop a vision of a better society, and act so as to bring that vision into existence. For example, a Social Reconstruction developer constructing a curriculum to educate sixth-grade students to help overcome the social crisis created by environmental pollution might include as part of his curriculum the following components: first, field trips to let students see the effects of pollution; second, classroom discussions using value clarification techniques to lead students to understand the dangers of pollution, to envision an environment without pollution, and to formulate strategies for ending pollution; and, finally, student action that takes place outside of the school context to educate "the masses" of their friends and parents to end pollution through social means, such as protests against polluters, circulation of petitions to be published in newspapers, or creation of environmental clean-up days. Or, for example, a Social Reconstruction developer constructing a curriculum to educate high school students to help overcome a social crisis created by a particular war, or war in general, might include as part of his curriculum the following components: the reading of famous war novels, the reading of current newspapers, the viewing of famous war movies, and the viewing of current television news broadcasts to enlighten students as to the nature of "war as a social phenomenon that has brought much misery and suffering into the world"[14]; such would be coordinated with consciousness raising classroom discussions designed to help students understand the nature of war, to formulate a vision of a world at peace, and to develop strategies to end war; and then there would follow student action that takes place outside the school context, action to educate and motivate "the masses" of their friends and parents to end war through social techniques such as discussion similar to classroom discussions, massive peace marches and sit-ins, or social disobedience such as draft card burning. What is important to note is that the teaching of courses such as those just described, the rebuilding of the school program, and

> the reconstruction of the curriculum . . . would not call for the addition of new subjects. Indeed, to superficial observation, *perhaps no important changes would be discernible*. The same disciplines would be taught; the same activities would be organized. Children would learn to read and write and figure; they would work and play together. *But the spirit, the approach, the orientation would be different*. Pupils and teachers might be doing the same things as before, but the motivation would follow unwonted channels. The appeal to the egoistic and possessive tendencies would be strictly subordinated; *the emphasis everywhere would be placed on the social and co-operative. . . .* From the earliest years the whole life of the school would be organized so

> as to bring out and strengthen these qualities. No
> individual would be rewarded for merely overcoming or
> surpassing another. . . . [In addition] the several
> divisions of subject matter composing the curriculum
> would be given a social meaning.[15]

The anti-pollution and anti-war curricula just described, for
example, might be taught as part of social science courses. In such
a case, part of what "would be different" is (a) that "the selection
and the organization of materials in the . . . social sciences . . . would be determined by the needs of a society [in
crisis] . . . and administered in terms of the interests of the masses
of the people"[16] rather than in terms of the scholarly academic
content of the social sciences themselves, (b) that the pedagogy of
the social sciences would be centered on classroom discussion
where the teacher would be more of a catalyst and companion to
students rather than an authority and giver of knowledge, and (c)
that the intent would not be to produce in students knowledge of
the social sciences but rather social action designed to reconstruct
society and by doing so eradicate its problems.

SOCIETY AND RECONSTRUCTION
Social Perspective

Social Reconstruction developers view their world within a
social perspective. The nature of society as it is and as it should be
become the determinants of most of their concepts and assumptions. For example, the following three crucial aspects of life are
socially defined. First, human experience is believed to be most
fundamentally shaped by cultural factors; meaning in man's life is
defined in terms of his relationship to society. Second, education
is viewed as a function of the society which supports it; it must be
interpreted within the context of a particular culture. Third, truth
and knowledge are interpreted as based in and defined by cultural
assumptions; they are idiosyncratic to each society and testable
with respect to criteria based in social consensus rather than
empirical or logical criteria.

As a result, Social Reconstruction developers believe that "there
is no *good individual* apart from some conception of the nature of
the *good society*. Man without human society and human culture
is not man."[17] They believe that "there is also no *good education*

apart from some conception of the nature of the *good society*. Education is not some pure and mystical essence that remains unchanged from everlasting to everlasting."[18] They believe that there is no *truth or knowledge* apart from some conception of the nature of the *good society*; "and the good society is not something that is given by nature: it must be fashioned by the hand and brain of man."[19] Of importance here is the belief in cultural relativity. The "good individual," the "good education," and "truth and knowledge" are defined by a particular culture and the only thing that gives them either meaning or value is the existence of that culture in a particular time and place. Counts implies this in speaking about education when he writes:

> The historical record shows that education is always a function of time, place, and circumstance. In its basic philosophy, its social objective, and its program of instruction, it inevitably reflects in varying proportion the experiences, the condition, and the hopes, fears, and aspirations of a particular people or cultural group at a particular point in history. In actuality it is never organized and conducted with sole reference to absolute and universal terms . . . education as a whole is always relative, at least in fundamental parts, to some concrete and evolving social situation. It possesses no inner logic or empirical structure of its own that dictates either its method or its content. In both its theoretical and practical aspects it expresses the ideals of some given society at some given period in time, either consciously with clear design or half-consciously with hidden and confused purpose. There can be no all-embracing educational philosophy, policy, or program suited to all cultures and all ages.

> Hence the problem of education assumes one form in ancient Athens in the time of Pericles, another in China during the Tang dynasty, another in Mediaeval Saxony, another in modern Japan, still another in Russia under the Communists, and yet another in twentieth-century America.[20]

What is important for the Social Reconstruction developer as a creature of a particular time, place, and circumstance is that since society is viewed as undergoing a crisis, it follows that the good man, the good education, and truth and knowledge are also undergoing a crisis. For stability to return it is necessary to develop a vision of the good society and to move the culture in the direction of that vision. From that vision will implicitly follow conceptions of the good man, the good education, and truth and knowledge; and from the reconstruction of society in accordance with that vision will come the actualization of these conceptions.

The Individual in Society

The Social Reconstruction concern is primarily with the forces at work in society that shape human experience, and secondarily with the individuals at work who shape society. The emphasis is upon economic, political, and educational forces that control the impact upon society of such varied things as social classes, scientific discoveries, moral trends, and aesthetic movements. The emphasis is upon the group rather than the individual: upon the whole versus its parts. Causal explanations proceed from dynamics of the society as a whole, to the dynamics of social subgroups, to the individual.[21] In this context, the individual is viewed as fulfilling his potential as a human being in relationship to social groups, in interaction with other men, and in interdependence with a human community. This does not mean that man is a creature of social determinism. Man is shaped by society and man can also shape society. However, it does mean that interpretations and intentions are expressed with respect to the social group rather than with respect to the individual.

Society, Change, and Crisis

The view of society utilized by Social Reconstruction developers is one of historic evolution: societies pass through periods of evolution, stability, and degeneration. One of the prime characteristics of our society is that it is undergoing change—that it is, as noted earlier, "passing through one of the greatest periods of transformation in the history of mankind."[22] During this period of change, society's very "survival . . . is threatened by an increasing number of unprecedented and, to date, insoluble problems"[23] that originate within the internal discontinuities of society itself. The social crisis, whether wrought by technological, economic, political, or psychological factors, has rendered virtually all of society's problem-solving strategies and institutions irrelevant. If society fails to detect that its problem-solving strategies and institutions—which were originally developed to conserve and transmit the culture during a previous period of relative stability— are irrelevant to the transformations being wrought upon itself, these strategies and institutions will become threats to its survival.[24]

The situation of society, however, is full of promise as well as menace. The changes wrought upon society by its internal dynamics have unfettered and extended the limits previously set by its structure so that "there lies within our grasp the most humane, the most beautiful, and the most majestic civilization ever fashioned by any people."[25] The possibility to significantly improve the total human societal condition lies within reach.

Hope exists, for it is believed that there is no deterministic, metaphysical design which prescribes the history of a society, even though societies are largely formed and limited by the characteristics of the period in which they exist. Society hammers out its own history through the thoughts and struggles of its members: "the course it takes and the goals it attains depend wholly upon the choice made and the failures and successes experienced by man."[26] As a result, the evolution of society is "bound merely by our ideals, our power of self discipline, and by our ability to devise social arrangements suited to"[27] the changes occurring within society.

Reconstruction and Vision

Faced with the crises of society, the Social Reconstruction developer devises a vision of a new, better society that lacks the problems of the existing society. He then develops educational programs that allow people to see the disparity between the crisis-ridden present society and the future utopian society and that motivate them to transform the present society into that future utopian society. The Social Reconstruction developer does not accept the present societal conditions as unalterable "givens." Nor does he accept the present conditions of society as factors to be improved through simple tinkering. He rejects the present crisis-ridden conditions of society, creates a vision of a better society distinct from the present one, and attempts to reconstruct the existing society by eradicating its imperfections and substituting in their place other social structures. That is, he attempts to build a new society out of the existing one, rather than attempting to perfect the best aspects of the existing society in hopes that this will make the present society more tolerable. The Social Reconstruction developer does not proceed in a legalistic manner of building onto already existing precedents to strengthen what exists. He proceeds in a revolutionary manner of creating new social arrangements that will replace those of the past.

In assuming that the way to overcome the present social crisis is through envisioning and implementing a future better society, the Social Reconstruction developer assumes that men need a "compelling and challenging vision of human destiny"[28] that points the way to better social conditions. Counts states:

> The times are literally crying for a new vision of American destiny. . . . Such a vision of what America might become in the industrial age I would introduce into our schools as the supreme imposition [indoctrination], . . . one to which our children are entitled—a priceless legacy which . . . should be the first concern of our [educational] profession to fashion and bequeath. . . . To refuse to face the task of creating a vision of a future America immeasurably more just and noble and beautiful than the America of today is to evade the most crucial, difficult, and important educational task.[29]

There are several important characteristics of the Social Reconstructionists' vision of the future good society. First, the vision of the future good society is not a finished vision that portrays a utopia in its ultimate state in precise detail. It is a directed vision that points the way in which society must move in order to reconstruct itself. It provides "a vision of the *possibilities* which lie ahead and endeavor[s] to enlist their [children's] loyalties and enthusiasms in the realization of the vision."[30] It does not provide a precise description of the *possibility* that lies ahead and does not attempt to enslave men into mindlessly working to institute that possibility. It designates the directions in which society should move in striving to reconstruct itself, rather than the endpoint which society should reach in order to achieve perfection.[31] In addition, the vision of the future good society does not hold inherent within it a clearly prescribed program of action that dictates how it is to be achieved. The exact details of the situations within which men find themselves must prescribe how men will act to reconstruct society. The vision of the future good society is a general one that provides value-laden standards for action and social acceptability. It is not a blueprint that dictates exactly how the future good society must be built and what it must look like. Indeed, it could not be such; for, if it were, it would negate the significance of social relativity and the uniqueness of the "particular time and place in history"[32] within which a man must act. Just as the Social Reconstruction developer views the present society from the position of cultural relativity, so too does he view his vision from the position of cultural relativity; and he insists that "it must be suited to a particular time and place in history"[33] and appropriately implemented within the limiting parameters of the particular context within which a certain group of people find themselves. Second, the vision of the future good society is created in response to existing social conditions; and, as such, it embodies within it both a picture of reality *as it is* and a vision of reality *as it ought to be*. Its power lies both in its ability to offer men salvation from an intolerable reality as it is, and in its ability to offer men a utopian vision of reality as it ought to be. Understanding the vision of the future good society carries inherent within it the requirement that one understand society as it is in order to fully appreciate the alternate society as it ought to be. Finally, the Social Reconstruction developer's vision of the future good society is a social rather than an individual vision. It is a vision that allows the masses of persons making up society to overcome their problems together and to collectively achieve the good life. It is not a vision that allows certain individuals to achieve the good life and escape from their problems at the expense of others.

The Social Reconstruction developer's vision of the future good society serves several functions in enabling the masses of people to reconstruct their society. First, it allows persons coming from diverse situations to rise above the unique particulars of their situations to see the social crises as a whole (as, for example, when

Blacks, Mexican Americans, and American Indians all see that they are oppressed ethnic groups lacking the power to determine their own destinies); allows them to collectively share in a common vision of a better life; and thus allows them to act together to fulfill common needs and to collectively—rather than individually—better themselves and thus better society as a whole. Second, the vision offers the masses an alternative to and thus possible escape from the crisis-ridden society within which they find themselves. Without the perception that their crisis-ridden world is a limiting situation that they can overcome, and not a closed world from which there is no escape, the masses would not be able to wage the struggle to reconstruct their society. By providing a viable alternative to existing living conditions, the vision of the future good society illustrates that the existing crisis-ridden society is a limiting condition that actually can be overcome. Third, the vision has values inherent in it, and these values allow men to see their problems *as problems* rather than to simply accept them as innate characteristics of the world within which they live. For example, someone who places no value on freedom and self-determination would not see oppression as a problem to be overcome. Educating men to value freedom so that they see the oppression around them prepares the way for dissatisfaction that can lead to action directed towards transforming what is into what ought to be. Thus, the vision acts to educate the masses to see their problems as problems. Fourth, the vision of the future good society offers the masses of society the hope of something better that motivates them to act in ways other than those normally expected of them. Giving men hope and courage that allow them to step outside of their normal social roles is crucial in motivating them to overcome the social crises within which they find themselves. Fifth, the vision gives the masses clear long-range goals to work for that offer direction to their thinking, so that they do not become distracted from their endeavors to reconstruct society by the immediacies of daily life. Short-range and vaguely defined goals will not suffice, for "it is now imperative that we know where we want to go—not only because seeking such knowledge will help us to know where we do and do not want to go, but because, so long as we do not know we shall be unprepared to go there."[34] And, sixth, the vision of the future good society defines the nature of the good individual, the good education, and worthwhile truth and knowledge. Without the ability to identify the good individual, the good education, and worthwhile truth and knowledge, the masses would not be able to cultivate them and make them multiply in ways that would help reconstruct society.

The emphasis upon developing a vision of a good society leads the Social Reconstruction developer into the mainstream of cultural utopianism. Here the distinction must be made between utopias of escape and utopias of reconstruction: "the first leaves the external world the way it is, the second seeks to change it so that one may have intercourse with it on one's own terms. In one we build impossible castles in the air; in the other we consult a surveyor and an architect and a mason and proceed to build a house which meets our essential needs."[35] Social Reconstruction developers insist that their visions be realizable, that they be utopias of reconstruction. The orientation about a utopian philosophy demands that the heart of the ideology be directed towards the future. This orientation towards the future is not an amorphous, diffuse orientation but a directed one that specifies those aspects of society which are undesirable and those which are desirable; that demands a value commitment on the part of its advocates; and that calls for aggressive behavior on the part of these advocates towards those not in sympathy with the vision.[36]

Social Dynamics

In viewing society in its stark reality, Social Reconstruction developers usually identify three types of social subgroups: there are "bad guy" subgroups, "good guy" subgroups, and the "masses." Both the "bad guy" and "good guy" subgroups are minorities which are attempting to control the "masses": the "bad guy" minorities perpetuate the status quo by supporting ideas and institutions suited to an age that is gone in order to exploit the "masses" for selfish reasons; the "good guy" minorities represent future-oriented forces attempting to bring into existence a better and more just society run for the benefit of the "masses." This view of social dynamics is characterized by Brameld:

> If the reconstructionist is prepared to argue that he is
> the minority spokesman for values that are already

cherished by the majority, whether consciously or not, he is equally prepared to show that another minority actually dominates the majority. This is the minority that now so largely controls the instruments of power and that has succeeded in persuading the majority that their own interests are best served by perpetuating those controls. Upon this point the task of reconstructionism is also that of a critical minority—the task of showing how frequently the majority of citizens exercise their franchise of the secret ballot not in behalf of their own interests—that is, their most cherished values—but rather in behalf of continued scarcity, chronic insecurity, frustration, and war. In this sense, indeed, one may say that the great political struggle that goes on in our democracy is not, after all, one between the majority and a minority—like most other great struggles of history, it is between at least two organized minorities. One minority is concerned with widening. ... The opposing minority works to narrow. ... [37]

Important to note in this statement are several assumptions. First, the "good guy" subgroups are out of power and the "bad guy" subgroups are in control of the "masses." As a result, responsibility for the ills of society is viewed as falling solely upon the shoulders of the "bad guy" subgroups. Second, the attitude prevails that the "good guy" subgroups are "the minority spokesmen for *values* that are *already cherished* by the *majority, whether consciously or not.*" This leads to the belief in a hierarchical set of values where some values are better than others for superhuman reasons; to the belief that the "good guy" subgroups possess the truth as represented in the superhuman values; to the belief that those values are good for the "masses" whether they are conscious of it or not; to the belief that it is permissible to indoctrinate the "masses," since one knows what is really good for them; and to the belief that it is permissible to control and manipulate the "masses" so long as it is for their own good. Third, society is viewed as engaged in a "great political struggle," with the "good and bad guy" subgroups waging war over the "masses." This war is treated as a holy war, a great crusade, where evil and good battle each other over issues that are value laden.[38] Further, the school is expected to be one of the weapons to be used in waging the war.[39] And, fourth, the emphasis in the war is upon forming a single unified "group mind"[40] that agrees upon what the true values of society are and what the vision of the future good society should be.

Social Philosophic Viewpoint

Social Reconstruction developers assume a social philosophic stance toward society. They assume that "If education is to grapple with a given social situation, it must incorporate a social philosophy adequate to that situation—a social philosophy that has substance as well as form—a social philosophy that represents great historical choices."[41] Although they begin by examining society and end by developing strategies for reconstructing that society, the core of the thinking of Social Reconstruction developers takes place within a level of philosophic discourse concerned as much with "what should be" as with "what is." Their vision for the future is based within a philosophic concern for the nature of the "good society." This philosophic approach tends to be eclectic, often including bits and pieces as well as major directions from a variety of diverse thinkers who are often in fields other than education. In fact, these developers usually assume that the major inspirations which affect their social philosophy *must* come from sources other than education, for they believe "that our present educational system is not viable and is certainly not capable of generating enough energy to lead to its own revitalization."[42] By acting as middlemen, philosophic synthesizers, these developers construct their beliefs by consulting a diverse set of "great thinkers." This gives their social philosophy what appears to be an open, evolving quality, even though that quality is bound and limited by social values held with great conviction. The quality of conviction underlying the Social Reconstruction developer's social philosophy is what differentiates the work of a philosopher from that of an ideologist.

RECONSTRUCTION THROUGH EDUCATION
The School as the Institution of Change

Working within this framework, the Social Reconstruction developer dedicates himself to the reconstruction of society. The approach taken consists of a reaction against the existing crisis-ridden society, the formation of a utopian vision, and action directed towards moving the existing society towards the future utopia. This approach is imbedded within a curriculum to be used in schools. The schools then become the social institution through which leadership is to be provided and action is to be initiated in reconstructing society.

The profession of education thus has the role of preparing man to transform the present crisis-stricken society into a future utopia. To accomplish this, educators "should deliberately reach for power and then make the most of their conquest. . . . To the extent that they are permitted to fashion the curriculum and the procedures of the school they will definitely and positively influence the social attitudes, ideals, and behaviors of the coming generation"[43] and through them enable the masses of society to reconstruct themselves, and by so doing reconstruct society. This means that "instead of shunning power, the profession [of education] should rather seek power and then strive to use that power fully and wisely and in the interests of the great masses of the people."[44] This calls for educators to take on new roles and new functions within our society, for at present they are but meek followers of social consensus rather than dynamic leaders who mold social attitudes.

In fact, education as it is presently conducted within schools must also take on entirely new functions and purposes. "That the existing school is leading the way to a better social order is a thesis which few informed persons would care to defend. . . . Only in the rarest of instances does it wage war on behalf of principle or ideal. Almost everywhere it is in the grip of conservative forces and is serving the cause of perpetuating ideas and institutions suited to an age that is gone."[45] As a result, schools as they presently exist are contributing to the social crisis and are out of touch with the needs of society. This is because the school has only been a follower of society and has simply reflected society's means of coping with what it perceives as reality. The school must now cast off the submissive reflective role and become the leader of society, for "If the schools are to be really effective, they must become centers for the building, and not merely for the contemplation of our civilization."[46] As Counts says, schools must

face squarely and courageously every social issue, come
to grips with life in all of its stark reality, establish an
organic relation with the community, develop a realistic
and comprehensive theory of welfare, fashion a compelling and challenging vision of human destiny, and become
somewhat less frightened than it is today of the bogeys
of imposition and indoctrination.[47]

This means that instead of reflecting society's present ineffective
social institutions the school must generate new strategies for
social survival and reconstruction, which the society will reflect.[48]
It must remake itself so that it will be in phase with the vision of
the future and in congruence with the changes underlying the
social crisis, so that it can prepare students to live in the society of
the future—getting them ready to remake the society of the
present into the society of the future. The way it can do this is by
developing, through the medium of its own personnel, curricula
designed within the context of the Social Reconstruction Ideology. The school then will become the catalyst that stimulates the
reconstruction of society.

Education as a Social Process

The primary aim of the Social Reconstruction developer is to
use education as a social process in order to reconstruct society.
His aim is to first educate society through the individual and then
to educate the individual through society. His concern is first with
the education of the group and then second with the education of
the individual. Within this context, learning experiences are
construed to be group experiences that take place through human
interaction; and the focus is on the "group mind" rather than the
"individual mind." The individual is important with the Social
Reconstruction Ideology. However, his happiness and fulfillment
are viewed as achievable only in relation to the group-centered
culture. Brameld places the individual in society when he writes:

The question of the importance of individual differences
will best be resolved, not by beginning with it, but by
ending with it. The point of departure should be human
similarities.... Once these have been agreed
upon ... we are then in a much more favorable position
to encourage those elements of individuality—those

deviations from the group pattern—that ultimately can
and should contribute to the attainment of that
design.[49]

One begins with questions of the group and ends with questions of
the individual; individual differences are defined as *deviations*
from the group; and elements of individuality are encouraged only
when they can and should contribute to the attainment of group
ends.

Here one speaks not of individual self-realization but of social
self-realization for both the society and the individual members of
society. The values of social self-realization became ones of
belonging to the group, appreciation by the group, and participation in the group.[50] Within this context social consensus plays a
central role; for it is believed that once a social consensus is
reached about the nature of the present society and the vision for
the future society, it will be possible for the "masses" to
appropriately reconstruct their society.[51] The aim is to fashion,
through education, a social consensus among the "masses" which
will by majority rule force the society to align itself with the
vision of the future utopia and thus eradicate the present social
crisis. It is thus through the creation of social consensus within
society that the developer hopes to achieve social reconstruction
both for society and by society.

Means of Education

The primary means of education used by the Social Reconstruction developer is the dialogue or group discussion. The dialogue is
a social means of educating a group of persons; it demands for its
use both a social context and human social interactions. The
dialogue is considered an ideal educational medium because it
makes use of language, which in its broad interpretation as "all
forms of symbolic codification"[52] places it in the position of
being "the mediator of all human perception,"[53] learning,
knowing, feeling, and acting.

The Social Reconstruction dialogue takes place among one or
more students and a teacher. The social interactions that take
place during the dialogue involve education being carried out by
the teacher in cooperation *with* the student. This means that the
teacher must be capable of learning what the student has to teach,

as well as the student learning what the teacher has to teach. It also means that the teacher must be capable of teaching what the student feels he needs to learn, as well as the student teaching the teacher what he needs to learn. The dialogue thus involves shared participation, responsibility, and interaction among its participants. The dialogue does not involve education being carried out by the teacher *for* the student, by the teacher *about* the student, or by the teacher *at* the student.

The Social Reconstruction dialogue at its best has three crucial dimensions: thought, commitment, and action. The potential for all three must be present in a dialogue for it to be vital. If a dialogue lacks the potential for action, then the thinking that takes place during the dialogue degenerates into useless verbalism. If a dialogue lacks the potential for thought, then the action that takes place as a result of the dialogue degenerates into meaningless activism.[54] If a dialogue lacks the potential for commitment, then the thinking that takes place during the dialogue will lack the power to be transformed into action. For a dialogue to be vital it must contain the potential for thought, action, and commitment tied together in interaction—if one is absent, then the others will suffer also. More precisely, if a dialogue does not have the potential for thought about society as it is and as it ought to be, the potential for commitment to transforming society as it is into society as it ought to be, and the potential for action directed toward such, then the dialogue is not vital within the context of the Social Reconstruction Ideology.

The content for a dialogue comes from those involved in the dialogue. It is a re-presentation to the group by its members of things they have experienced and now want to know more about or want to know in a new way. Thus, the actual experiences of those involved in the dialogue are crucial. The dialogue is defined by those experiences and must take into account those experiences as the persons who have had them perceive them. Although the dialogue is defined by the perceived experiences of its participants, it is important to note that it is not limited by those experiences. This is because the social interactions that take place during a dialogue can expand on the experiences of its participants (as when two people's thoughts are joined together to generate a new thought neither would have been capable of generating alone) and because the group can re-present the experiences of a participant back to him so that he can see them in a new way and thus re-perceive or re-experience them anew (as when one person's interpretation of the meaning of a particular experience allows another person who has had a similar experience to understand that experience in a way he had not previously understood it). What is important here is the centrality of the experiences of those participating in the dialogue to the dialogue. Anything said during the dialogue as well as any inputs into the dialogue from sources such as outside experts, books, movies, or the like must directly relate to the experienced difficulties, needs, and interests of those involved in the dialogue. If they do not, they will not be meaningful to those taking part in the dialogue and will not be able to be meaningfully discussed during the dialogue.

As a result, one must start a dialogue where the participants *are*. One must start a dialogue with what people have experienced to be their difficulties, needs, or interests as they themselves perceive them. This "starting where the people are"[55] is central not only to the dialogue, but is also central to the overall efforts of the Social Reconstruction developer while creating curricula. The Social Reconstruction developer believes that if education is to be meaningful to a person it must relate directly to his experiences. As a result, in creating a curriculum the Social Reconstruction developer must either find a way to tap the experiences of those who will be exposed to his curriculum or find a way of giving them the experiences he will build upon. It is from one's experiences *with* the existing social crisis and in response to a perceived difficulty that one has experienced *within* the existing social crisis that one is motivated to understand the nature of the existing society, to envision a future better society, and to act so as to transform the existing society into the future better society.

Within the context of the dialogue, there are two pedagogical techniques that the Social Reconstruction developer usually builds into his curriculum: (1) an "expository" technique in which students are intellectually converted to accept the developer's analysis of the present social crisis and vision of the future utopia, and (2) a "conditioning" technique in which students are subconsciously conditioned to live in the developer's future utopia and abhor the ills of the present crisis-ridden society. The former technique rests upon the belief that the student should be aware of the circumstances under which he lives and should be led to consciously reject the existing society and embrace the society of the future: that the decisions and choices must be consciously and cognitively accepted by the student and that he must be aware of what is happening to him. The latter technique rests upon the belief that the best way to reconstruct society is to simply condition people to live in the society of the future: that every society indoctrinates its members into it without the members having any real choice in the matter or understanding of the indoctrination; and that since the behaviors desirable in citizens of the future are known, they should simply be programmed into students of the present.

When using the expository technique, the dialogue tends to proceed by having students—as individuals and as a group which formulates and agrees upon a consensus—verbally analyze society, formulate a vision of a utopian society in which the faults and weaknesses of the present society are eradicated, develop a social conscience which impels them to commit themselves to transform the existent society into the future utopia, and decide how to act so as to implement the future utopia. This mode of education is dependent upon the power of ideas to move men to act so as to reconstruct themselves and society. The belief is that if a person thinks in terms of a reconstructed society, he will act in such a manner as to bring into existence a reconstructed society.

When using the conditioning technique, the dialogue process itself and the environment surrounding the dialogue mold the student to act in accordance with the values and modes of behavior inherent in the curriculum developer's vision of the future utopian society. Thus, if sharing behavior is valued within the future utopia, sharing behavior—in contrast to competitive behavior—would be directly conditioned into the student during the dialogue by having him conform to discussion norms which demand sharing behavior and censor competitive behavior. In this case, the norms of the discussion and the behaviors expected before, during, and after the discussion, as built into the discussion process itself by the curriculum developer, become the forces which mold the education of the student. Here the assumption is that the best way to get the student to live in accordance with the vision of the future is actually to have him live in accordance with that vision. It is by *living* the good life that one will learn to live the good life—not merely by *thinking* about the good life.

Both the expository and conditioning techniques of educating students during a dialogue are used simultaneously and in such a way as to reinforce each other.

EDUCATION THROUGH INDOCTRINATION

The question of how the Social Reconstruction developer—whose point of view is always and necessarily a minority point of view within society—is to convince society what is best for it and thus bring into existence the desired social consensus raises questions about the civic responsibility of the educator to the society he serves and questions about the indoctrination of a majority group by a minority. These questions arise because the developer believes that his insight into the nature of society and what is good for the "masses" is superior to and different from that of the "masses," and because he believes that it is his job to transform society's values so that they accord with his own.

Civic Responsibility

Does the curriculum developer have the right to attempt to change the social patterns of a culture against the will of the members of the culture? Does the developer have the right to educate children to live in a world that is alien to that of their parents and of which their parents do not approve? What civic responsibility does the educator have to the society he serves?

From the Social Reconstruction perspective, the educator has the civic responsibility not to simply reflect the wishes of his society but to do what is best for his society. In fact, "Representing as they do, not the interests of the moment or of any special class, but rather the common and abiding interests of the people, [educators and] teachers are under heavy social obligation to protect and further those interests."[56] If this involves educating the children of a culture in such a way that they will reject the existing culture in reconstructing it, it is necessary to do so for the good of the culture. Educators are not to be simply reflectors of the culture but leaders of the culture. They must be innovators in analyzing the culture to find out what is best for the culture and in acting to achieve that which is best for the culture. It is always the educator's responsibility to do what *he* believes is best for his culture, independent of what the *culture* believes is in its best interests. This role for the educator is different from the role he has had in the past. It is a role that requires that the good educator be one who can change society in line with his beliefs about society. No longer is the educator simply charged with the responsibility of inculcating in children the myths of their society or developing within children their ability to dispassionately analyze social history. The Social Reconstruction educator must take a stance with respect to the current social crisis and educate students in such a way that they too adopt that stance and go out among the masses of society to work to reconstruct society in line with the requirements of that stance. This means that:

> Always and everywhere genuine education is a form of practical endeavor—a form of social action. This means that the educator fails in his line of duty if he refuses to step out of academic cloisters, . . . reject the role of a disinterested spectator, take an active part in shaping events, make selections among social values, and adopt, however tentatively and broadly, some conception of social welfare and policy.[57]

Indoctrination

In order to accomplish what he believes is best for his society, the curriculum developer can use whatever means he requires, society will tolerate, and his vision will support. But the type of means one uses to accomplish preconceived ends—as inherent in the developer's biased vision of the future good society—raises the question of indoctrination. Does the educator have the right to indoctrinate students, either with or without their consent? The answer is, yes! Education must "become less frightened than it is today of the bogies of imposition and indoctrination"[58] and deliberately use them openly and forthrightly during instruction.

There are many reasons why the Social Reconstruction developer condones the use of indoctrination. Central to them all is the belief that indoctrination is unavoidable and that education cannot avoid being biased. The Social Reconstruction developer holds that indoctrination is an inevitable consequence of living in social groups. As Counts phrases it: "The most crucial of all circumstances conditioning human life is birth into a particular culture. By birth one becomes a Chinese, an Englishman, a Hottentot, a Sioux Indian, a Turk, or a . . . American. . . . By being nurtured on a body of culture, however . . . the individual is at once imposed upon"[59] and indoctrinated. To grow from infancy to adulthood within a culture is to become indoctrinated to and by that culture. In fact, "the induction of the immature individual into the life of the group"[60] is the traditional role of the school. And "education, in discharging its function of inducting the child into the life of the group, stands at the focal point in the process of cultural evolution—at the point of contact between the older and the younger generation where values are selected and rejected."[61] As such, the school necessarily acts as an agent of society in indoctrinating the child into society's approved modes of behavior and thought. As Counts phrases it:

> I am prepared to defend the thesis that all education contains a large element of imposition [or indoctrination], that in the very nature of the case this is inevitable, that the existence and evolution of society depend upon it, that it is consequently eminently desirable, and that the frank acceptance of this fact by the educator is a major professional obligation. I even contend that the failure to do this involves the clothing of one's own deepest prejudices in the garb of universal truth.[62]

From the Social Reconstruction point of view, bias and partiality are inherent in the very nature of *all* education. On the less obvious level, the questions the teacher asks have embedded in their language cultural biases, and the social interactions acceptable within the school—respect for teachers, for example—have embedded within them cultural biases. On the more obvious level, the questions of who will teach, what to teach, where to teach, and how to teach all involve value decisions that make impartiality utterly impossible—for "in the making of the selection the dice must always be weighted in favor of this or that."[63] Educators who believe themselves impartial and neutral transmitters of instruction are viewed by Social Reconstruction developers as sorely ignorant of the nature of their endeavors. Impartiality within the schools, therefore, is impossible; indoctrination is an integral and essential part of education.

What is really at issue is not whether indoctrination will take place in schools or whether schools will be biased. What is at issue is whether a social minority will use indoctrination for purposes other than those of simply getting the individual to fit into and adjust to society as it is. That is, what is at issue is whether a social minority will indoctrinate the masses of society through the schools—at the point "where values are selected and rejected"—to use new modes of behavior and ways of thinking that are now foreign to them. The Social Reconstruction developer's answer is clear: "Neutrality with respect to the great issues that agitate society, while perhaps theoretically possible, is practically tantamount to giving support to the forces of conservatism."[64] And to give support to the forces of conservatism is to perpetuate the existing social crisis that threatens society's very existence. Thus, educators must not only use indoctrination, but they must also use it in the cause of social reconstruction in order to overcome the existing social crisis.

Once the issue of whether or not the Social Reconstruction developer can use indoctrination within the schools to change the nature of society is settled, other questions arise. These questions include: From what sources should the indoctrination come? Toward what ends should the indoctrination serve? How will the indoctrination be imposed? Meaningful answers to these questions must derive from the particulars of the situation: the social crisis the developer is struggling to overcome, his vision of the future utopian society, and the time, place, circumstances, and people being dealt with. However, the following statement by George Counts gives the flavor of how social bias can be introduced into the school through indoctrination:

> The several divisions of subject matter composing the curriculum would all be given a social meaning. This may be illustrated by reference to geography, science, and art. Geography would be taught and studied, not merely as a body of information useful and interesting to the individual, but as the physical basis for the building of a finer civilization and culture. The natural

resources of the nation would actually be regarded as possessions of the nation—as the source of a richer and more abundant common life, rather than as fields for the operation of profit-seeking enterprise and the accumulation of great private fortunes. In similar manner, science and technology would be looked upon neither as a leisure-time activity of a special class nor as an instrument for personal aggrandizement, but rather as the spear-point of man's age-long struggle with nature. And art would be taught primarily, not as a vehicle of individual expression, as important as that is, but as a means of enriching and beautifying the common life. Instead of spending itself in museums and galleries and the private homes of the rich, it would bring beauty of line and form and color to factories, cities, highways, parks, great public buildings, the objects of ordinary use, and the dwellings of the people. All of the subjects of study would be integrated by the mighty and challenging conception of the building of a great industrial civilization conceived in terms of the widest interests of the masses.[65]

Note in this statement how school subjects are used for purposes other than those (supposedly) inherent in the school subject itself.

Social Reconstruction Slogans

Several practices utilized by Social Reconstruction developers to bring about a better society reside under the slogans of "crap detecting," "the medium is the message," and "relevance."

"Crap detecting" is a slogan which refers to the analysis of the faults of society.[66] "Crap detecting" is to develop "in youth the attitudes and skill of social, political, and cultural criticism"[67] that will provide "the young with a 'What is it good for?' perspective on its own society."[68] Social Reconstruction developers believe that "If the school is to function at all in the betterment of the social order, it must expose pitilessly and clearly the shortcomings in contemporary society."[69] To accomplish this the skill of "crap detecting" is taught to students in order to provide them with a "set of criteria by which our present culture can be judged, and a set of tools with which"[70] to uncover its shortcomings. The goal during "crap detecting" is not only to examine society but also to examine the meanings one has accumulated about the nature of society so that those meanings may be subjected to testing, verifying, reordering, and reclassifying. It is hoped that "crap detecting" will enable the participants to unlearn the irrelevant problem-solving strategies taught them by an obsolete society. From crap detecting one is to move to "utopia construction."

"The medium is the message" is a slogan utilized to insist that the environment in which one learns and the process by which one learns have a profound effect upon what one learns. " 'The medium is the message' implies that the invention of a dichotomy between content and method is both naive and dangerous. It implies that the critical content of any learning experience is the method or process through which the learning occurs"[71] and the nature of the environment within which the learning occurs. The "medium" here refers to the process by which one learns and the environment within which one learns. The " 'message' here means the perceptions you are allowed to build, the attitudes you are enticed to assume, the sensitivities you are encouraged to develop—almost all of the things you learn to see and feel and value."[72] Social Reconstruction developers manipulate environmental and methodological variables to shape the beliefs, attitudes, and knowledges of students in order to achieve the desirable social consensus. Techniques include the use of sensitivity groups to teach responsiveness to the "group mind" and "social consensus." Field experiences, such as participation in labor disputes, clean-up of polluted environments, and work within poor neighborhoods are designed to teach students "appropriate" and "inappropriate" values by having them experience conditions brought into existence through the lack of the appropriate values. Town meetings and student-governed schools are often designed to emphasize the role of social consensus, and are often used to mold student opinion about what is in the best interest of the group.

"Relevance" is a slogan used to emphasize that what is to be learned is most easily acquired by the learner if it has an immediate emotional attraction to him and if it is identifiable by him as important to him and stimulating to his interest. Social Reconstruction developers assume that "There is no way to help a learner to be disciplined, active, and thoroughly engaged unless *he* perceives a problem to be a problem or whatever is to-be-learned as worth learning, and unless he plays an active role in determining the process of solution."[73] "Relevance" is interpreted to mean that education must start where the people are, for "people will learn, and put to effective use, only what they themselves determine is necessary."[74] That is, it is assumed that education moves people to think and commit themselves to action only "in response to a perceived difficulty,"[75] need, or interest. This means that the curriculum developer must discover what the needs, difficulties, and interests of the people are in order to motive them to reflect upon the nature of the present social crisis, to envision a future utopian society, and to act so as to transform the present society into the future utopia. It means that the Social Reconstruction developer must "learn from the people [the nature of their needs as they perceive them]; start their education where they are,"[76] "and let the [curricular] program grow out of the people's needs."[77] As such, the Social Reconstruction developer must link his vision of a reconstructed society to the needs of the masses. All work done *for* the masses must start from their needs, in such a way that the masses come to see that the work *must* be done and that it can only be done by *them*. Society cannot be changed in accordance with the Social Reconstruction developer's vision until, through the developer's work, the masses have become conscious of the need to change society in terms of their own felt needs and are willing and determined to do so. Note that "relevance" does not refer to assumptions about appropriateness of content to the level of student maturity. It does not refer to developmental issues. It refers to *motivational* issues.

Let us now turn from an examination of beliefs affecting the general context within which the Social Reconstruction developer works to an examination of several concepts affecting the manner in which the developer creates curricula. This includes an examination of the developer's conceptualization as to his aims as a curriculum developer, the child, learning, teaching, knowledge, and evaluation.

AIMS OF THE CURRICULUM DEVELOPER

The aim of the Social Reconstruction developer is to eliminate from his culture those aspects which he believes undesirable, to substitute in their place social values which he believes desirable, and by so doing to reconstruct his culture so that it and its constituent members "shall attain maximum satisfaction of their material and spiritual wants."[78] As such, he wishes to redirect the growth of his society toward a utopian vision which he believes to be more just and satisfying than the realities which presently control society.

To accomplish this the developer directs his energy towards creating a social consensus which rejects the faults of the existent society and accepts the virtues of the future utopia. To develop the social consensus, the developer attempts to manipulate society at the point where it inducts the child into the life of the culture—at the point "where values are selected and rejected." This takes place within the context of society's educational system. By educating youth to live in a society superior to the existing one, it is hoped that societal growth can be redirected so as to bring into existence a better society.

To accomplish this the developer builds a socio-educational program—a curriculum—which prepares people to live in the future utopian society and which gets them ready to actively manipulate the destiny of society.

Within this context there exist many different visions of the nature of the future utopian society, and many different strategies which dictate the type of curriculum necessary to transform the existent society into the future utopian society. The overall orientation, however, as illustrated in Figure 5.1, is one which begins with analysis of existing objective social reality, moves to a projection of a subjective future utopia, and then moves back to manipulation of the existing objective social reality in order to transform it into the subjective future utopia.

THE CHILD
The Child as an Agent of the Developer's Utopia

The child is viewed as a potential contributing member of society who will stimulate the reconstruction of the society. As such, the child is not viewed as a child, as an individual, or as a person who defines his own meaning. Rather he is seen as a potential member of society and as a person who exists to further

Figure 5.1

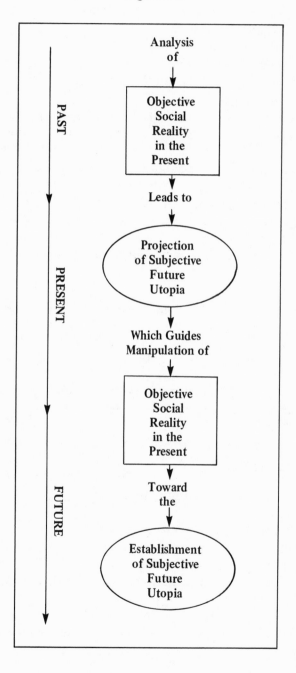

an end external to himself. The child is not intrinsically defined but is extrinsically defined as a derivative of the developer's concept of his utopian society.[79]

At birth the child is viewed as being by nature "neither good nor bad; he is merely a bundle of potentialities which may be developed in manifold directions."[80] It is the role of education to guide the development of those potentialities so that they contribute to the functioning of the good society which will in turn give value to the developed potentialities.[81] The child "is born helpless":[82] as he grows, develops his potentialities, and becomes inducted into his culture, he attains the power and freedom to mold the world within which he lives. It is the role of education to guide the development of the child's growth so that he appropriately uses his freedom and power to mold the existent society into the best possible future society.[83] At birth the child is viewed as a meaning making organism who has little meaning within himself. As he grows, the child takes on meaning by actively interpreting the world to himself. It is the role of education to shape the meaning created by the child and the ways in which the child makes meaning so that they are in conformity with the vision of the utopian society.[84] As the child grows, he is viewed as linearly progressing towards an educated state from which he can contribute to the reconstruction of society: he is not viewed within a developmental context which emphasizes the child living fully within each of the developmental stages through which he passes.[85] It is the role of education to speed the child towards his educated state of being so that he can actively participate in the reconstruction of society. As such the child is not viewed as an agent of himself but rather as an agent of the developer's vision of the future utopian society.

The Child as a Meaning Maker

The child is viewed as a maker of meaning. He makes meaning for himself as the result of being stimulated by the environment within which he lives. The view that the child is a meaning maker is summed up in the following passage:

> We now know that each man *creates his own unique world*, that he, and he alone, *generates whatever reality he can ever know.* . . . . It turns out, too, that language is

far from being neutral in the process of perceiving, as well as in the process of evaluating perceptions. We have been accustomed to thinking that language "expresses" thought and that it "reflects" what we see [and experience within our environment]. We now know that this belief is naive and simplistic, that our languaging process is fully implicated in any and all of our attempts to assess reality . . . *we do not "get" meaning from things, we assign meaning.* But beyond this . . . the meaning we assign is a function of the pattern or system of symbols through which we order and relate whatever it is we are dealing with. In other words, *whatever is out there [in our environment] isn't anything until we make it something, and then it "is" whatever we make it.*[86]

There are four corollaries to the assumption that man is a meaning maker. First, Social Reconstruction developers distinguish between subjective reality within the learner and objective reality outside the learner. Second, Social Reconstruction developers assume that meaning resides within the individual and his subjective reality and not outside of the individual within objective reality. Third, it is believed that the child makes meaning as a result of being stimulated by his environment. Fourth, it is assumed that it is the child who actively makes meaning for himself; that he is not a passive absorber of meaning conveyed to him by an agent external to himself. This view of the child as a meaning maker is portrayed in Figure 5.2.

Figure 5.2

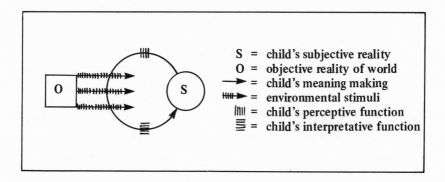

S = child's subjective reality
O = objective reality of world
→ = child's meaning making
⊪► = environmental stimuli
⊪ = child's perceptive function
≣ = child's interpretative function

In viewing the child as a meaning maker, four different aspects of the child's mind are distinguished. First, the contents of the child's mind are noted. Herein entitled the child's "meaning," this includes such factors as the beliefs, facts, theories, affiliations, fears, hopes, etc., which are stored within the child's mind. Second, the organization of the child's knowledge is noted. Entitled the child's "meaning structure"—popularly called by such names as knowledge structure, life space, and frame of reference— this designates at least the organization of meaning within the child's mind and the storage and retrieval functions governing the intake, output, and redistribution of meaning within the child's mind. Third, the perceptual filters which control the types of stimuli the child perceives from among the many sensations that impinge upon him are noted; they are herein entitled the "perceptive function." They control the manner in which the child perceives reality. (They are portrayed by the vertical crosshatching on the meaning making arrow in Figure 5.2.) Fourth, the mental mechanisms which control the meaning which is given to the sensations the child perceives are noted. Such are herein entitled the "interpretative function" and control the manner in which the child interprets reality. (They are portrayed by the horizontal crosshatching on the meaning making arrow in Figure 5.2.)

Two things are important to note in the Social Reconstruction developer's view of the child as a meaning maker. First, the child is viewed somewhat as a computer simulation that is activated by itself. As such, while creating curricula, the developer works as if he can see within the child's mind—as if the child's mind can be rewired and reorganized—and behaves towards the child as though he is an instrument that can be manipulated to carry out an end external to himself. Second, the child's mind is viewed as containing several types of knowledge: it contains meaning, meaning structures, perceptual functions, and interpretative functions. The child's perceptive function, interpretative function, and meaning structure are important because they affect the manner in which the child perceives, interprets, and organizes reality. They affect, for example, whether or not the child hears certain overtones in peoples' complaints about society, how he interprets the overtones he hears, and how he gives meaning to that information by fitting it into his meaning structure.

The Child in Society

The child is not viewed as an individual but as a member of a social group. He can only realize his potential as a human being in social interaction with others, can only be educated in a human community, and can only act to bring into existence the future utopian society in communal relationship with a group of other human beings. The child is defined, to a very large degree, by the social situations in which he finds himself. He is defined by social situations as they affect him and as he affects them. He is educated through social situations as they affect him and as he affects them and through his ability to understand the nature of the interactions that take place and through his ability to act upon his understanding within social situations. In other words, *"Men are because they are in a* [social] *situation."*[87] And they will further actualize their potential as human beings the more they understand the nature of their social predicament and act upon it.

There are two different types of social communities to which the child belongs that are of interest to the Social Reconstruction developer: the community outside the school, within which the child spends most of his life and upon which the child is to act to reconstruct society, and the community within the school over which the developer exercises control. For the Social Reconstruction developer, the extent to which he can merge these two types of communities is the extent to which he will be successful in providing a meaningful education. That is, the extent to which the developer will be able to educate the child to reconstruct society is viewed as related to the extent to which he is capable of using the time the school has with the child to educate the child *about* his community outside school, *within* his community outside school, *in terms of* his community outside school, and *through* his community outside school. This involves dealing with all aspects of the child's life as they will be lived within the community outside school: it involves dealing "with not only the development of intellectual powers, but also the formation of character, the acquisitions of habits, attitudes, and dispositions suited to a given set of living conditions, a given level of culture, and a given body of ideals and aspirations."[88] When the Social Reconstruction developer sees the child, he sees the "whole child": he sees all aspects of the child's thinking, feeling, relating, and acting *in interaction with each other* and as they will function in the situations within which the child will find himself outside of the school.

LEARNING
Meaning and Structure

The curriculum developer working within the Social Reconstruction Ideology views learning as active assimilation of new experience into the learner's meaning structure in such a way as to force his meaning structure to accommodate to the new experience. There are two significant components of this view of learning. The first hinges upon the phrase meaning making: learning is thought of in terms of the learner making meaning out of his sensations. Learning is a process of actively assimilating and accommodating experience in such a way that it makes sense to the learner. The second component of this view of learning depends upon the concept of meaning structure: learning occurs with respect to what one already knows about the world, and it is meaningful only when it can be accommodated to one's overall conception of reality. As a result, learning involves learning things within the context in which they occur and in terms of what one already knows.

Meaning Making

The learner is viewed as an active agent in his learning. Learning is not a passive process of incorporating objective reality into the mind by simple absorption. It is an active process during which the learner chooses from among his many sensory experiences those with which he will become cognizant (the perceptive function), and interprets those sensations into perceptions which have meaning in relation to his existing meaning structure (the interpretative function). That is:

> We do not get our perceptions from the "things" around us. Our perceptions come from us. This does not mean that there is nothing outside of our skins. It does mean that whatever is "out there" can never be known except as it is filtered through a human nervous system. We can never get outside of our own skins. "Reality" is a perception, located somewhere behind the eyes. . . .

What we perceive is largely a function of our previous experiences, our assumptions, and our purposes (i.e., needs). In other words, the perceiver decides what an object is, where it is, and why it is according to his purpose and the assumptions that he makes at any given time. You tend to perceive what you want and need to perceive, and what your past experience has led you to assume will "work" for you. . . . If rain is falling from the sky, some people will head for shelter, others will enjoy walking in it. Their perceptions of "what is happening" are different as reflected in the fact that they "do" different things. The fact that both groups will agree to the sentence "It is raining" does not mean they will perceive the "event" in the same way.[89]

Both the choices of which sensation to perceive and how to interpret those perceptions are active functions on the part of the learner which are uniquely determined by the learner's existing meaning structure. Meaning is actively created by the learner and not passively absorbed by him: the subjective reality that he comes to know results from personally impressing meaning onto objective reality.

It is important to note that what the learner comes to know is not nature itself but nature actively interpreted through such things as his language. The learner incorporates into himself the stimuli impinging upon him by passing it through his perceptive and interpretative functions, while applying meaning giving filters to it such as his language and modes of thinking. In McLuhanesque terms, the medium (the mind) is the message (what one knows) in the sense that the operators governing the working of the mind actively mold psychological sensations into mental perceptions. The works of Edward Sapir and Benjamin Lee Whorf, for example, are often used to illustrate how the structure and lexicon of an individual's language mold the manner in which the individual uniquely perceives reality.[90]

Meaning Structure

One learns things in terms of what one already knows and within the context in which they occur. It is believed, first, that learning can take place *only* in relation to what one already knows. For experiences to make sense to the learner, they must be capable of being accommodated into the learner's meaning structure. This means that they must be of a form and contain a content that relates to both the learner's personality structure and his totality of past learning experiences. The mere occurrence of a "psychological fact" does not result in learning. It is only when the occurrence is related to other phases of the learner's experience and capable of being related to and incorporated into the learner's meaning structure that learning takes place.

It is, in fact, the learner's meaning structure which gives import to what a learner perceives. The significance of this is that whatever the learner hears or sees will be meaningful to him only on his own terms and not on the terms of the emitter of the information: what he learns will be a function of his past experiences, his assumptions, and his purposes—and not those of the stimulator of his sensations.

Second, it is believed that things must be learned within the context in which they occur for valid meaning to be infused into them. The concern is with learning taking place in terms of total patterns of events, with respect to gestalts of occurrences, and in organic relatedness, rather than in atomic unrelatedness. As Patty puts it: "The task is not to get the facts, noetic elements, and then to organize them—not to let someone else do all or part for us; it is to get the facts-in-organization and to experience the whole learningfully."[9][1] To be valid and meaningful, learning must be the product of insight into the patterns or gestalts relating the parts of an event to the total occurrence of the event.

Nature of Learning

There are a number of important interrelated characteristics of the nature of learning. First, Social Reconstruction developers are primarily concerned with learning as a social rather than an individual act. They are concerned primarily with social groups rather than with individuals learning something. Learning, in both process and product, in both means and ends, aims at "social self-realization" rather than individual self-realization.[9][2] As such, learning not only requires that a social group acquire knowledge but also that it reach a consensus about both the nature and truth of the knowledge acquired. Learning is always directed towards reaching social consensus or agreement. In fact, "the objective of the entire [learning] process is to attain a consensus upon which the group can depend and from which it can act"[93] to reconstruct society.

Second, learning is to take place "both in the classroom and the community."[94] Learning requires immersion in and interaction with a social group that "extends beyond the school proper into the community"[95] outside the school. This means that Social Reconstruction curricula require two separate social settings within which learning takes place: within the school and outside the school. The learner needs to interact with both of these communities for learning to be real and vital.

Third, learning takes place through communication. Communication can include such things as singing, acting, sociodrama, group processing, or values clarification. The group discussion or dialogue is the most commonly used form of communication. From a practical point of view, learning through communication

means, to begin with, that the traditional classroom becomes completely transformed. Instead of communication being limited to the imparting of indirect evidence from textbooks, pictures, or lectures, learning takes place by the reciprocal expression among students and teachers alike. The effort to *articulate* interests [feelings or thoughts] is encouraged and respected. Likewise the effort to *interpret* all evidence provided by science, art, or history replaces the passive recitation, which does virtually nothing to bring such evidence into vital relationship with one's own experience. The more that genuine back-and-forth communication takes place, the more spontaneous it becomes, and the more facile and precise the meanings that emerge.[96]

Fourth, learning involves some form of direct experience: "fundamental to learning is the kind of evidence about our wants which springs from our own experience, and of which we ourselves become directly aware. Education that fails to provide generous opportunity for such experience . . . cannot hope to reach successful practice of social consensus."[97] Learning is not limited to firsthand experiences, but the Social Reconstruction developer tries to keep learning as close to firsthand experience as possible.

Thus, if a group is to learn something like history, about which they cannot have firsthand experiences, the curriculum developer attempts to provide firsthand accounts of what happened (rather than colorless descriptions of descriptions of descriptions of what occurred).

Fifth, valuable learning requires not just thought, but also an emotional response to what has been understood that includes commitment to one position or another and action directed towards reconstructing society. Counts hints at this tripartite nature of learning as thought, commitment, and action when he writes that society requires learners who, while "capable of gathering and digesting facts, are at the same time able to think in terms of life, make decisions, and act."[9][8]

Sixth, learning requires interaction of the learner with the environment outside himself. Learning is meaning making that is initiated by an active learner. However, the learner must interact with someone or some situation to make meaning. In terms of Figure 5.2, the learner (S) does not learn in isolation from stimuli coming from a reality outside himself (O). Rather, he learns as a result of his meaning making endeavors, engaging and interacting with stimuli from an outside source. That is, there must be a learner (S) actively interacting with a reality outside himself (O) for meaning to be made and learning to take place within the learner. If the learner does not actively interact with something—as when a teacher lectures *at* the learner rather than discussing *with* the learner—meaning making, and thus learning, is not viewed as taking place. In the case of the teacher lecturing at the student, information may be processed through the student or even stored within the student; but if the student is not actively making meaning, he is not viewed as learning. (At a later point the learner might call up out of his memory what the teacher lectured about to "discuss it with himself" so that then he can make meaning and thus learn; however, this requires a strained social interaction taking place within a single person.) Learning through interaction takes place within a social group where both the group affects the learner and the learner affects the group. Here it is important that "Children should continually share in a social environment which they enrich by that sharing, and which enriches them,"[9][9] for learning requires a two-way process of affecting and being affected by a social group—and through that process a coming to learn about the nature of the interactions taking place.

TEACHING

The intent of teaching is to indoctrinate students into the developer's view of the nature of the existing society and vision of the future utopia, and by so doing to motivate them to reconstruct society. Those aspects of the student which teaching is to affect include the student's meaning structure, the student's modes of perceiving and interpreting events within his environment, and the accumulation of particular meanings which the student holds to be true. By appropriately molding these aspects of the student's mind, it is hoped that the student will learn to act and think in such a way as to support the transformation of the existing society into the future utopia.

The Social Reconstruction developer can utilize a variety of different forms of teaching to accomplish his ends. The two which will be discussed here are called the discussion method and the experience method. Both depend upon the technique of having the student learn indirectly through the medium-experiences which he encounters while engaging in an activity whose visible message is not necessarily the most important aspect of the curriculum.

The Discussion Method

The discussion method of teaching involves engaging a group of students in a conversation while the teacher elicits "from students the meanings that they have already stored up so that they may subject those meanings to a testing and verifying, recording and reclassifying, modifying and extending process."[100] The topic about which the discussion is held is not the important part of the teaching. The important part is the process of having the students examine their meanings, their meaning structure, their perceptive functions, and their interpretative functions while discussing a topic. The content of the discussion is, in a sense, the knowledge and ways of knowing already accepted by the student; the student is assumed to learn in relation to what he already knows. The assumption underlying this mode of teaching is that in order to mold the knowledge and ways of knowing already accepted by the student, such must be regurgitated by the student so that they can be examined and reconstructed. The discussion process allows the teacher to get the student to expose his meanings to the class so that the class—through the guidance of the teacher—can guide the student, through peer-group pressure, to reconstruct his meanings.

This mode of teaching is characterized in Figure 5.3 and Figure 5.4. Figure 5.3 shows the student engaging in a discussion. By exposing his meanings to the discussion group, he thus opens himself up to having his meanings reconstructed through the discussion process. During the discussion process, the teacher does not impart information directly to the students, as portrayed in Figure 5.4 (a). Rather, the teacher engages in reciprocal expression

Figure 5.3

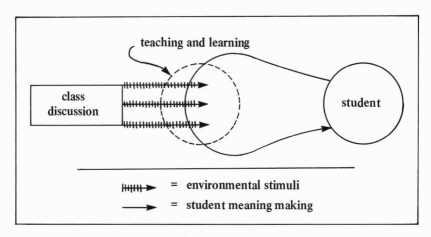

with students, while providing the rules for the discussion and the model for the mode of thinking that is to take place, as portrayed in Figure 5.4 (b) and (c).

The instructive function during this reciprocal expression, where the teacher acts more as a colleague than a prophet or judge, is imbedded in the type of language the teacher uses and urges students to use by example. The types of questions, the types of evidence, the types of value judgments, the modes of argumentation, and the criteria of relevance the teacher uses during discussion, become models of behavior for the student to imitate. Here it is the medium (the discussion itself) that is designed to provide the teaching, more than the message (the topic of discussion).

Figure 5.4

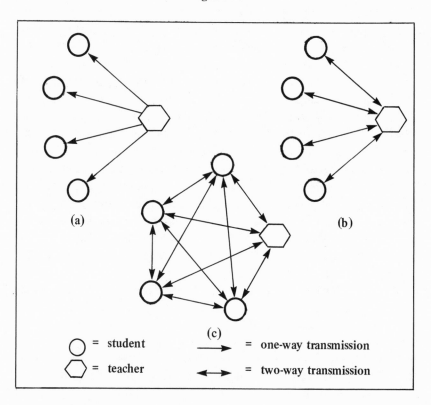

(a)

(b)

(c)

◯ = student   ⟶ = one-way transmission

⬠ = teacher   ⟷ = two-way transmission

The Experience Method

The experience method of teaching involves placing students in an environment so that they can learn from those who usually function within that environment. Experiences provided students may range from participation in picket lines and union strikes to ecological restoration, political campaigning, or rural commune living. The environments within which students are placed and those alongside of whom they work are especially chosen so as to indoctrinate the student into some particular aspect of the developer's view of the nature of the existing society or vision for the future utopia. It is assumed that the student will absorb the attitudes and values, modes of perception and interpretation, and "world view" of those normally engaged in the environment: this is because they will experience firsthand the reasons for the existence of such knowledges and ways of knowing, and because they will get caught up in the immediacy of the situation and be carried away by it in such a manner that they will mold themselves to be like the people who normally function within the environment in order to survive. The experience method of teaching thus involves using an approximation of an apprentice system of education to indoctrinate the student into the developer's view of the existing society and vision of the future utopia, instead of to teach a trade. Here teaching involves providing the students with placements in environments sufficiently extreme to cause the desired learning to take place, but not so foreign to students that they develop counter-reactions; it involves providing the students with counseling sessions designed to help the students adjust to the environment in which they find themselves; and it involves providing the students with discussion sessions similar to those used within the discussion method of teaching. Note that the counseling and discussion sessions are a crucial part of the experience method—it is in these sessions that the students and teacher engage in mutual meaning making (learning) under the careful guidance of the teacher. Within the experience method, the teacher is not an imparter of information but a colleague who can be trusted and confided in as a friend. This puts the teacher and the class on the same side of the experience and allows them to share meaning structures.

Both the experience and discussion methods of teaching make use of the techniques of group dynamics to teach the student sensitivity and responsiveness to individuals within the group and to group pressures. In such a context, learning through group dynamics is a powerful means of subliminally teaching such social self-realization values as belonging to the group, appreciation by the group, and participation in the group.[101] It is important to teach such values because the aim of the developer is not to simply educate individuals but to educate a social consensus within society.

Characteristics of Teaching
Several characteristics of what Social Reconstruction developers consider to be good teaching are common among both the discussion and experience methods of teaching. First, both are

group methods, making use of group pressures to mold the student to conform to a preconceived standard. Not only are the visible messages often social, but also the medium used to convey the invisible messages is a social medium. Second, both methods demand and make use of relevance to the life of the student as a motivating factor. Within the discussion method, the topics discussed often come from the expressed concerns of the students, in order to be appealing enough to them so that they will become engaged in the discussion and expose themselves; while, within the experience method, relevance comes from the immediacy of the situation in which the student finds himself. Third, both methods make use of the teacher as a colleague or companion to be looked up to by students, rather than as an authority who has control over students. The teacher and the students are viewed as on the same side of either the discussion or the experience: they are allied against the evils of the world, and they complement rather than combat each other. As a result, teaching is not an oppressive endeavor: it is not the case that the teacher knows everything and the students know nothing; rather, both bring experiences to share with each other during instruction. It is not the case that the teacher actively thinks and the students passively absorb; rather, both actively engage in meaning making in the presence of each other. It is not the case that the teacher talks and the students listen; rather, both talk and listen as partners in a mutual endeavor. It is not the case that the teacher chooses content and the students accept it; rather, both have experiences that contribute to the content of instruction. And, fourth, the important learnings in both methods are subliminal learnings that are not easily specified or even visible. Such learnings are conveyed through the learning medium—such as the standards of proper discussion—and involve manipulation and indoctrination of the student by the learning medium.

Social Reconstruction developers view the attitudes, interpretations, and visions of teachers to be of crucial importance during teaching. They believe that *"there can be no significant innovation in education that does not have at its center the attitude of teachers*, and it is an illusion to think otherwise. The beliefs, feelings, and assumptions of teachers are the air of a learning environment; they determine the quality of life within it."[102] So important are the personal attributes and philosophy of the teacher that during teacher training for the use of a new curriculum more emphasis is usually placed on appropriately developing the personality and philosophic vision of the teacher than on training the teacher in the technical skills of teaching.

In addition, Social Reconstruction developers believe that teachers should be "genuinely qualified to provide American communities with a vigorous, enlightened, and public-spirited type of leadership, ready and competent to challenge the power of selfish interests and to champion the cause of the masses of the people."[103] This means both that teachers must be "people on fire with an awareness of injustice and the determination to correct it"[104] and that "teachers should deliberately reach for power and then make the most of their conquest."[105]

KNOWLEDGE
Types of Knowledge

For curriculum developers working within the Social Reconstruction Ideology, knowledge is made up of three categories of elements: personal meanings, perceptive and interpretative functions, and meaning structures. Personal meanings include such things as facts, assumptions, hopes, fears, and information. Perceptive and interpretative functions designate the operators which govern the manner in which the child perceives and interprets reality. Meaning structures designate the organizations of personal meaning within the child's mind and the operators which relate personal meanings to each other.

Knowledge and Value

Knowledge embodies both truth and value: it embraces both intelligence and a corresponding moral stance with respect to that intelligence (whether in the form of meaning, functions, or structures). There is thus an interdependence among knowledge and values.[106] This interdependence has its origin within the Social Reconstruction developer's view of reality from the perspective of a future utopia. By processing reality through the vision of a future utopia—which to the developer becomes "an object of religious faith"[107]—intelligence becomes good or bad, moral or immoral, as it supports or refutes the developer's utopian vision. As a result, values and intelligence are viewed as real in the same way; and little differentiation is made between the questions "Is x real?" and "Is x moral?" A scientific fact (political interpretation, religious hope, or affiliative emotion) is viewed from the perspective of "Is it worthwhile intelligence with respect to the analysis of the existing society and projection of the future society?" Knowledge is always good knowledge or evil knowledge, worthwhile knowledge or worthless knowledge, moral knowledge or immoral knowledge. Knowledge is not an impartial quantity and knowing is not a neutral affair.[108] Knowledge is of worth because it contributes to the attainment of the future social utopia; and knowledge-getting is a moral activity inseparable from the cultural activity of searching for and implementing a satisfactory vision for the future good society.

Knowledge and Reality

The Social Reconstruction curriculum developer distinguishes between subjective reality and objective reality and believes that worthwhile knowledge resides within the subjective reality of both individuals and society. He believes that:

> There is no such thing as "subject matter" in the abstract. "Subject matter" exists in the minds of perceivers. And what each one thinks it is, is what it is. We have been acting in schools as if knowledge lies outside the learner, which is why we have the kinds of curricula, syllabi, and texts we have. But knowledge ... is what we know *after* we have learned. It is an outcome of perception and is as unique and subjective as any other perception.[109]

Knowledge does not reside outside of men in such things as books or magazines. It does not reside in "words" separate from people, but in the meaning people create for themselves. Knowledge is defined in terms of the subjective meaning it has to its possessors. For the Social Reconstruction developer, it is more important what society and people believe to be true and valuable than what might be true or valuable in any absolute sense.

As such, knowledge resides within its possessor and originates within that possessor's interaction with his environment. It is a personally held article of faith; and, as such, impersonal information has little value. Knowledge is what each person interprets knowledge to be within the context of a relativistic social consensus. Here is a crucial assumption. Knowledge's truth and worth are verifiable through social consensus. What the majority of the members of a society believe to be true *is* true for those persons making up the society. That is:

> the truth of those experiences most vital in the social life of any culture are determined, not merely by the needful satisfactions they produce, but also by the extent to which they are *agreed upon* by the largest possible number of the group concerned. Without this factor of agreement or consensus, the experience simply is not "true."[110]

As a result, knowledge is relativistic in nature, and its truth and value depend upon the society within which it exists. For the Social Reconstruction developer, there is no such thing as absolute knowledge that is true for all peoples under all circumstances in all cultures.

This does not mean that some knowledge is not better for certain purposes and certain peoples than other knowledge. In particular, that knowledge which accords with the developer's vision of the future utopia is the knowledge of most worth for him; and it is that knowledge which the developer desires his society to accept as meaningful through social consensus and to acquire.

Creation of Knowledge

In discussing the creation of knowledge, two cases need to be distinguished: the creation of knowledge by members of society and the creation of curricular knowledge. Knowledge held by the persons making up society is actively created by those persons who possess it. Knowledge does not come into existence by itself and passively reside within objective reality. It comes into existence when someone actively impresses meaning on sensory data, and it resides within the subjective consciousness of its possessor. The process by which a person actively loads meaning and value onto sensory data is the process by which knowledge is created. Sensory data or objective information without meaning and value loaded upon them by a person are not called knowledge.

As such, the meaning structure, the perceptive functions, and the interpretative functions of a person are crucial to the Social Reconstruction developer. They are the operators which in turn give meaning and value to the subsequent knowledge the person creates. In many ways, in fact, it is these meaning-giving operators which the developer wishes to orient towards his future utopia. In so doing, the developer brings the knower to share his vision of the future utopia, rather than simply to be knowledgeable about his vision.

The knowledge which the curriculum developer imbeds within his curriculum has its source within his subjective interpretation of the nature of society in the past, present, and future. It derives from the developer's personal analysis of his world. It is chosen for inclusion within the curriculum because it acts to convert the child into a participant in the developer's vision of the future utopia. It is imbedded within the curriculum with the intention of aligning the child's knowledge and ways of knowing with those of the developer and with the intention of activating the child to reconstruct society. This view of the source of curricular knowledge is portrayed in Figure 5.5. Important to note here is that curricular knowledge has its origin within the developer's subjective view of society and that it is specifically directed towards affecting the subjective consciousness of the child so as to make him into a change agent who swells the social consensus which will

Figure 5.5

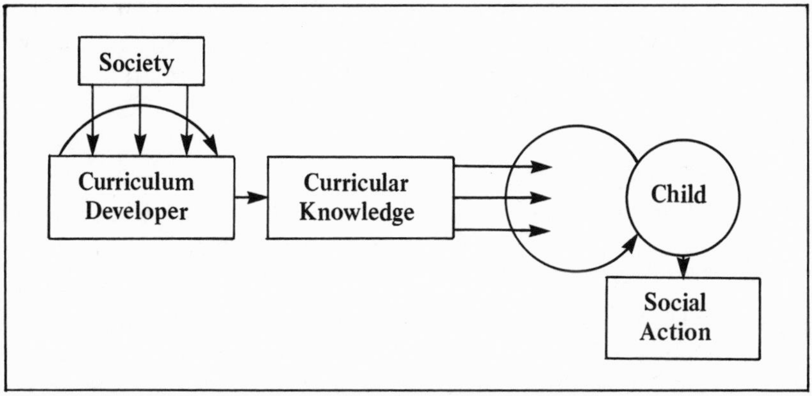

in turn hopefully align society with the developer's vision. Thus, objective information such as that possessed by the academic disciplines is of little use to the developer except as value can be loaded upon it so that it supports his vision of the future utopia.

Characteristics of Knowledge

Four other attributes of knowledge need to be briefly mentioned. First, knowledge is not viewed as a purely intellectual quantity. Both man's "gut" knowledge and his "intellectual" knowledge are viewed as important and interdependent. Both his "unrational" (subconscious) and his "rational" (conscious) knowledges and awarenesses are of concern to the curriculum developer.[111] Second, knowledge is not just a cognitive affair, but also an experiential affair. Knowledge is not just "information about," but also "experience with," the subject matter studied. Knowledge is based both in man's experiences with his environment and in his ability to understand things about his environment in terms of those experiences. Third, although knowledge is a personal attribute of the perceiver, the knowledge with which the Social Reconstruction developer is primarily concerned is the knowledge possessed by society. The developer wishes to reconstruct society by reconstructing the social consensus of the "masses." This means reconstructing the summative total of the knowledges—the gestalt of knowledges—held by the many individuals who, taken summatively, make up society. Fourth, the approach to knowledge is a gestalt approach which views knowledge in relation to other knowledge. Knowledge has meaning and value because it fits into a structure or pattern, both within the individual's intelligence and within the individual's view of objective reality. Individual bits of information, atomistically out of relation to any organizing theme, have little value.

EVALUATION

Curriculum developers working within the Social Reconstruction Ideology do not make use of formal objective evaluation. Rather, they use subjective evaluation based upon their personal opinions. They recommend a gestalt field theory approach to the evaluation of both curricula and students. Questions asked are not of the form "How does curriculum z or student y measure up to standard m?" but rather of the form "How does curriculum z or student y measure up to standard m given the circumstances within which they find themselves?" Evaluation is not a simple comparison of expected outcomes to achieved outcomes, but rather a comparison of the evaluee—whether curriculum or student—to both expectations and to the field within which the evaluee functions. (See Figure 5.6.) In the case of curricular evaluation this involves taking account of the social environment

Figure 5.6

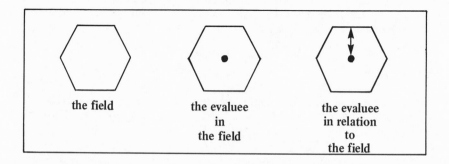

the field	the evaluee	the evaluee
	in	in relation
	the field	to
		the field

within which the curriculum is examined. In the case of student evaluation, this involves taking account of both the student's performance and the student's ability to perform. For example, in evaluating a child's self-concept with respect to the variable "power over environment," one would use a function including the parameters: the power the child exhibits, the power the child is capable of possessing, the power the child thinks other children have, and the power the child thinks he has. Here the relation is between (1) the power the child possesses with respect to what is available to him, and (2) the power the child thinks he has with respect to the power he thinks he is capable of possessing.[112]

For Social Reconstruction developers, student evaluation and curriculum evaluation are inextricably tied together within the evaluative forum of the particular social environment within which the student lives. As Horton says, the measure of a curriculum's "effectiveness—perhaps the only valid one—comes when a work-shop participant returns home. Many never become active. Others become devoted to fundamental social change."[113] Here the curriculum is evaluated through the students' performance or lack of such outside of the school. The same holds true for student evaluation. What a student has learned is thought to be testable only within his everyday life outside of the school as he works to reconstruct society in light of the curriculum's vision of the future good society.

Notes

[1] Neil Postman and Charles Weingartner. *Teaching as a Subversive Activity.* New York: Delacorte Press, 1969, p. xi. Copyright ©1969 by Neil Postman and Charles Weingartner. Reprinted by permission of Delacorte Press.

[2] *Ibid.*

[3] George S. Counts. "Dare Progressive Education Be Progressive?" *Progressive Education*, Vol. IX, No. 4 (April, 1932), pp. 260-261. Reprinted by permission of The John Dewey Society.

[4] George S. Counts. *The Social Foundations of Education.* New York: Charles Scribner, 1934, p. 533. From THE REPORT OF THE COMMISSION OF THE SOCIAL STUDIES, Part IX: THE SOCIAL FOUNDATIONS OF EDUCATION by George S. Counts. Copyright © 1934 by Charles Scribner's Sons. Reprinted by permission of Charles Scribner's Sons.

[5] Frank Adams. "Highlander Folk School: Getting Information, Going Back, and Teaching It." *Harvard Educational Review*, Vol. 42, No. 4 (November, 1972), p. 516.

[6] Myles Horton. "The Highlander Folk School." *The Social Frontier* (January, 1936), p. 117.

[7] *Ibid.*, p. 118.

[8] Myles Horton. "An Interview with Myles Horton: 'It's a Miracle—I Still Don't Believe It.'" *Phi Delta Kappan*, Vol. XLVII, No. 9 (May, 1966), p. 492.

[9] *Ibid.*

[10] *Ibid.*

[11] Frank Adams with Myles Horton. *Unearthing Seeds of Fire: The Idea of Highlander*. Winston-Salem: John F. Blair, 1975, p. 213.

[12] *Ibid.*, p. 214.

[13] Adams. "Highlander," *loc. cit.*, p. 501.

[14] Counts. *The Social Foundations, loc. cit.*, p. 550.

[15] *Ibid.*, pp. 544-545, 546. (The italics are mine.)

[16] *Ibid.*, p. 548.

[17] Counts. "Dare Progressive Education," *loc. cit.*, p. 258. (The italics are mine.)

[18] *Ibid.* (The italics are mine.)

[19] George S. Counts. *Dare the School Build a New Social Order*. New York: John Day and Co., 1932, p. 15.

[20] Counts. *The Social Foundations, loc. cit.*, p. 1.

[21] Theodore Brameld. *Toward a Reconstructed Philosophy of Education*. New York: The Dryden Press, 1956, pp. 43 and 224.

[22] *Ibid.*, p. 3.

[23] Postman and Weingartner, *loc. cit.*, p. xi.

[24] *Ibid.*, p. 208.

[25] Counts. *Dare the School, loc. cit.*, p. 35.

[26] Brameld. *Toward, loc. cit.*, pp. 60-61.

[27] Counts. "Dare Progressive Education," *loc. cit.*, p. 260.

[28] *Ibid.*, p. 259.

[29] Counts. *Dare the School, loc. cit.*, pp. 54, 55.

[30] *Ibid.*, p. 37. (The italics are mind.)

[31] The danger inherent in a fixed vision is that as society reconstructs itself the dynamics underlying it may shift so as to make the original

"finished vision" obsolete. This doesn't happen with a directed vision, for the vision constantly adjusts itself to the critical dynamics of society.

[32] Counts. *The Social Foundations, loc. cit.*, p. 534.

[33] *Ibid.*

[34] Brameld. *Toward, loc. cit.*, p. 76.

[35] Lewis Mumford. *The Story of Utopias.* London: Liveright, 1933, p. 15.

[36] Counts. *The Social Foundations, loc. cit.*, p. 536; Counts. "Dare Progressive Education," *loc. cit.*, pp. 257-258; and Brameld. *Toward, loc. cit.*, pp. 24, 76, 112, 246.

[37] Brameld. *Toward, loc. cit.*, pp. 129-130.

[38] *Ibid.*, p. 246.

[39] Counts. *Dare the School, loc. cit.*, p. 5.

[40] Brameld. *Toward, loc. cit.*, p. 247.

[41] Counts. *The Social Foundations, loc. cit.*, p. 534.

[42] Postman and Weingartner, *loc. cit.*, p. xv. Postman and Weingartner give the following examples of sources of such an eclectic social philosophy: McLuhan's *Understanding Media*; Weiner's *The Human Use of Human Beings*; Rogers' *On Becoming a Person*; Korzybski's *Science and Sanity*; and Richards' *Practical Criticism.*

[43] Counts. *Dare the School, loc. cit.*, pp. 28-29.

[44] *Ibid.*, pp. 29-30.

[45] *Ibid.*, pp. 4-5.

[46] *Ibid.*, p. 37.

[47] Counts. "Dare Progressive Education," *loc. cit.*, p. 259.

[48] William H. Kilpatrick. "Launching the Social Frontier." *The Social Frontier: A Journal of Criticism and Reconstruction*, Vol. 1, No. 1 (October, 1934), p. 2; Goodwin Watson. "Education Is the Social Frontier." *The Social Frontier*, Vol. 1, No. 1 (October, 1934), p. 22.

[49] Brameld. *Toward, loc. cit.*, p. 268.

[50] *Ibid.*, pp. 118, 119, 172, 174.

[51] *Ibid.*, p. 107.

[52] Postman and Weingartner, *loc. cit.*, p. 122.

[53] *Ibid.*

[54] Paulo Freire. *Pedagogy of the Oppressed.* New York: Seabury Press, 1970, pp. 75-76. Reprinted by permission of The Seabury Press, Inc.

[55] Horton. "Highlander," *loc. cit.*, p. 516.

[56] Counts. *Dare the School, loc. cit.*, p. 29.

[57] Counts. *The Social Foundations, loc. cit.*, pp. 2-3.

[58] Counts. *Dare the School, loc. cit.*, pp. 9-10.

[59] *Ibid.*, p. 13.

[60] Counts. *The Social Foundations, loc. cit.*, p. 536.

[61] *Ibid.*, p. 532.

[62] Counts. *Dare the School, loc. cit.*, p. 12.

[63] *Ibid.*, p. 19.

[64] *Ibid.*, p. 54.

[65] Counts. *The Social Foundations, loc. cit.*, p. 546.

[66] The journal of the Social Reconstruction Ideology during the 1930's included in its title the statement that one of its functions was to be a social critic. It was called *The Social Frontier: A Journal of Educational Criticism and Reconstruction.*

[67] Postman and Weingartner, *loc. cit.*, p. 2.

[68] *Ibid.*, p. 13.

[69] Counts. *The Social Foundations, loc. cit.*, p. 552.

[70] Brameld. *Toward, loc. cit.*, p. 109.

[71] Postman, *loc. cit.*, p. 19.

[72] *Ibid.*, p. 17.

[73] *Ibid.*, p. 52.

[74] Adams, *Unearthing Seeds of Fire, loc. cit.*, p. 213.

[75] *Ibid.*, p. 208.

[76] *Ibid.*, p. 206.

[77] Horton. "A Interview," *loc. cit.*, p. 494.

[78] Brameld. *Toward, loc. cit.*, p. 18.

[79] *Ibid.*, pp. 108, 119, 286, 355.

[80] Counts. *Dare the School, loc. cit.*, p. 15.

[81] *Ibid.*

[82] *Ibid.*, p. 13.

[83] *Ibid.*, pp. 13-15.

[84] Postman and Weingartner, *loc. cit.*, ch. 6.

[85] Counts. *Dare, loc. cit.*, pp. 14-16; and Brameld, *loc. cit.*, p. 355. It is also worth noting that one curricular implication of this is that children are often placed in adult roles where the appropriate behavior for the child to follow is predetermined in the hope that such will influence his overall behavior. Such roles include teaching younger children, joining picket lines, or campaigning for political candidates.

[86] Postman and Weingartner, *loc. cit.*, pp. 98-99. (The italics are mine.)

[87] Freire, *loc. cit.,* p. 100.[

[88] Counts. *The Social Foundations, loc. cit.*, p. 536.

[89] Postman and Weingartner, *loc. cit.*, pp. 90, 91.

[90] *Ibid.*, p. 101.

[91] William L. Patty. *A Study of Mechanism in Education: An Evaluation of the Curriculum-Making Devices of Franklin Bobbitt, W.W. Charters, and C.C. Peters from the Point of View of Relativistic Pragmatism.* New York: Teachers College Press, 1938, p. 86.

[92] Theodore Brameld. *Patterns of Educational Philosophy.* New York: World Book Company, 1950.

[93] *Ibid.*, p. 546.

[94] *Ibid.*, p. 567.

[95] *Ibid.*, p. 533.

[96] *Ibid.*, p. 542.

[97] *Ibid.*, p. 540.

[98] Counts. *Dare the School, loc. cit.*, p. 22.

[99] Brameld. *Patterns, loc. cit.*, p. 533.

[100] Postman and Weingartner, *loc. cit.*, p. 62.

[101] Brameld. *Toward, loc. cit.*, pp. 118, 119, 174, 189.

[102] Postman and Weingartner, *loc. cit.*, p. 33.

[103] Counts. *The Social Foundations, loc. cit.*, p. 558.

[104] Adams. "Highlander Folk School," *loc. cit.*, p. 501.

[105] Counts. *Dare the School, loc. cit.*, p. 28.

[106] Brameld. *Toward, loc. cit.*, p. 111.

[107] *Ibid.*, p. 243.

[108] *Ibid.*, p. 246.

[109] Postman and Weingartner, *loc. cit.*, p. 92.

[110] Brameld. *Patterns, loc. cit.*, p. 456.

[111] Brameld. *Toward, loc. cit.*, p. 83.

[112] The following diagram attempts to illustrate different possibilities: in (a) the child thinks that not much power is available and that he has little power; in (b) the child thinks that not much power is available but that he has a lot; and in (c) the child thinks that he has the same amount of power as in (b) but that the amount of power available to him is much greater. In each case the bearing upon the evaluation of the child's self-concept will be quite different.

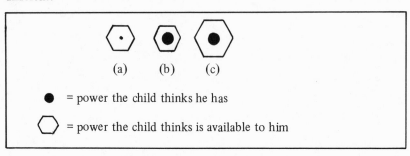

(a)   (b)   (c)

● = power the child thinks he has

⬡ = power the child thinks is available to him

[113] Adams. *Unearthing Seeds of Fire, loc. cit.*, pp. 215-216.

6.
Curricular Ideologies:
An Overview

This study has provided a description of four curricular ideologies: the Scholar Academic Ideology, the Social Efficiency Ideology, the Child Study Ideology, and the Social Reconstruction Ideology. In exploring each ideology, several aspects of the conceptual framework within which the developer works have been singled out for examination. These include the professional aims of the curriculum developer, the developer's conception of knowledge, the developer's view of learning, the developer's posture toward childhood, the developer's conception of teaching, and the developer's beliefs about evaluation. Thus far these topics have been separately investigated within the context of each ideology. They will now be examined with a comparative intent. This examination will provide the reader with a comparative study of these topics as they cut across all four ideologies. It will also focus the reader's attention upon some of the particular issues that should be considered when comparing the ideologies.

After this comparative examination is completed, several as yet unmentioned aspects of the ideologies will be briefly speculated upon, primarily to emphasize that this study has not exhausted all possible topics that need consideration.

COMPARATIVE SUMMARY
Aims of the Developer

Every curriculum developer has professional aims that give meaning to his endeavors. At least four questions can be posited about those professional aims: What does the developer conceive of his professional aims as being? For what kind of client or ideal does the developer conceive of himself as working? Where do the developer's vested interests lie? And, does the developer see himself as responsible to a client whose vested interests are other than his own? The following discussion briefly answers these questions with respect to curriculum developers working within each ideology. In doing so the discussion makes explicit some of the differences among the ideologies.

The aim of the Social Efficiency developer in creating curricula is to efficiently and scientifically carry out a task for a client (usually taken to be society). The developer conceives of himself as an unbiased agent of his client whose vested interests are other than his own. The Social Efficiency developer considers his vested interests to lie in how efficiently and scientifically he accomplishes his task, rather than in what the task is that he accomplishes.

The aim of the Scholar Academic developer in creating curricula is to perpetuate the existence of his discipline both by guaranteeing that there will exist future members of the discipline (who will in turn carry on its traditions and further its epistemic development), and by building literacy about the discipline within the general public (so that the public will support the endeavors of the discipline and benefit from its discovered truths). This aim usually takes the form of extending the discipline by transmitting its essence to students. The developer conceives of himself as working within his academic discipline in such a way that his own endeavors in creating curricula and the endeavors of his academic community coincide.

The aim of the Child Study developer in creating curricula is to stimulate the growth of children by designing experiences from which children can learn, fulfill their needs, and pursue their interests. This aim includes within it the secondary aim of stimulating his own growth and the growth of teachers, both of whom support the growth of children. The Child Study developer does not view himself as responsible to a client, but as serving the ideal of growth of the child. He conceives of his vested interests as being identical to those of the child at the level of generalities, albeit with the recognition that individuals grow in idiosyncratic ways, and thus have very different types of vested interests at the level of particulars.

The aim of the Social Reconstruction developer in creating curricula is to eliminate the undesirable aspects of his culture and substitute in their place more desirable ones. He tries to reconstruct his culture in such a way that its members will attain maximum satisfaction of their material and spiritual needs. The Social Reconstruction developer conceives of himself as working for those downtrodden members of society, whose material and spiritual needs are not being met. However, he sees himself as responsible primarily to his vision of the future utopia. As such, the Social Reconstruction developer's vested interests (his vision of the future utopia) are often very different from those of the downtrodden members of society for whom he is working (who often believe that things are presently as good as can be expected). The developer tries to change this difference of opinion over vested interests through the use of indoctrination.

Knowledge

One of the most important factors underlying the intent and behavior of any curriculum developer resides in his concept of curricular knowledge. Making sense out of the positions taken by curriculum developers with respect to knowledge and being able to decode the different ways in which the word knowledge is used by developers is crucial to understanding their behavior.

Let us review the position held by curriculum developers with respect to the following questions concerning curricular knowledge: (1) What is the nature of knowledge? (2) What kinds of abilities does knowledge give to a person? (3) What is the source of knowledge? (4) From where does knowledge derive its authority? (5) How is its truth verified? Such questions will allow us to review the overall position of each ideology towards knowledge, and will allow us to pinpoint and compare their differences with respect to specific issues.

For developers who embrace the Social Efficiency Ideology, knowledge has the nature of a capability for action. Knowledge gives the child the ability to do certain things. It has its source in normative objective reality as interpreted by the members of society; it derives its authority from the impact it has in perpetuating society by providing individuals with the skills that they need to function within society; and its truth is verified through a congruence method of checking to see if it corresponds to empirical reality as interpreted by members of society.

Knowledge, for developers of the Scholar Academic Ideology, has the nature of didactic statements and modes of thinking. Knowledge gives the child the ability to understand certain things. It has its source in objective reality as interpreted by the academic disciplines; it derives its authority from the academic discipline to which it belongs; and its truth is verified through a congruence method of checking to find the degree to which it reflects the essence of the academic discipline to which it belongs.

Within the Child Study Ideology, knowledge has the nature of personal insights that reflect the "quality of being" of the individual possessing the knowledge. Knowledge gives the child the ability to be himself at his highest level of self-actualization. It has its source in the individual child's direct experience with the world and his personal creative self-expression in response to experience as directed by his felt needs and personality structure; it derives its authority from the meaning it has to its possessor; and its truth is verifiable through the personal insight of the individual possessing it. In a sense, curricular knowledge is not a major concern of the Child Study developer—it is a first derivative of learning and a second derivative of growth, each of which is respectively more important than knowledge.

Developers working within the Social Reconstruction Ideology view knowledge as having a nature which expresses both truth and value: both intelligence and a moral stance. Knowledge gives the child the ability to interpret and to reconstruct his society. It has its source within the developer's interpretation (and, through the developer's interpretation, the child's interpretation) of the past, present, and future of society; it derives its authority from the developer's vision of the future utopia (and, through the developer's vision, the child's vision of the future utopia); and its truth is verified through the developer's conviction regarding its ability to improve the existing social context in reference to the vision of the future utopia.

Figure 6.1 sets forth in tabular form the answers given by each of the four curricular ideologies to the five questions just posed about the nature of knowledge. Examining this figure allows one to see clearly the differences between the ideologies with respect to questions about the nature of knowledge.

Figure 6.1

	Nature of knowledge	Knowledge gives the person the ability	Source of knowledge	Knowledge derives its authority from	Knowledge's truth is verified by
Scholar Academic	didactic statements and modes of thinking	"to understand" certain things	objective reality as interpreted by the academic discipline	the academic discipline to which it belongs	checking to find the degree to which it reflects the essence of the academic discipline to which it belongs
Social Efficiency	a capability for action	"to do" certain things	normative objective reality as interpreted by members of society	the impact it has in perpetuating society by providing individuals with the skills they need to function within society	checking to see if it corresponds to society's view of the nature of empirical reality
Child Study	personal insights	"to be oneself" at one's highest level of self-actualization	the individual's personal creative response to his direct experience in his world	the meaning it has to its possessor	through the personal insights of the individual possessing it
Social Reconstruction	intelligence and a moral stance	"to interpret" and "to reconstruct" one's society	the individual's interpretation of the past, present, and future of society	the individual's vision of the future "good society"	through the individual's belief in its ability to improve the existing society

Let us now examine the position held by curriculum developers with respect to their concepts of the nature of knowledge by posing two more questions: (1) Where does worthwhile knowledge reside, within the individual or outside the individual? (2) What is more important about knowledge, the source from which it originates or the use to which it can be put? The answers to these questions allow us to see differences among the ideologies and to see them in relation to each other with respect to their relative value systems. Underlying these two questions is an implicit distinction between objective reality and subjective reality. Objective reality refers to things within the real world whose existence and nature can be impartially perceived and verified. Subjective reality refers to things within the mind of a person which result from his own uniquely personal observations, thoughts, feelings, temperaments, etc. Objective reality refers back to those things (i.e., objects) independent of the mind of the perceiver; subjective reality refers back to conceptions, meanings, or perceptions within a person's (i.e., subject's) mind.

Curriculum developers working within any one of the four ideologies believe that worthwhile curricular knowledge has its origins in either objective reality or subjective reality. Scholar Academic developers and Social Efficiency developers believe that knowledge originates and has a separate existence outside of the individual, i.e., that it exists within the objective, publicly accessible world of reality. In contrast, Child Study developers and Social Reconstruction developers believe that knowledge originates and exists within the subjective mind of the individual, and that knowledge is dependent upon the subjective understanding of that individual. As a result, Scholar Academic developers and Social Efficiency developers believe that knowledge is universal and that anyone can come to understand it in its true form, while Child Study developers and Social Reconstruction developers consider knowledge to be idiosyncratic to the individual who possesses it—idiosyncratic to the extent that each individual understands knowledge in his own uniquely personal way that is not easily accessible or comprehensible to anyone other than that individual. Thus, even though Scholar Academic developers believe that knowledge has its origins in the objective interpretations of the academic disciplines, and Social Efficiency developers believe that knowledge has its origins in the normative reality of society, they both act on the belief that knowledge originates outside the individual. Similarly, even though Child Study developers believe that knowledge has its origins in the individual's creative response to his personal experiences, while Social Reconstruction developers believe that knowledge has its origins in the individual's interpretation of social events, they both act on the belief that knowledge is created by the individual who possesses it and that it has its origins in subjective reality.

We can also differentiate between curriculum developers according to whether they value knowledge primarily because of the source from which it originates or because of the uses to which it can be put. Scholar Academic developers believe that knowledge's value comes primarily from the fact that it has its origins in the academic disciplines, while Child Study developers believe that knowledge is valuable primarily because it was created by the person who possesses it. In both cases, knowledge is believed to be valuable because of its origins and not because of its uses. In contrast, Social Efficiency developers and Social Reconstruction developers value knowledge primarily for the uses to which it can be put. Social Efficiency developers believe that knowledge is useful and thus important because of its ability to sustain and perpetuate the best of our present society. Social Reconstruction developers believe that knowledge is useful and thus important because it allows individuals to act so as to bring into existence a society better than the present one.

If we cross-correlate the question "Are the origins of knowledge in objective or subjective reality?" and the question "Does knowledge's importance come from its source or its use?" we will obtain a four-cell matrix. This matrix illustrates the relationship between the ideologies, since one and only one ideology falls within each cell of the matrix. See Figure 6.2. Within this matrix the ideologies can be compared according to whether their position is to the right or left of the vertical axis, or whether their position is above or below the horizontal axis. Figure 6.3 appropriately substitutes in the place of the name of each ideology a visual model of the essence of the views of developers regarding the dynamic relationships between subjective and objective reality.

Figure 6.2

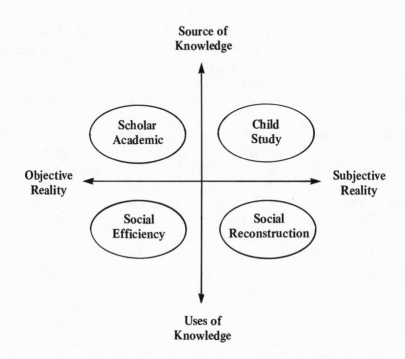

Vertical Axis: Is knowledge valued primarily because of the source
                   from which it originates or primarily because of the uses
                   to which it is put?

Horizontal Axis: Is knowledge believed to have its origin in objective
                   reality or subjective reality?

Figure 6.3

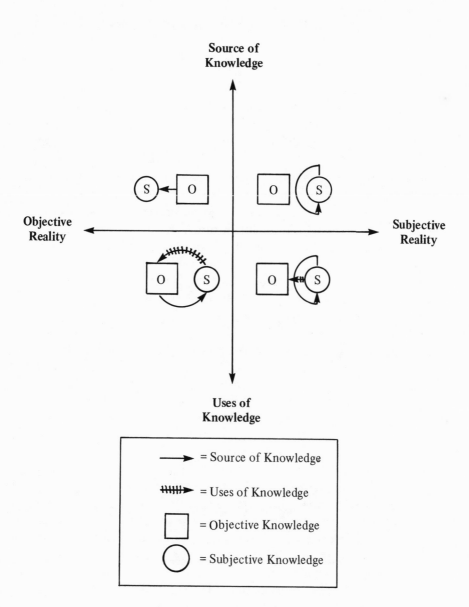

In each visual model, the relation between object (O) and subject (S), the origin of the source of knowledge (plain arrow), and the existence and direction of the uses of knowledge (slashed arrow) reflect the dynamic relationships among these elements as conceived by each ideology.

Learning

Curriculum developers within each of the ideologies have differing views as to the nature of learning. Developers working within the Social Efficiency Ideology view learning as a process by which the learner is shaped within a stimulus-response environment by an agent outside of himself—shaped in such a manner that a change in organization of mind manifests itself as a change in behavior. Developers within the Scholar Academic Ideology view learning from the perspective of the transmitter of what is to be learned—who is the active agent during learning—rather than from the perspective of the receiver of learning, who is viewed as having a passive role during learning. Within the Child Study Ideology, learning is viewed as the undergoing phase of man's growth during which the child makes meaning through creative self-expression— as a result of organically interacting with his environment in a mode which is in congruence with his needs, personality, and stage of epigenetic development. Within the Social Reconstruction Ideology, learning is viewed as indoctrination into a way of viewing events within one's environment through an intelligence oriented around a vision of a future utopia; that allows one to learn things both in relation to what one already knows and within the context in which they occur.

We can posit several questions which may help make explicit some of the differences among the ideologies with respect to their views as to the nature of learning. Such questions are: (1) Is learning viewed from the perspective of the receiver or the transmitter of the learnings? To put it another way, does the curriculum developer view learning through the eyes of the teacher (adult) or through the eyes of the learner (child)? (2) Is learning viewed primarily as a natural function of growth or as an artificial function of societal transmission? Here the question is one of whether the developer believes that the type of learning his curriculum provides for is the same as or different from the type of learning the child can naturally acquire while growing up outside of the formal schooling context. (3) Is learning treated as an integrated process or as an atomistic process? That is, can one break the learning process down into individual and disjoint (i.e., atomistic) acts or must one treat the learning process in a holistic (i.e., integrated) manner? (4) Is learning primarily a process of changing mind or changing behavior? (5) Is the desired result of learning a change of mind or a change in behavior? (6) Is the primary actor during learning the learner himself or some agent outside of the learner who does something to the learner? (7) Is there a concern with formal learning theory? What type of learning theory does the developer utilize, whether or not he is concerned with formalized learning theories? (8) How is the issue of readiness for learning treated? (9) How is individualized instruction visualized? Or, is the individual learner taken into account while the developer is planning his curriculum? Answers to these questions with respect to the positions held by curriculum developers are cross-correlated to the four ideologies and presented in tabular form in Figure 6.4.

The Child

The individual towards which education is usually directed is the child. As such, the way the curriculum developer conceives of the child and childhood and the way he imbeds these conceptions in his curriculum tells us much about his conception of education. Developers working within each of the four ideologies view the nature of the child and childhood differently. Let us briefly summarize the four views with respect to the nature of the child and then analyze these views in some detail.

Developers working within the Social Efficiency Ideology view childhood as a stage of learning that has meaning because it leads to adulthood. It is in this latter period that man is seen as a constructive member of society. The child is viewed as a raw material to be shaped into a finished product, a product which will possess well-developed behavioral capabilities. The developer focuses on the action capabilities of the child rather than on the child as an actor within his world.

Developers within the Scholar Academic Ideology view the child as a neophyte within the hierarchical community of the

Figure 6.4

LEARNING	Scholar Academic	Social Efficiency	Child Study	Social Reconstruction
Is learning viewed from the perspective of the receiver or transmitter of the learnings?	transmitter	transmitter	receiver	transmitter
Is learning primarily a "natural" function of growth or an "artificial" function of societal transmission?	artificial	artificial	natural	natural
Is learning treated as an integrated process or as an atomistic process?	atomistic	atomistic	integrated	integrated
Is learning primarily a process of changing mind or changing behavior?	mind	behavior	mind	mind
Is the desired result of learning a change in mind or behavior?	mind	behavior	mind	behavior

Figure 6.4 (Continued)

LEARNING	Scholar Academic	Social Efficiency	Child Study	Social Reconstruction
Is the prime actor during learning the learner himself or some agent outside of the learner that does something to the learner?	agent	agent/learner	learner	learner/agent
Is there a concern with formal learning theory? (What type of learning theory is used?)	No (of disciplines)	Yes (behaviorist)	No (genetic epistemology)	Yes (psychoanalytic, gestalt, cultural anthropology)
How is the issue of readiness treated?	as direct simplification of difficult topics	with respect to prior capabilities accumulated	from the view of epigenetic stages of growth	within the context of the individual gestalts of prior understandings and experience
How is individualized instruction visualized?	ignored (heterogeneous grouping with respect to academic excellence)	to teach a standardized task to each child at his own rate and sometimes via different routes	to help an idiosyncratic being become more so	ignored (use individual interests to mold a common consensus)

academic disciplines. The child is viewed as lacking something which exists outside of his mind within the developer's discipline, something which is capable of being transmitted into his mind by that discipline. The developer focuses on two qualities of the child's mind: memory (which can be filled) and reason (which can be trained).

Developers utilizing the Child Study Ideology view the whole child as an integrated organism possessing natural goodness, as a self-propelled agent of his own growth, and as a self-activated maker of meaning. The focus is on the person in contrast to the acts or attributes of the person; and on the uniqueness of the individual as he is during childhood rather than as he might be during adulthood. These developers are concerned with processes internal to the child, such as mental health and self-esteem, and talk as though they can visualize the inner working of the child's mind during his epigenetic development.

Developers working within the Social Reconstruction Ideology view man as a social being whose nature is defined by the society within which he lives. As such, the concern is with the child as a maturing member of society who can act upon society to redefine his own nature and the nature of that society.

We can pose, in analyzing the relationship of the curricular ideologies to their respective concepts of the child and childhood, the following ten questions: (1) Is the child treated as an active or passive agent in his world? (2) Is the child viewed as having something of worth or as missing something of worth? (3) Is the developer's concern with processes internal to the child or with processes external to the child? (4) Is the developer's concern focused primarily on the child's mind or primarily on the child's behavior? (5) Is the child viewed as an integrated organism or as an atomized and partitionable organism? (6) Does the developer focus his efforts on the child himself or on the acts or attributes of the child? (7) Is the concern with the child as he or she is or with the child as he or she ought to be? (8) Is the child thought to exist for himself or to further an end external to himself? (9) Is each child viewed as a unique individual or is each child viewed as he or she relates to standardized norms? (10) Is the child viewed within a social context (and if so of what type) or is the child viewed outside of and independent of a social context? Answers to these questions as they relate to each of the four ideologies are given in Figure 6.5.

The answers to two of these questions are worthy of particular comment. The questions are: "Is the child viewed as having something of worth (that gives him value as a child) or is the child viewed as missing something of worth (which he must acquire in order to have value)?" and "Is the developer's concern with processes internal to the child or with processes external to the child?" If we cross-correlate the question "Does the child have something of worth or is the child missing something of worth?" and the question "Is the concern with processes internal to or external to the child?" we obtain a four-cell matrix. This matrix illustrates the relationships between the ideologies, since one and only one ideology falls within each cell of the matrix. See Figure 6.6. Within this matrix the ideologies can be compared according to whether their position is to the right or left of the vertical axis or whether it is above or below the horizontal axis. In addition, the position of the ideologies within this matrix can be compared with the position of the ideologies in the matrix in Figure 6.2 (which depicts the relative positions of the ideologies towards the issue of knowledge). Although the definitions of the axis have been changed, the relative position of the ideologies remains the same. This constancy offers some hints as to how the developer's views of the nature of the child and childhood relate to his views of the nature of knowledge. For example, the question might be raised as to the relation of the variables on the horizontal axis of Figure 6.2 and Figure 6.6, respectively: "Do the origins of knowledge reside within subjective reality or objective reality?" and "Is the child viewed as having something of worth or missing something of worth?" Here, as one might expect, the view of the child as having something of worth corresponds to the belief that the origins of knowledge reside within his subjective reality; while the view of the child as missing something of worth corresponds to the belief that the origins of knowledge lie outside of the child, within objective reality.

Teaching

Curriculum developers, as we have made clear, have fundamentally different views about teachers and teaching. Because

Figure 6.5

THE CHILD	Scholar Academic	Social Efficiency	Child Study	Social Reconstruction
Is the child an active or passive agent in his world?	passive	active	active	active
Is the child viewed as having something of worth or missing something of worth?	missing	missing	having	having
Is the concern with processes internal to the child or external to the child?	internal	external	internal	external
Is the concern with the child's mind or the child's behavior?	mind	behavior	mind	behavior
Is the child viewed as an integrated organism or an "atomized," "partitionable" organism?	atomized	atomized	integrated	integrated

Figure 6.5 (Continued)

THE CHILD	Scholar Academic	Social Efficiency	Child Study	Social Reconstruction
Is the focus on the child or on the acts or attributes of the child?	attributes	attributes	child	attributes
Is the concern with the child "as is" or as he "ought" to be?	ought	ought	as is	ought
Is the child thought to exist "for himself" or to further an end external to himself?	external	external	himself	external
Is the child viewed as a unique individual or in conformity to standardized norms?	norms	norms	individual	norms
Is the child viewed within a social context or outside of a social context?	in context (of the discipline)	in context (of the present society)	out of context	in context (of the future society)

Figure 6.6

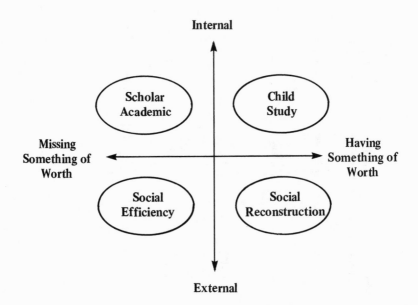

<table>
<tr><td>Vertical Axis:</td><td>Is the concern with processes internal to or external to the child?</td></tr>
<tr><td>Horizontal Axis:</td><td>Is the child viewed as having something of worth (that gives him value as a child) or as missing something of worth (which he must acquire in order to have value)?</td></tr>
</table>

teachers are the persons who use curricula in the instructional arena, they hold a crucial position in contributing to a curriculum's success or failure when it is used with children (versus its success or failure as an object before instructional interactions begin). As such, a developer's views about teachers are important, because those views can greatly affect whether or not the curriculum is implemented in accordance with the developer's intent. (Failure of a curriculum due to improper use by teachers is one of the greatest dangers faced by curriculum workers.) Let us briefly summarize the views about teachers and teaching held by curriculum developers within each of the four curricular ideologies and then proceed to analyze them in detail.

Within the Social Efficiency Ideology, the teacher is viewed as a manager or supervisor of the learning conditions and materials designed by a developer. The teacher is to act in strict accordance with the directions provided by the developer. The teacher is to serve in the dual roles of preparing the stimulus conditions within which the student will learn and supervising the student as he learns within those conditions.

Scholar Academic developers view teaching as that function of their discipline responsible for initiating novices into the discipline by transmitting that which is known to those who do not already know it. The teacher is conceived as an authority who is to get the knowledge of the discipline into the minds of students in the manner prescribed by the developer within his curriculum.

Child Study developers view teachers as aids to growing children. Their task is twofold: to facilitate the child's learning by presenting him with opportunities for experience from which he can make meaning, and to intervene between the child and such opportunities in order to facilitate his learning. The opportunities for experience and modes of intervention are selectively chosen by the teacher from among those created by developers, selected so that they will match the needs of each child.

For developers working within the Social Reconstruction Ideology, teaching involves guiding the learning of students in such a way that the students become indoctrinated into the mode of knowing and acting prescribed by the curriculum developer's vision of the future utopian society. Teachers are to act as companions to students, while using group pressures and the

Figure 6.7

TEACHING	Scholar Academic	Social Efficiency	Child Study	Social Reconstruction
What is the role of the teacher (with respect to students)?	transmitter	manager	facilitator	colleague
Is the primary job of the teacher one of "preparing" and "supervising an educational environment or "delivering" learnings?	deliver	prepare	prepare	prepare
According to what standard is teacher effectiveness measured?	accurateness in presenting discipline	efficiency in getting students to achieve goals	facilitating growth and development	get student to accept and act upon utopian vision
Is the teacher to stimulate diversity or uniformity among students?	uniformity	uniformity	diversity	uniformity
Is the teacher viewed primarily as an "implementer of the developer's curriculum as is" or as a "creative adapter of the developer's curriculum to his own situation"?	implementer	implementer	adapter (based on present child needs)	adapter (based on current social issues)
Is it the job of the teacher or developer to plan for individual differences among students?	neither	teacher	both	teacher

Figure 6.7 (Continued)

TEACHING	Scholar Academic	Social Efficiency	Child Study	Social Reconstruction
What medium is usually used during teaching?	didactic discourse	programed teacher and instruction	child-environment interaction	group dynamics
What is the intent of teaching?	advance the student within the discipline	prepare children to perform skills needed by a client (society)	further child growth according to the needs of each child	indoctrinate students into a vision of a better society
Is the teacher to be concerned with the whole child (cognitive, affective, etc.) or only a single aspect of the child?	not whole child (cognitive)	not whole child (skills)	whole child	whole child
Does the developer view the attitudes, beliefs, interpretations and visions of teachers to be of crucial importance?	No	No	Yes	Yes
Is it part of the teacher's job to do research into such things as the nature of children or appropriate learnings for children to acquire?	No	No	Yes	Yes

medium within which the student learns to mold the student's learning.

Again, we can gain additional insight into the positions implicit in the ideologies by asking several questions concerning the developer's views about teachers and teaching: (1) What is the role of the teacher (specifically with respect to students)? (2) Is the primary job of the teacher one of preparing and supervising an educational environment or one of delivering learnings? (3) According to what standard is teacher effectiveness measured? (4) Is the teacher to stimulate diversity or uniformity among students? (5) Is the teacher viewed primarily as an implementer of the developer's curriculum as it is or primarily as a creative adapter of the developer's curriculum to his or her own situation? At issue here is whether the developer does or does not try to create a "teacher proof" curriculum. (6) Is it the job of the teacher or developer to plan for individual differences among students? (7) What type of media are usually employed during teaching? (8) What is the intent of teaching? (9) Is the teacher to be concerned with the whole child (e.g., cognitive, affective, social, or physical attributes) or only with a single dimension of the child? (10) Does the developer view the attitudes, beliefs, interpretations, and visions of teachers to be of crucial importance? (11) Does the developer believe that part of the teacher's job is to do research into such things as the nature of children or appropriate learnings for children to acquire? Answers to these questions as they relate to each of the four ideologies are tabulated in Figure 6.7.

Evaluation

Developers have differing views about evaluation. Social Efficiency developers atomistically evaluate curricula and students with respect to an *a priori* standard that is based in normative values. They evaluate in order to scientifically determine quality control. In doing so, they use a binary criterion that determines acceptance or rejection (pass or fail) of that which they are evaluating. Scholar Academic developers evaluate student success in running a curriculum through the use of objective statistical instruments that are designed to measure the extent to which students can re-present to members of the discipline that which has been transmitted to them. Students are evaluated with respect to an *a posteriori* standard in order to rank order them within the discipline's hierarchy for prestige purposes. Evaluation of curriculum comes from the opinion of scholars within the discipline as to how well the curriculum reflects the essence of the discipline and how well it prepares students to pursue future work within the discipline. Child Study developers attempt to use evaluation solely for the benefit of the person or curriculum being evaluated. Evaluation is assumed to take on a reflective quality devoid of "moral loading." The intent is to enable the evaluee, be he student, teacher, or curriculum developer, to learn from his mistakes. Moreover, it is believed within this ideology that evaluative feedback should come directly from the materials with which the evaluee is interacting, rather than from or through an outside authority. Developers within the Social Reconstruction Ideology take a subjective, holistic approach to evaluating the evaluee in relation to the field within which he exists.

In analyzing in greater detail the differing views about evaluation that are held by curriculum developers, a distinction must be made between evaluation that is primarily designed to give information about the students who are undergoing the curriculum and evaluation that is primarily designed to give information about the nature and effectiveness of the curriculum itself. The former will be called student evaluation and the latter will be called curriculum evaluation.

The answers to several questions which touch on each ideology make explicit some of the differences among the ideologies with respect to their views of student evaluation. Such questions are: (1) What is the purpose of student evaluation as it relates to the person who receives the results of the evaluation? (2) What is the intent of student evaluation as it relates to the evaluee? (3) Is the development of formal evaluative measures for student evaluation considered to be an integral part of the curriculum development process? (4) What is the nature of the evaluative instruments used in evaluating students? (5) Are subjective or objective instruments used to evaluate students? (6) Is student evaluation viewed from an atomistic or holistic perspective? (7) To whom are the results of student evaluation to be directed or beneficial? (8) During student evaluation is the focus on the individual, group norms, or a fixed criterion? (9) Does student evaluation take place during

Figure 6.8

STUDENT EVALUATION	Scholar Academic	Social Efficiency	Child Study	Social Reconstruction
What is the purpose of student evaluation as it relates to the person who receives the results of the evaluation?	rank order evaluees for future advancement in the discipline	certify to a client that a student has certain skills	diagnose student's abilities so as to facilitate their growth	to measure a student's progress with respect to his/her abilities
What is the intent of student evaluation as it relates to the evaluee?	test one's ability to re-present what has been transmitted to him	to test one's ability to perform a specific task	to reflect to the evaluee his progress	to allow the student and his teacher and peers to question the student's meaning and values
Is the development of formal evaluative measures for student evaluation considered an integral part of the curriculum development process?	No	Yes	No	No
What is the nature of the evaluative instruments used in evaluating students?	norm referenced	criterion referenced	informal subjective diagnosis	informal subjective diagnosis

Figure 6.8 (Continued)

STUDENT EVALUATION	Scholar Academic	Social Efficiency	Child Study	Social Reconstruction
Are subjective or objective instruments used to evaluate students?	objective	objective	subjective	subjective
Is student evaluation viewed from an atomistic or holistic perspective?	atomistic	atomistic	holistic	holistic
To whom are the results of student evaluation to be directed or beneficial?	the academic disciplines (academicians, administrators)	the developer's client (society, administrators, parents)	child only	teacher
During student evaluation is the focus on the individual, group norms, or a fixed criterion?	group norms	criterion	individual	individual with respect to a criterion
Does student evaluation take place during the instructional process or after the instructional process?	after	after	during	during
When are the criteria for successful student work defined?	after evaluation	before evaluation	never	never

the instructional process or after the instructional process? (10) When are the criteria for successful student work defined? Answers to these questions are cross-correlated to the four ideologies and are presented in tabular form in Figure 6.8.

A further distinction needs to be made in order to discuss the differing views of curriculum developers about curriculum evaluation. The distinction must be made between evaluation that takes place during the curriculum development process which is designed to give the curriculum developer information that will help him improve his curriculum and evaluation that is designed to provide information to potential users of a curriculum on either the curriculum's overall worth and effectiveness with respect to its own goals or the curriculum's comparative worth and effectiveness with respect to the goals of several different competing programs. The former is called formative curriculum evaluation, and the latter is called summative curriculum evaluation. Answering the following thirteen questions with respect to each ideology makes explicit some of the differences among the ideologies with respect to their views of curriculum evaluation: (1) Is the development of formal evaluation measures for the purpose of curriculum evaluation considered an integral part of the curriculum development process? (2) Is formative evaluation of curriculum considered important? (3) Why is formative evaluation considered important? (4) Is accountability a central issue during formative evaluation? If yes, to whom? (5) Are subjective or objective instruments used during formative curriculum evaluation? (6) Are the norms for formative curriculum evaluation determined before, during, or after evaluation takes place? (7) Is formative evaluation primarily conducted in an atomistic or holistic manner? (8) What type of information results from formative evaluation: binary "it's OK or it needs revision" information or specific information on the individual successes and failures of each component of the curriculum? (9) What methodology or criteria are used to determine a curriculum's success or failure during formative evaluation? (10) Is summative curriculum evaluation considered important? (11) Why is summative evaluation considered important? (12) Are subjective or objective instruments used during summative curriculum evaluation? (13) Is accountability a central issue during summative curriculum evaluation? Answers to these questions as they pertain to each of the four ideologies are given in tabular form in Figure 6.9.

OTHER PARAMETERS
Freedom

Curriculum developers like to use the word freedom, but a developer can mean many different things when he speaks of giving the child freedom. Developers within the Social Efficiency Ideology wish to give the student *freedom to* constructively contribute to and function within adult society in the manner he desires by providing him with the variety of social behaviors and technical skills he will need to do so. Scholar Academic developers wish to give the student *freedom from* the restrictions of society and nature by giving him knowledge about society and nature which will allow him to understand them and thus avoid the ways in which they control him. Child Study developers wish to provide the student with *freedom from* the influences and controls of society so that he can develop naturally in accordance with his organic self. Developers within the Social Reconstruction Ideology wish to give the student *freedom to* control society and the destiny of society.

Time

Developers within each ideology orient their efforts within different temporal frameworks. Their endeavors tend to be directed towards different temporal orientations, even though each is in some way concerned with the past, present, and future. Scholar Academic developers look towards the knowledge which has already been accepted by their discipline as important while they create curricula—they look to the past for guidance. Social Efficiency developers look towards the present needs of society (or some other client) to guide them in their endeavors to create curricula to meet those present needs in the very near future. Child Study developers attempt to know only the present as seen through the eyes of the child. Social Reconstruction developers unavoidably make use of the past and present as they analyze the nature of society while intently focusing their attention upon the future.

Figure 6.9

CURRICULUM EVALUATION	Scholar Academic	Social Efficiency	Child Study	Social Reconstruction
Is the development of formal evaluation measures for curriculum evaluation considered an integral part of the curriculum development process?	No	Yes	No	No
Is formative evaluation of curriculum considered important?	Yes	Yes	Yes	No
Why is formative evaluation considered important?	(a) to make sure the curriculum reflects the discipline, (b) to see if the curriculum is teachable	to conform to scientific procedures and demonstrate accountability to the client	to give the developer information that will allow him to develop the best curriculum possible	—
Is accountability a central issue during formative evaluation? If yes, to whom?	Yes (to discipline)	Yes (to client)	Yes (to self, as developer)	—
Are subjective or objective instruments used during formative curriculum evaluation?	Subjective (teacher reports) (scholar examination)	Objective	Subjective (developer, observation)	—

Figure 6.9 (Continued)

CURRICULUM EVALUATION	Scholar Academic	Social Efficiency	Child Study	Social Reconstruction
Are the norms for formative curriculum evaluation determined before, during, or after evaluation takes place?	after	before	during	—
Is formative evaluation primarily conducted in an atomistic or holistic manner?	holistic, with respect to overall effects of units	atomistic	atomistic and holistic	—
What type of information results from formative evaluation: (a) binary "its OK or it needs revision" information or (b) specific information on the individual success and failures of each component of the curriculum?	binary	binary	specific information about each curriculum component	—
What methodology/criteria are used to determine a curriculum's success or failure during formative evaluation?	(a) logical analysis in terms of presenting discipline accurately, (b) teacher reports as to teachability	objective criterion referenced data on student success in achieving goals	observational data as to student involvement in and growth from the curriculum	—

Figure 6.9 (Continued)

CURRICULUM EVALUATION	Scholar Academic	Social Efficiency	Child Study	Social Reconstruction
Is summative curriculum evaluation considered important?	Necessary, not important	Yes	No	No
Why is summative curriculum evaluation considered important?	to sell the curriculum on the market place	conform to scientific procedures; accountability to the client	—	—
Are subjective or objective instruments used during summative curriculum evaluation?	objective (achievement tests)	objective	subjective testimonials	—
Is accountability a central issue during summative curriculum evaluation?	No	Yes	No	No

Social Improvement

Developers within each ideology have their own ideas of how to improve society. Developers within the Social Efficiency Ideology wish to accentuate the best of the past and present in training man to perpetuate the existing social order. Developers within the Social Reconstruction Ideology wish to break with the past and present and reconstruct society with respect to a vision of a utopian society. Scholar Academic developers wish to improve society by educating an intellectual elite so that scholar kings can rule society through knowledge. Child Study developers are concerned with the development of the individual man under the assumption that only better men will make a better society.

Clientele

To some extent, it can be said that developers within each ideology conceive of themselves as best serving a certain clientele. Social Efficiency developers best serve the middle class, which will perpetuate the functioning of the existing society. Scholar Academic developers serve best the intellectually talented. Child Study developers conceive of themselves as best serving the pure and uncontaminated child. The Social Reconstruction developers have in the past desired to serve the downtrodden silent masses, although they usually seem to best serve the upper-middle class vocal masses.

Values

Perhaps one of the most difficult, as well as one of the most interesting, issues open for investigation is the nature of the value systems guiding the programmatic efforts of developers within each curricular ideology. Developers within the Social Efficiency Ideology seem to be ruled by a technological value system. Developers using the Scholar Academic Ideology may have their programmatic efforts guided by a scientific-humanistic value sytem. Child Study developers may be adhering to a value system based in ethical-aesthetic principles. Social Reconstruction developers may be guided by a value system essentially political and anthropological in nature.

Images and Classrooms

There is always a point where we should abandon words,

Figure 6.10

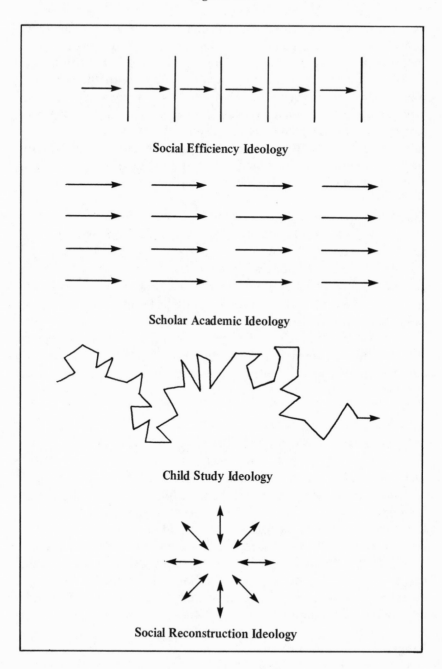

Figure 6.11

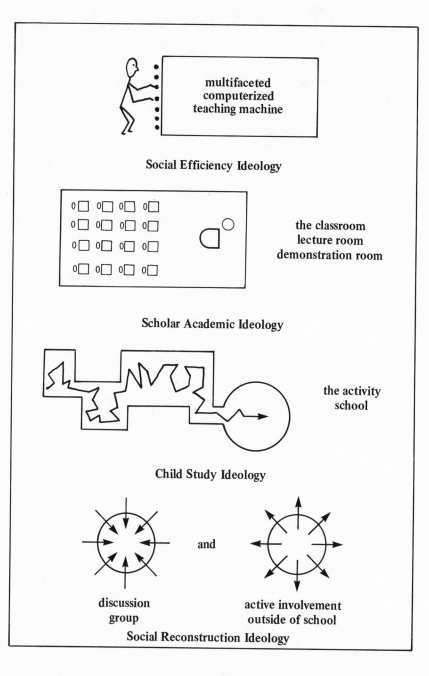

multifaceted
computerized
teaching machine

Social Efficiency Ideology

the classroom
lecture room
demonstration room

Scholar Academic Ideology

the activity
school

Child Study Ideology

discussion
group

and

active involvement
outside of school

Social Reconstruction Ideology

diagrams, and tables for purer images. Figure 6.10 provides an attempt to present the essence of the different curricular ideologies discussed herein in pictorial form through the use of vectors. Hopefully the direction and placement of the vectors with respect to each other give a flavor for the endeavor engaged in by developers working within each ideology. There is also a time to give pure images some relationship to reality. Figure 6.11 attempts to portray the nature of the instructional arena as developers within the different ideologies might conceive such to appear.

Bibliography

Adams, Frank. "Highlander Folk School: Getting Information, Going Back, and Teaching It." *Harvard Educational Review*, Vol. 42, No. 4 (November, 1972).

Adams, Frank and Myles Horton. *Unearthing Seeds of Fire: The Idea of Highlander*. Winston Salem: John F. Blair, 1975.

Aiken, Wilford M. *The Story of the Eight Year Study*. New York: Harper and Brothers, 1942.

American Association for the Advancement of Science Commission on Science Education. *The Psychological Bases of Science—A Process Approach*. Washington, D.C.: AAAS, 1965.

American Association for the Advancement of Science. *Guide for Inservice Instruction: Science—A Process Approach*. Washington, D.C.: AAAS Miscellaneous Publication 67-9, 1967.

American Association for the Advancement of Science. *Science—A Process Approach: Purposes, Accomplishments, Expectations*. Washington, D.C.: AAAS Miscellaneous Publication 67-12, 1967.

American Association for the Advancement of Science, Commission on Science Education. *Science—A Process Approach: An Evaluation Model and Its Application: Second Report*. Washington, D.C.: AAAS Miscellaneous Publication 68-4, 1968.

American Association for the Advancement of Science. *Science—A Process Approach*. New York: Xerox Corporation, 1968.

American Educational Research Association Monograph Series on Curriculum Evaluation No. 1: Perspectives on Curriculum Evaluation. Chicago: Rand McNally, 1967.

Anderson, Vernon E. *Principles and Procedures of Curriculum Improvement*. New York: The Ronald Press, 1965.

Ardrey, Robert. *The Territorial Imperative*. New York: Atheneum, 1966.

Armington, David. "Letter of Kallet, Hull, and Sealey." Newton: Educational Development Corporation, unpublished mimeograph, June 7, 1967.

Atkin, J. Myron. "Behavioral Objectives in Curriculum Design: A Cautionary Note." *The Science Teacher,* Vol. 35 (May, 1968).

Barth, Roland S. *Open Education and the American School*. New York: Agathon Press, 1972.

Beauchamp, George A. and Kathryn E. Beauchamp. *Comparative Analysis of Curriculum Systems*. Wilmette, Ill.: Kagg Press, 1967.

Bell, Daniel. *The Reforming of General Education*. New York: Columbia University Press, 1966.

Bellack, Arno A. "The Structure of Knowledge and the Structure of the Curriculum." In Dwayne Huebner (Ed.) *A Reassessment of the Curriculum*. New York: Teachers College Press, 1964.

Blackie, John. *Inside the Primary School*. New York: Schocken Books, 1971.

Bobbitt, Franklin. "The Elimination of Waste in Education." *The Elementary School Teacher*, Vol. 12, No. 6 (February, 1912).

Bobbitt, Franklin. "Some General Principles of Management Applied to the Problems of City School Systems." In *Twelfth Yearbook of the National Society for the Study of Education Part I*. Chicago: University of Chicago Press, 1913.

Bobbitt, Franklin. *The Curriculum*. Boston: Riverside Press, 1918.

Bobbitt, Franklin. "The Objectives of Secondary School Education." *The School Review*, Vol. 28, No. 10 (December, 1920).

Bobbitt, Franklin. *How to Make a Curriculum*. Boston: Houghton Mifflin Co., 1924.

Bobbitt, Franklin. "Education as a Social Process." *School and Society*, Vol. 21 (April, 1924).

Bobbitt, Franklin. "The New Technique of Curriculum Making." *The Elementary School Journal*, Vol. 25, No. 1 (September, 1924).

Bobbitt, Franklin. "What Understanding of Human Society Should Education Develop?" *The Elementary School Journal*, Vol. 25, No. 4 (December, 1924).

Bobbitt, Franklin. "Discovering the Objectives of Health Education." *The Elementary School Journal*, Vol. 25, No. 10 (June, 1925).

Bobbitt, Franklin. "The Orientation of the Curriculum-Maker." In *The Foundations of Curriculum Making: Twenty-Sixth Yearbook of the National Society for the Study of Education, Part II.* Bloomington, Illinois: Public School Publishing Company, 1927.

Bobbitt, Franklin. *Curriculum Investigations.* Chicago: University of Chicago Press, 1926.

Bowers, C.A. *The Progressive Educator and the Depression: The Radical Years.* New York: Random House, 1969.

Brameld, Theodore. *Patterns of Educational Philosophy (First Edition).* New York: World Book Company, 1950.

Brameld, Theodore. *Philosophies of Education.* New York: Holt, Rinehart, and Winston, 1955.

Brameld, Theodore. *Toward a Reconstructed Philosophy of Education.* New York: The Dryden Press, 1956.

Brauner, Charles J. *American Educational Theory.* Englewood Cliffs: Prentice-Hall, 1964.

Broudy, Harry S. *Building a Philosophy of Education (Second Edition).* Englewood Cliffs: Prentice-Hall, 1961.

Brown, Mary and Norman Precious. *The Integrated Day in the Primary School.* New York: Agathon Press, 1969.

Bruner, Jerome. *The Process of Education.* Cambridge: Harvard University Press, 1960.

Bruner, Jerome. "Needed: A Theory of Instruction." *Educational Leadership*, Vol. 20, No. 8 (May, 1963).

Bruner, Jerome. *Toward a Theory of Instruction.* Cambridge: Belknap Press, 1966.

Burnham, W.H. "Education from the Genetic Point of View." *Proceedings of the National Education Association*, 1905.

Bussis, Anne and Edward Chittenden. *Analysis of an Approach to Open Education.* Princeton: Educational Testing Service, 1970.

Butler, J. Donald. *Four Philosophies and Their Practice in Education and Religion.* New York: Harper, 1951.

Callahan, Raymond E. *Education and the Cult of Efficiency.* Chicago: University of Chicago Press, 1962.

Charters, W.W. *Methods of Teaching.* Chicago: Row, Peterson, and Co., 1909.

Charters, W.W. *Curriculum Construction.* New York: Macmillan, 1923.

Charters, W.W. *Teaching of Ideals.* New York: Macmillan, 1927.

Commission on the Reorganization of Secondary Education. *Cardinal Principles of Secondary Education.* Washington, D.C.: U.S. Bureau of Education Bulletin No. 35, 1918.

Connelly, F. Michael. "Conceptual Structures in Ecology with Special Reference to an Enquiry Curriculum in Ecology." Chicago: University of Chicago unpublished doctoral dissertation, 1968.

Connelly, F. Michael. "Philosophy of Science and the Science Curriculum." *Journal of Research in Science Teaching,* Vol. 6 (January, 1969).

Counts, George S. "Dare Progressive Education Be Progressive?" *Progressive Education,* Vol. 9, No. 4 (April, 1932).

Counts, George S. *Dare the School Build a New Social Order?* New York: Arno Press, 1932.

Counts, George S. *The Social Foundations of Education.* New York: Scribner, 1934.

Craig, Gerald Spellman. *Certain Techniques Used in Developing a Course of Study in Science for the Horace Mann Elementary School.* New York: Teachers College Press, 1927.

Cronbach, Lee J. "Course Improvement Through Evaluation." *Teachers College Record,* Vol. 64, No. 8 (May, 1963).

Dapper, Gloria and Barbara Carter. "Jerrold Zacharias: Apostle of the New Physics." *Saturday Review* (October 21, 1961).

Davis, Robert B. "Discovery in the Teaching of Mathematics." In Lee S. Shulman and Evan R. Keislar (Eds.) *Learning by Discovery: A Critical Appraisal.* Chicago: Rand McNally, 1966.

Delima, Agnes. *Our Enemy the Child.* New York: New Republic, Inc., 1926.

Dewey, Evelyn and John Dewey. *Schools of Tomorrow.* New York: E.P. Dutton and Company, 1915.

Dewey, John. *The Child and the Curriculum.* Chicago: University of Chicago Press, 1902.

Dewey, John. *Reconstruction in Philosophy.* New York: Henry Holt and Co., 1920.

Dewey, John. *Human Nature and Conduct.* New York: The Modern Library, 1922, 1957.

Dewey, John. "Progressive Education and the Science of Education." *Progressive Education*, Vol. V, No. 3 (July-September, 1928).

Diederich, Mary E. "Physical Sciences and Processes of Inquiry: A Critique of CHEM, CBA, and PSSC." *Journal of Research in Science Teaching,* Vol. 6, No. 4 (February, 1969).

Elam, Stanley (Ed.) *Education and the Structure of Knowledge.* Chicago: Rand McNally, 1964.

Elementary Science Study. *Introduction to Elementary Science Study.* Newton, Ma.: Education Development Center, 1966.

Elementary Science Study. *The ESS Reader.* Newton, Ma.: Education Development Center, 1970.

Erikson, Erik H. *Childhood and Society.* New York: W.W. Norton, 1963.

Featherstone, Joseph. "A New Kind of Schooling." *The New Republic*, Vol. 158, No. 9 (March, 1968).

Ferris, Frederick L. "Testing in the New Curriculum: Numerology, Tyranny, or Common Sense." *The School Review*, Vol. 70 (Spring, 1962).

Flavell, J.H. *The Developmental Psychology of Jean Piaget.* New York: D. Van Nostrand, 1963.

Ford, G.W. and Lawrence Pagno (Eds.) *The Structure of Knowledge and the Curriculum.* Chicago: Rand McNally, 1964.

Foshay, Arthur W. "How Fare the Disciplines?" *Phi Delta Kappan*, Vol. 51, No. 7 (March, 1970).

Fraser, Dorothy M. *Current Curriculum Studies in Academic Subjects.* Washington, D.C.: NEA, 1962.

Freire, Paulo. *Pedagogy of the Oppressed.* New York: Seabury Press, 1970.

Freud, Sigmund. *The Standard Edition of the Complete Psychological Works of Sigmund Freud.* London: Hogarth, 1964.

Furth, Hans G. *Piaget and Knowledge.* Englewood Cliffs: Prentice-Hall, 1969.

Gagné, Robert M. "The Acquisition of Knowledge." *Psychological Review*, Vol. 69, No. 4 (July, 1962).

Gagné, Robert M. "The Learning Requirements for Inquiry." *Journal of Research in Science Teaching*, Vol. 1, No. 2 (September, 1963).

Gagné, Robert M. "Learning and Proficiency in Mathematics." *The Mathematics Teacher,* Vol. 56, No. 8 (December, 1963).

Gagné, Robert M. "Educational Objectives and Human Performance." In J.D. Krumboltz (Ed.) *Learning and the Educational
Process*. Chicago: Rand McNally, 1965.

Gagné, Robert M. *The Conditions of Learning* (First Edition).
New York: Holt, Rinehart, and Winston, 1965.

Gagné, Robert M. "Elementary Science: A New Scheme of
Instruction." *Science*, No. 151 (January, 1966).

Gagné, Robert M. "The Analysis of Instructional Objectives for
the Design of Instruction." In Robert Glaser (Ed.) *Teaching
Machines and Programmed Learning II: Data and Directions*.
Washington, D.C.: National Education Association, 1965.

Gagné, Robert M. *Science—A Process Approach: Purposes, Accomplishments, Expectations*. Washington, D.C.: AAAS Miscellaneous Publication 67-12, 1967.

Gagné, Robert M. "Curriculum Research and the Promotion of
Learning." In *American Educational Research Association
Monograph Series on Curriculum Evaluation: Perspectives on
Curriculum Evaluation*. Chicago: Rand McNally, 1967.

Gagné, Robert M. *et al.* "The Individual Basis of Scientific
Inquiry." In *The Psychological Bases of Science—A Process
Approach*. Washington, D.C.: American Association for the
Advancement of Science Miscellaneous Publication 65-8, 1965.

Gagné, Robert M. *The Conditions of Learning: Second Edition*.
New York: Holt, Rinehart, and Winston, 1970.

Gagné, Robert M., J.R. Mayor, H.L. Gerstens, and N.E. Paradise.
"Factors in Acquiring Knowledge of Mathematical Tasks."
Psychological Monograph, No. 76, 1962.

Gillet, Harry O. and William C. Reavis. "Curriculum-Making in the
Laboratory Schools of the School of Education, The University
of Chicago." *The Twenty-Sixth Yearbook of the National
Society for the Study of Education*. Bloomington: Public
School Publishing Co., 1927.

Glaser, Robert (Ed.) *Teaching Machines and Programmed Learning
II: Data and Directions*. Washington, D.C.: National Education
Association, 1965.

*Goals for School Mathematics: The Report of the Cambridge
Conference on School Mathematics*. Boston: Houghton Mifflin,
1963.

Goodlad, John I. *School Curriculum Reform in the United States*.
New York: Fund for the Advancement of Education, 1964.

Goodlad, John I. *The Changing School Curriculum*. New York: The Fund for the Advancement of Education, 1966.

Goodlad, John I. *School, Curriculum, and the Individual*. Waltham, Ma.: Blaisdell, 1966.

Goodlad, John I. "Curriculum: A Janus Look." *The Teachers College Record*, Vol. 70, No. 2 (November, 1968).

Graham, Patricia Albjerg. *Progressive Education: From Arcady to Academe: A History of the Progressive Education Association: 1919-1955*. New York: Teachers College Press, 1967.

Grannis, Joseph C. "The School as a Model of Society." *Harvard Graduate School of Education Bulletin*, Vol. 12, No. 2 (Fall, 1967).

Grobman, Arnold B. *The Changing Classroom: The Role of the Biological Sciences Curriculum Study*. New York: Doubleday, 1969.

Grobman, Hulda. *Developmental Curriculum Projects: Decision Points and Processes*. Itasca, Ill.: F.E. Peacock Publishers, 1970.

Harvard Project Physics. *Harvard Project Physics: Newsletter 1*. Cambridge: Harvard Project Physics, 1964.

Hawkins, David. "On Living in Trees." Newton, Ma.: Elementary Science Study, unpublished mimeo No. 5143165, 1964.

Hawkins, David. "Messing About in Science." *Science and Children*, Vol. 2, No. 5 (February, 1965).

Hein, George E. *Open Education: An Overview*. Newton, Ma.: Education Development Center, 1975.

Holland, James G. "Teaching Machines: An Application of Principles from the Laboratory." *Journal of the Experimental Analysis of Behavior*, No. 3 (1960).

Holland, James G., Carol Solomon, Judith Doran, and Daniel A. Frezza. *The Analysis of Behavior in Planning Instruction*. Reading, Ma.: Addison-Wesley, 1976.

Horton, Myles. "The Highlander Folk School." *The Social Frontier*, Vol. 2, No. 4 (January, 1936).

Horton, Myles. "An Interview with Myles Horton: 'It's a Miracle— I Still Don't Believe It.' " *Phi Delta Kappan*, Vol. XLVII, No. 9 (May, 1966).

Howard, Leo M. "The Developmental Classroom." Boston: Office of Program Development, unpublished miemo, 1968.

Howe, Nancy. Interview by Francis Litman reported at the Harvard Graduate School of Education, May 1969.

Huebner, Dwayne (Ed.) *A Reassessment of the Curriculum*. New York: Teachers College Press, 1964.

Instructional Aids, Materials, and Supplies—Guidelines. Newton, Ma.: Education Development Center, 1972.

Introduction to the Elementary Science Study. Newton, Ma.: Education Development Center, 1966.

Isaacs, Susan. *The Children We Teach*. London: University of London Press, 1967.

Jersild, Arthur T. *Child Development and the Curriculum*. New York: Teachers College Press, 1946.

Johnson, Marietta. "The Educational Principles of the School of Organic Education Fairhope, Alabama." In *Twenty-Sixth Yearbook of the National Society for the Study of Education*. Bloomington: Public School Publishing Company, 1927.

Johnson, Marietta. *Thirty Years with an Idea: The Story of Organic Education*. University, Alabama: University of Alabama Press, 1974.

Keppel, Francis. "Foreword" to *Goals for School Mathematics: The Report on the Cambridge Conference on School Mathematics*. Boston: Houghton Mifflin, 1963.

Kerr, Clark. "The Multiversity: Are Its Several Souls Worth Saving?" *Harpers*, No. 227 (November, 1963).

Kilpatrick, William H. *The Project Method*. New York: Bureau of Publications, Teachers College, 1918.

Kilpatrick, William H. "Launching the Social Frontier." *The Social Frontier*, Vol. 1, No. 1 (October, 1934).

King, Arthur and John A. Brownell. *The Curriculum and the Disciplines of Knowledge*. New York: Kreiger, 1966.

Kliebard, Herbert M. "The Curriculum Field in Retrospect." In Paul Witt (Ed.) *Technology and the Curriculum*. New York: Teachers College Press, 1968.

Kliebard, Herbert M. "Bureaucracy and Curriculum Theory." In Vernon F. Haubrich (Ed.) *Freedom, Bureaucracy, and Schooling*. Washington, D.C.: Association for Supervision and Curriculum Development, 1971.

Kohlberg, Lawrence. "Moral Education in the School: A Developmental View." *School Review*, Vol. 74, No. 1 (September, 1966).

Kohlberg, Lawrence. "The Child as Moral Philosopher." *Psychology Today*, Vol. 2, No. 4 (September, 1968).

Kolesnick, Walter B. *Mental Discipline in Modern Education.* Madison: University of Wisconsin Press, 1962.

Krieghbaum, Hillier and Hugh Ranson. *To Improve Secondary School Science and Mathematics Teaching.* Washington, D.C.: U.S. Government Printing Office, 1968.

Krug, Edward A. *The Shaping of the American High School: 1880-1920.* Madison: University of Wisconsin Press, 1969.

Kuhn, Thomas S. *The Structure of Scientific Revolutions.* Chicago: University of Chicago Press, 1962.

Leitman, Allan. "Travel Agent." *Housing for Early Childhood Education.* Washington, D.C.: A.C.E.I., 1968.

Lindvall, C.M. and John O. Bolvin. "Programed Instruction in the Schools: An Application of Programing Principles in 'Individually Prescribed Instruction.' " In *The Sixty-Sixth Yearbook of the National Society for the Study of Education: Part II, Programed Instruction.* Chicago: University of Chicago Press, 1967.

Lukinsky, Joseph Sander. " 'Structure' in Educational Theory." *Educational Philosophy and Theory,* Vol. 2, No. 2 (October, 1970).

MacDonald, James B. and Robert R. Leeper (Eds.) *Language and Meaning.* Washington, D.C.: Association for Supervision and Curriculum Development, 1966.

Mager, Robert F. *Preparing Instructional Objectives.* Palo Alto: Fearon Publishers, 1962.

Mager, Robert F. and Kenneth M. Beach. *Developing Vocational Instruction.* Palo Alto: Fearon Publishers, 1967.

"Man: A Course of Study." Cambridge, Ma.: Miscellaneous publication of Educational Development Corporation, Social Studies Project, 1969.

Marrow, H.I. *A History of Education in Antiquity.* New York: Mentor, 1964.

Martin, Jane R. "The Disciplines and the Curriculum." *Educational Philosophy and Theory,* Vol. 1, No. 1 (1969).

Mayhew, K.C. and A.C. Edwards. *The Dewey School.* New York: Atherton Press, 1966.

Miel, Alice. "Reassessment of the Curriculum—Why?" In Dwayne Huebner (Ed.) *A Reassessment of the Curriculum.* New York: Teachers College Press, 1964.

Monroe, Paul and E.L. Thorndike. "Research Within the Field of Education: Its Organization and Encouragement." *The School Review Monographs: No. 1*. Chicago: University of Chicago Press, 1911.

Monroe, Walter S. "Projects and the Project Method." *University of Illinois Bulletin*, Vol. 23, No. 30 (March 29, 1926).

Morrison, Philip. "The Curricular Triangle and Its Style." *ESI Quarterly Report* (Summer-Fall, 1964). Reprinted in *The ESS Reader*. Newton, Ma.: Education Development Center, 1970.

Mumford, Lewis. *The Story of Utopias*. London: Liveright, 1933.

National Education Association. *Report of the Committee of Ten on Secondary Schools*. New York: American Book Company, 1894.

Parker, Chester S. "The Present Status of Education as a Science." In *The School Review Monographs: No. II*. Chicago: University of Chicago Press, 1912.

Parker, Francis W. *Talks on Pedagogics*. New York: E.L. Kellogg, 1894.

Passow, A. Harry. *Curriculum Crossroads*. New York: Teachers College Press, 1962.

Patty, William L. *A Study of Mechanism in Education: An Examination of the Curriculum-Making Devices of Franklin Bobbitt, W.W. Charters, and C.C. Peters, from the Point of View of Relativistic Pragmatism*. New York: Teachers College Press, 1938.

Peters, Charles C. *Foundations of Educational Sociology*. New York: Macmillan, 1930.

Peters, Charles C. *Objectives and Procedures in Civic Education*. New York: Longmans, Green, and Co., 1930.

Peterson, Francis E. *Philosophies of Education Current in the Preparation of Teachers in the United States*. New York: Teachers College Press, 1933.

Phenix, Philip H. "The Disciplines as Curriculum Content." In A. Harry Passow (Ed.) *Curriculum Crossroads*. New York: Teachers College Press, 1962.

Phenix, Philip H. *Realms of Meaning*. New York: McGraw Hill, 1964.

Phenix, Philip H. "The Architectonics of Knowledge." In Stanley Elam (Ed.) *Education and the Structure of Knowledge*. Chicago: Rand McNally, 1964.

Phenix, Philip H. "Curriculum and the Analysis of Language." In James B. MacDonald and Robert R. Leeper (Eds.) *Language and Meaning*. Washington, D.C.: Association for Supervision and Curriculum Development, 1966.

Phenix, Philip H. "The Use of Disciplines as Curriculum Content." In Frank C. Steeves (Ed.) *The Subjects in the Curriculum*. New York: Odyssey Press, 1968.

Plowden, Lady Bridget *et al. Children and Their Primary Schools: A Report of the Central Advisory Center for Education*. London: H.M.S.O., 1967.

Postman, Neil and Charles Weingartner. *Teaching as a Subversive Activity*. New York: Delacorte Press, 1969.

Process Hierarchy Chart for Science—A Process Approach, Parts A-D. New York: Xerox Education Division, 1967.

Rathbone, Charles H. "The Implicit Rationale of the Open Education Classroom." In Charles H. Rathbone (Ed.) *Open Education: The Informal Classroom*. New York: Citation Press, 1971.

Rathbone, Charles H. *Open Education: The Informal Classroom*. New York: Citation Press, 1971.

Richardson, Elwyn. *In the Early World*. New York: Random House, 1964.

Rudolph, Frederick. *The American College and University*. New York: Knopf, 1962.

Rugg, Harold Ordway. "The Foundations and Techniques of Curriculum Construction." *The Twenty-Sixth Yearbook for the National Society for the Study of Education: Volumes I and II*. Bloomington, Ill.: Public School Publishing Co., 1927.

Rugg, Harold Ordway. *Foundations for American Education*. New York: World Book Co., 1947.

Rugg, Harold Ordway and John Roscoe Clark. "Scientific Method in the Reconstruction of Ninth-Grade Mathematics: A Complete Report of the Investigation of the Illinois Committee on Standardization of Ninth-Grade Mathematics: 1913-1918." *Supplementary Educational Monographs*, Vol. II, No. 1 (April, 1918).

Rugg, Harold Ordway and Ann Schumaker. *The Child Centered School*. New York: Arno Press, 1928.

Ryle, Gilbert. *The Concept of Mind*. London: Hutchinson, 1949.

Schaefer, Robert. "Retrospect and Prospect." *The Seventieth Yearbook for the National Society for the Study of Education: Part I.* Chicago: University of Chicago Press, 1971.

Scheffler, Israel. "Philosophical Models of Teaching." *Harvard Educational Review*, Vol. 35, No. 2 (Spring, 1965).

Schwab, Joseph J. "The Concept of the Structure of a Discipline." *The Educational Record*, Vol. 43, No. 3 (July, 1962).

Schwab, Joseph J. *BSCS Biology Teachers Handbook.* New York: John Wiley, 1964.

Schwab, Joseph J. "The Structure of the Natural Sciences." In G.W. Ford and Lawrence Pagno (Eds.) *The Structure of Knowledge and the Curriculum.* Chicago: Rand McNally, 1964.

Schwab, Joseph J. "Problems, Topics, and Issues." In Stanley Elam (Ed.) *Education and the Structure of Knowledge.* Chicago: Rand McNally, 1964.

Science: A Process Approach. "Hierarchy Chart." New York: Xerox Education Division, no date.

Sealey, L.G.W. "Looking Back on Leicestershire." *ESI Quarterly Report* (Spring-Summer, 1966). Newton, Ma.: Education Development Center, 1966.

Seguel, Mary Louise. *The Curriculum Field: Its Formative Years.* New York: Teachers College Press, 1966.

Shulman, Lee S. "Psychological Controversies in the Teaching of Science and Mathematics." *The Science Teacher*, Vol. 35, No. 6 (September, 1968).

Shulman, Lee S. and Evan R. Keislar (Eds.) *Learning By Discovery: A Critical Appraisal.* Chicago: Rand McNally, 1966.

Silberman, Arlene. "The School of Your Child's Dreams." *Good Housekeeping* (March, 1971).

Silberman, Charles (Ed.) *The Open Classroom Reader.* New York: Vintage Books, 1973.

Silverman, Robert E. "Using the S-R Reinforcement Model." *Educational Technology*, Vol. 8 (March 15, 1968).

Sizer, Theodore R. *Secondary Schools at the Turn of the Century.* New Haven: Yale University Press, 1964.

Skinner, B.F. *Beyond Freedom and Dignity.* New York: Knopf, 1972.

Smith, Eugene Randolph. "The Principles of Curriculum-Making in the Beaver Country Day School." *The Twenty-Sixth Year-*

book of the National Society for the Study of Education. Bloomington: Public School Publishing Company, 1927.

Steeves, Frank L. (Ed.) *The Subjects in the Curriculum*. New York: Odessey Press, 1968.

Stout, John Elbert. *The Development of High School Curricula in the North Central States from 1860 to 1918*. Chicago: University of Chicago Press, 1921.

Sully, James. *Teachers Handbook of Psychology*. New York: Appleton, 1886.

Taba, Hilda. *Curriculum Development*. New York: Harcourt, Brace, and World, 1962.

Taylor, F.W. *Principles of Scientific Management*. New York: Harper and Brothers, 1911.

The ESS Reader. Newton, Ma.: Education Development Center, 1970.

The Provincial Committee on Aims and Objectives of Education in the Schools of Ontario. *Living and Learning*. Toronto: Ontario Department of Education, 1968.

The Scholars Look at the Schools: A Report of the Discipline Seminar. Washington, D.C.: National Education Association, 1962.

The Twenty-Sixth Yearbook of the National Society for the Study of Education: Volumes I and II. Bloomington: Public School Publishing Co., 1927.

Thorndike, Edward L. *Education*. New York: Macmillan, 1912.

Tippett, James S. *et al. Curriculum Making in the Elementary School*. Boston: Ginn and Co., 1927.

Twelfth Yearbook of the National Society for the Study of Education: Part I. Chicago: University of Chicago Press, 1913.

Tyler, Ralph W. *Basic Principles of Curriculum and Instruction*. Chicago: University of Chicago Press, 1950.

Waddle, Charles Wilkin. *An Introduction to Child Psychology*. New York: Houghton Mifflin, 1918.

Walberg, Herbert. *Characteristics of Open Education*. Newton, Ma.: Education Development Center, 1971.

Walberg, Herbert J. and Susan Christie Thomas. *Characteristics of Open Education: Toward an Operational Definition*. Newton, Ma.: Education Development Center, 1971.

Walters, E.H. *Activity and Experience in the Infant School*. London: National Froebal Foundation, no date.

Watson, Fletcher. "Approaching the Design of Science Curricula." Cambridge: unpublished paper at the Harvard Graduate School of Education, 1962.

Watson, Goodwin. "Education Is the Social Frontier." *The Social Frontier*, Vol. 1, No. 1 (October, 1934).

Watson, James Dewey. *The Double Helix*. New York: Atheneum, 1969.

Watson, John. "Psychology as the Behaviorist Views It." *Psychological Review*, Vol. 30 (April, 1913).

Weber, Lillian. *The English Infant School and Informal Education*. Englewood Cliffs, New Jersey: Prentice-Hall, Inc., 1971.

Whitfield, Richard C. (Ed.) *Discipline of the Curriculum*. London: McGraw Hill, 1971.

Witt, Paul (Ed.) *Technology and the Curriculum*. New York: Teachers College Press, 1968.

Index